SPINOZA: New Perspectives

SPINOZA: New Perspectives

edited by Robert W. Shahan and J. I. Biro

University of Oklahoma: Norman

Edited by Robert W. Shahan

Bonaventure and Aquinas: Enduring Philosophers (with Francis J. Kovach; Norman, 1976)

David Hume: Many-sided Genius (with Kenneth R. Merrill; Norman, 1976)

American Philosophy: From Edwards to Quine (with Kenneth R. Merrill; Norman, 1977)

Spinoza: New Perspectives (with J. I. Biro; Norman, 1978)

Library of Congress Cataloging in Publication Data

Main entry under title:
Spinoza.
 Bibliography: p.
 1. Spinoza, Benedictus de, 1632–1677—Addresses, essays, lectures.
I. Shahan, Robert W., 1935–   II. Biro, John Ivan, 1940–
B3998.S744   199'.492   77–18541

Copyright © 1978 by the University of Oklahoma Press, Publishing Division of the University. Manufactured in the U.S.A. First edition, 1978; second printing, 1980.

Preface

When Hume called Spinoza "universally infamous" and talked of the "absurdities" and "hideous hypothesis" of this "famous atheist," he was reflecting the general estimate of Spinoza's philosophy that prevailed for more than a hundred years after the latter's death.

The story of how this atheist and materialist of the seventeenth and eighteenth centuries became the "gottrunkener Mensch" of Novalis and the romantics need not be detailed here. We mention it only to illustrate the variety of interpretations to which Spinoza's thought has been subject both in his lifetime and since.[1] The continuing vitality of the former conception of Spinozism in present-day Soviet philosophy[2] is one proof that these varied approaches represent what might be called perennial possibilities of interpretation, rather than temporary and idiosyncratic aberrations.[3] The range of interests, methods of treatment, and, indeed, styles represented in this book is another. These essays show that there is hardly any question of interpretation—be it one of over-all conception or of intricate detail—which can be regarded as settled. Yet they also show that in spite of this, or perhaps because of it, contemporary philosophers continue to be interested in this enigmatic figure—the most inaccessible representative of a generally inaccessible and, to twentieth-century minds, uncongenial age—and they have not lost their appetite for the task of making him speak to us about matters which concern us in language we can understand.

The irony of our honoring the author of "these gloomy and obscure" speculations not a year after paying tribute to his critic Hume would not be lost on the latter. But we cannot help feeling that he would regard it as a healthy thing, were he to share with us the advantage of sophisticated and sympathetic scholarship of the sort exemplified in these essays.

It is a pleasure to record our thanks to the authors and to the others who have helped in the preparation of this book. These include the staff at the University of Oklahoma Press, our secretary, Nancy Johnson, and our copy editor, Jeanne Crabtree. A special word of thanks is owing to Peter Hutcheson, who both devised and implemented the system of references employed in the volume and also prepared the index.

We are grateful to the organizers of the 1977 Oklahoma Conference on Philosophy for permission to include the papers by Professors Curley, Mark, and Parkinson, which were read at that conference; and to Dr. Paul Sharp, President of the University of Oklahoma, for his assistance in making possible the publication of this volume.

ROBERT W. SHAHAN

J. I. BIRO

Norman, Oklahoma

1 See "Fragmente der letzten Jahre," in Paul Kluckhohn (ed.), *Novalis Schriften* (Leipzig, 1928), Vol. III, p. 253. For a brief sketch of this story, see Frederick M. Barnard's article in *The Encyclopedia of Philosophy*. A useful collection of passages, representing comments on Spinoza both by contemporaries and by later writers, is to be found in Ernst Altkirch, *Maledictus und Benedictus—Spinoza im Urteil Des Volkes und der Geistigen bis auf Constantin Brunner* (Leipzig, 1924).

2 See G. L. Kline, *Spinoza in Soviet Philosophy* (London, 1952).

3 In 1910, at a time when idealism reigned in Spinoza studies, Santayana could say, "It is consonant with the spirit of Spinoza's religion, politics and ethics that the highest part of his philosophy should not lie in them, but in his physics." (Introduction to *The Ethics of Spinoza*, Everyman's Library, London and New York, 1910).

CONTENTS

The following abbreviations are employed for references to Spinoza's works within the text and footnotes:

E: *Ethica Ordine Geometrico Demonstrata* (A=axiom; C=corollary; Df.=definition; Dm.=demonstration; L=lemma; Post.=postulate; P=proposition; S=scholium.)

CM: *Cogitata Metaphysica*

E*p*: *Epistolae*

KV: *Korte Verhandeling van God, de Mensch en deszelfs Welstand*

PP: *Renati Des Cartes Principia Philosophiae*

TdIE: *Tractatus de Intellectus Emendatione*

TP: *Tractatus Politicus*

TTP: *Tractatus Theologico-Politicus*

Whenever an author cites a specific edition or translation of Spinoza's works (except in the case of references to Spinoza's *Ethics*), it is indicated within the reference according to the following abbreviations:

Boyle: *Spinoza's Ethics and "De Intellectus Emendatione,"* trans. A. Boyle (London: J. M. Dent & Sons, Ltd., 1910).

Elwes: *The Chief Works of Benedict de Spinoza*, trans. R. H. M. Elwes, 2 vols. (New York: Dover Publications, 1955).

Gebhardt: *Spinoza Opera*, ed. Carl Gebhardt, 4 vols. (Heidelberg: Carl Winter, 1925).

Gutmann: *Ethics Preceded by On the Improvement of the Understanding*, ed. James Gutmann (New York: Hafner, 1949).

Hayes: *Earlier Philosophical Writings*, trans. Frank A. Hayes (Indianapolis: Bobbs-Merrill, 1963).

Land: *Benedicti de Spinoza Opera, Quotquot Reperta Sunt*, ed. J. van Vloten and J. P. N. Land, 3rd edition, 4 vols. in 2 (The Hague: Martinus Nijhoff, 1914).

Wild: *Spinoza Selections*, ed. John Wild (New York: Charles Schribner's Sons, 1930).

Wolf (a): *The Correspondence of Spinoza*, trans. & ed. A. Wolf (London: Frank Cass, 1966).

Wolf (b): *Spinoza's Short Treatise on God, Man, and His Well-Being*, trans. & ed. A. Wolf (New York: Russell & Russell, 1963).

Here are some examples of abbreviated references to Spinoza's works:

E IV, P59, Dm. (part 4, proposition 59, demonstration).

E II, L7, S (part 2, lemma 7, scholium).

E I, A6 (part 1, axiom 6).

E II, P6, C (part 2, proposition 6, corollary).

TdIE, Boyle, IX. 70 (section 9 of *TdIE* in Boyle's translation, passage number 70).

PP, Gebhardt I, 127 (volume 1 of Gebhardt's edition, page 127)

Ep. 32, Wolf(a), 210 (letter 32, page 210 of Wolf's translation of Spinoza's correspondence).

KV II, chap. 19, Land, 72–3, Wolf(b), 120–21 (part 2, chapter 19, pages 72 and 73 of van Vloten and Land's edition, pages 120 and 121 of Wolf's translation of *KV*).

Truth and Adequacy in Spinozistic Ideas

THOMAS CARSON MARK
University of California, San Diego

I wish to discuss the concepts of truth and adequacy in Spinoza's philosophy. It is often supposed that in linking adequate ideas with true ideas Spinoza is doing something similar to what Descartes does in linking clear and distinct ideas with true ideas, namely offering adequacy as a criterion for truth. To be sure, Spinoza's definitions of adequacy and truth, together with some of the ways he talks about ideas and their objects, can be taken so as to suggest that the relation of truth to adequacy in Spinoza is like the relation of truth to clearness and distinctness in Descartes. I believe that this appearance is misleading. But the relationship between truth and adequacy cannot be made clear without some discussion of the nature of ideas and their relation to the mind, and in order to bring out the distinctive features of Spinoza's position on these questions it will be useful to call to mind certain fundamental Cartesian theses. I shall then argue that although Spinoza accepts some elements of the Cartesian view, he rejects others, and the result is a position farther from that of Descartes than is typically recognized. I must make clear, however, that although I speak of Spinoza's rejecting this or that Cartesian doctrine, such talk is strictly an expository device, not a claim about Spinoza's development. I do not intend to make any assertions in this paper concerning the precise route by which Spinoza came to hold the views I shall attribute to him.

I.

The Cartesian theses which are relevant to our discussion are these:

1. The entities which serve as bearers of truth or falsity—those to which the predicates "true" and "false" apply—are ideas.

2. Clearness and distinctness are internal characteristics of ideas.

3. Truth consists in a particular relation (often called "agreement") in which bearers of truth may stand to the things which make them true.

4. The truth relation is external to ideas in the sense that their truth or falsity cannot be ascertained simply by inspecting their internal

properties (at least not without some external argument to show that those properties count as a criterion).

5. Ideas are objects of awareness.

6. Ideas (or other mental entities) are the only objects of direct awareness.

The theses listed above are intimately related to Descartes' conception of ideas as representational entities. The representational character of ideas is sometimes described by Descartes in a technical terminology of "objective" and "formal" reality, whereby "formal" reality has to do with the real nature of a thing and "objective" reality with the way things are represented by ideas.[1] This terminology is found occasionally in Spinoza also, but with altered significance, as we shall see.

Two additional features of this general position should be stressed. First, the total cognitive situation involves three elements: besides the objective reality, which can be likened to the descriptive content of an idea and which serves as the object of awareness when the mind contemplates its ideas, and the formal reality with which it may or may not agree, there is a third element, which is the apprehending consciousness, the mind or ego. The relation between the mind and its ideas is one of direct awareness or apprehension, the relation between the idea or objective reality and the world or formal reality is one of representation, and between the mind and the world there is no direct relation at all. Second, because ideas are the only objects of direct awareness and truth is a relation between an idea and something which is not an object of awareness, establishing a criterion of truth becomes a problem. An idea cannot be directly compared with what it represents, so how can one discover whether it is true? The problem of the criterion is an inevitable consequence of the above theory about the nature of ideas and the mind's relation to them, and if Spinoza shares Descartes' views on these matters, then he, too, must face it.

I am not concerned to defend the preceding sketch as an interpretation of Descartes. Other views are expressed in his writings, particularly on the status of ideas, which are sometimes said to be acts or dispositions as well as objects of awareness,[2] and several of the theses listed can be accepted only with qualifications as giving Descartes' opinions.[3] Perhaps the position described should be presented as just one of several that can be found in Descartes. Nevertheless, it has *some* plausibility as an interpretation (it is prominent in the Second and Third Meditations), and it is what I shall have in mind when I refer in what follows to the Cartesian picture. Its real interest for us is as a background for Spinoza.

Taking adequacy to be similar to clearness and distinctness, there can be no doubt that of the six theses listed above Spinoza accepts the first three. The conceptions of truth as agreement and of adequacy as an internal, truth an external, characteristic of ideas are explicitly stated in Axiom 6 of Part I of the *Ethics* and in the definition of adequate ideas. Thus:

A true idea must agree with that of which it is the idea $(E \text{ I, A6})$[4]

and:

> By adequate idea I understand an idea which, in so far as it is considered in itself, without reference to the object, has all the properties or internal signs of a true idea. Explanation: I say internal, so as to exclude that which is external, the agreement, namely, of the idea with its object. $(E \text{ II, Df. 4})$[5]

But Spinoza denies or qualifies the last three theses, at least so far as they relate to *adequate* ideas (and we shall be concerned in this paper almost exclusively with adequate ideas). Rejection of the fourth thesis, which asserts that the truth of an idea cannot be recognized just by inspection without an externally grounded criterion of truth, is implied by Spinoza's denial that truth requires a sign $(TdIE, \text{ Gutmann, 13})$[6] and his claim that truth is its own criterion $(E \text{ II, P43, S})$. The positive interpretation of this claim of Spinoza's will be brought out in what follows; for the moment we simply note that he denies that truth requires a criterion of the Cartesian sort. As for the last two theses, Spinoza rejects them both. Ideas in Spinoza's philosophy should be taken primarily as acts of apprehension, not as objects of awareness; also, the immediate objects of the mind are not necessarily mental.

That Spinozistic ideas should be conceived as active in some sense or other is fairly widely conceded. A number of commentators have emphasized the point, and there are such obvious texts as the definition of "idea," along with its explanation:

> By idea I understand a conception of the mind which the mind forms because it is a thinking thing.
>
> Explanation: I use the word "conception" rather than "perception" because the name perception seems to indicate that the mind is passive in its relation to the object. But the word conception seems to express the action of the mind. $(E \text{ II, Df. 3})$

It is less obvious just how we should construe the activity which is here made a part of the notion of idea, and some writers take it simply to mean that ideas are more nearly analogous to propositions than to concepts. But I think that this is not to go far enough. Propositions are like Cartesian ideas in that their truth or falsity depends on an external relation, the occurrence of which cannot be ascertained just by understanding the proposition. Thus, propositions require the external sign that Spinoza denies is necessary for true ideas, which is to say that for him they share the undesirable features of images or "dumb pictures" (E II, P43, S); the "dumbness" of pictures consists, I believe, precisely in this need for an external sign.

The reply, of course, will be that adequate ideas are for Spinoza like *analytic* propositions, whose truth *can* be ascertained by inspection. But this suggestion is a departure from Spinoza because it is not clear that the truth of an analytic proposition lies in its agreement with an object, and Spinoza does assert that truth involves agreement. A more plausible reply is that ideas are for Spinoza like true (but not analytic) propositions only.[7] But if the concept of truth is built into the definition of "idea" then the status of false ideas becomes a problem, and although there are traditional lines along which the problem could be resolved (some of which are echoed in Spinoza's writing, e.g., E II, P38), we have at least departed from the Cartesian concept of truth as an external relation. Departure from the Cartesian concept is not a decisive objection; I also shall urge that the Cartesian concept is not Spinoza's. But if offered as a full account of Spinoza's view of ideas, the analogy with true propositions is deficient in another way: it leaves out the notion of mind. The significance of this omission will emerge as we proceed.

To say that the activity of ideas is not sufficiently explained by assimilating ideas to propositions is not yet to show that we should explain that activity by regarding ideas as acts of apprehension. Spinoza does not use the terminology, "act of apprehension," but he does talk of "knowing" things, and knowing a thing is frequently made equivalent to having an idea of the thing. The equivalence is most striking in the central propositions of Part II, where Spinoza himself calls attention to it by his frequent use of the phrase "the idea or knowledge" of a thing (E II, P19, 20, 23, 24, 25) and by arguments in which to show knowledge of something it is sufficient to show possession of the idea of that thing, and conversely, arguments in which from possession of an idea one can infer knowledge of the object of the idea. (E II, P19, 22, 23)

Now, the assimilation of "having an idea" to "knowing" is *also* not enough to establish that ideas should be construed as acts of apprehension, for "having an idea" is ambiguous between having a certain mental content—an idea—before the mind and performing an act of apprehension, and "knowing" is similarly ambiguous. But notice that in the central propositions of Part II, having an idea and knowing are both assimilated to yet a third concept, namely mind. The mind is by definition an idea (E II, P11), and the three-way equivalence of mind, idea, and knowledge is explicit in E II, P19, Dm.: "The human mind is the idea itself or the knowledge of the human body." Ideas and knowing are thus to be linked with the mind itself, not with its objects, and so the reading of "idea" which makes it an object before the mind can be rejected, and we are left with the view whereby ideas are actions of the mind. This is the point I believe Spinoza to be making when he says that to have a true idea is "to know a thing perfectly or as well as possible. No one, in fact can doubt this unless he supposes an idea to be something dumb, like a picture on a tablet and not a mode of thought, that is to say, the very act of understanding." (E II, P43, S)[8]

It may seem tempting at this point to construe ideas as judgments, which *would* make of them a kind of mental act. But judgments share with propositions the features that their truth or falsity cannot be internally determined, which is to say that they are "dumb" in the way that pictures are "dumb." I conclude that ideas should be taken not as acts of the mind, but as acts of perceiving or apprehending. Spinoza frequently uses the word "perceive" in describing the mind's relation to its object; the relation, I believe, is modeled on that between vision and its objects. Having an idea is not seeing, but it is *like* seeing, and the "act of understanding" with which Spinoza identifies an idea is an act of mental seeing or apprehending.[9]

To show that Spinoza rejects the sixth Cartesian thesis, thus denying that the direct objects of the mind must be mental, does not require extended argument; the mind is after all defined as an idea, so that if the objects of ideas are occasionally not mental, then the same may be true of the objects of the mind.[10] But it is patent that ideas *do*, sometimes, have physical things for their objects, and this *is* the case with the idea which is identified with the mind: "The object of the idea constituting the human mind is a body, or a certain mode of extension actually existing. . . ." (E II, P13) Again: "the body is the object of the mind." (E II, P21, Dm.) If the mind were aware only of objects which were also mental, how account for E II, P22: "The human mind not only perceives the modifications of the body, but also the ideas of these modifications of the body"? Is Spinoza speaking with uncharacteristic imprecision, intending to say that the human mind not only perceives the ideas of the modifications of the body, but also the ideas of the ideas of these modifications? Surely that is absurd. Spinoza has the vocabulary (ideas of ideas) to speak of the apprehension of mental contents if he wishes, and he uses that vocabulary with some care in the portion of Part II which we are considering, so there is no reason not to take him literally when he talks of the mind perceiving bodily modifications or of the mind having the body as its object.[11] (Of course, it does not follow that the mind can apprehend *only* bodies or modifications of bodies; there *are* ideas of ideas.)[12]

The real significance of the passages considered in the previous few paragraphs is this: the relationship between an idea and its object is made identical with the relationship between the mind and what the mind apprehends and also with the relationship between knower and known. *What* is perceived or apprehended may be conceived through Thought or through Extension, but in either case what is apprehended is the same as what is known. This means that in his analysis of knowing Spinoza does away with the three-level Cartesian analysis and invokes instead a two-level analysis in which there is no intermediate entity between the mind and what is known and in which what is apprehended is not the representation of something else which is inaccessible.[13] This is most evident in the case of the third kind of knowledge. Spinoza refers to knowledge of the third kind as "knowledge of individual objects" in E V, P36, but the point I am making is much more explicitly stated by him in the *Short Treatise*: "This kind of knowledge does not result from something else, but from a direct revelation of the object itself to the understanding" (*KV*, Wolf(b), 133), and again: "We call that *clear knowledge* which comes, not from our being convinced by reasons, but from our feeling and enjoying the thing itself, and it surpasses the others by others by far." (*KV*, Wolf(b), 69)

I do not say that the notion of representation is entirely absent from Spinoza's philosophy; it does occur, but its epistemological role is severely restricted.[14] Representation has to do only with those ideas which represent to us external objects (i.e., finite physical objects other than our own bodies). Spinoza calls these idea "images of things" (E II, P17, S), and they are necessarily inadequate. (E II, P26, C) Thus, knowing by means of representative entities is confined to what Spinoza calls the first kind of knowledge, which is necessarily false. (E II, P41)[15] The point on which I am insisting is that in those forms of knowledge involving truth—the second and third kinds of knowledge— knowledge is analyzed as a two-term relation between the mind and what is known, and what is known is not a representation but the thing itself.

III.

An immediate consequence of Spinoza's analysis of the cognitive situation in terms of two elements instead of three, is that the relation between idea and object and the relation between knower and known collapse into one relation. That this occurs is well known, but it is usually presented as an objection and described as a source (or an example) of confusion in Spinoza's epistemology.[16] But it is possible to criticize too hastily, for it is not that Spinoza treats ideas and their objects now one way, now another, unable to make up his mind, with resultant confusion. That would be a description of his procedure only if one presumes that it is the Cartesian picture he is trying to present, without succeeding very well. Whereas the real point should be that he *rejects* the Cartesian picture and the different relationships mentioned above are for him different ways of describing one and the same thing. To recognize this is to put ourselves in a position to reach a deeper grasp of his conceptions of truth and knowledge, which differ profoundly from our own. It does not follow that he is confused, unless to differ from us is in itself evidence of confusion.

As the two-term analysis of knowledge implies, there are many Spinozistic concepts which combine what we can call a psychological element—something having to do with a mental state—with an element which we would nowadays prefer to treat in nonpsychological terms. An example can be seen in the passages where Spinoza equates the relation between an objective essence and the formal essence which is its object with the relation between understanding and what is understood. Talking of something which in its real nature (*quoad suam essentiam formalem*) is intelligible—capable of being understood—he explains this possibility by pointing out that the thing can be the object of some objective essence. Thus, the idea of a circle "will be something intelligible through itself, that is, the idea in its formal essence, can be the object of another objective essence." (*TdIE*, Gutmann, 11–12) Similarly, the idea of Peter will be "capable of being understood—that is of being the object of another idea which will contain objectively all that the idea of Peter contains formally." (*TdIE*, Gutmann, 12) Notice that although Spinoza uses the phrase "objective essence," he gives it a sense rather different from what it has in Descartes. For Spinoza, the objective essence of Peter"; (*TdIE*, Gutmann, 12) "truth, or the objecsion," or simply the "idea" of a thing: "The true idea of Peter is the objective essence of Peter"; (*TdIE*, Gutmann, 12) "Truth, or the objective essences of things, or ideas (all these mean the same thing)." (*TdIE*, Gutmann, 13) Thus, a Spinozistic objective essence, unlike a Cartesian one, is not something about which it is possible to wonder whether it agrees with its object. Nevertheless, the Spinozistic objective

17

essence retains what we might call a "referential" dimension: to call an idea an objective essence is to emphasize the content of the idea, to think of it as the idea *of* some particular thing.

Another example of the assimilation of psychological and nonpsychological concepts can be seen in Spinoza's treatment of the notion of certainty. Spinoza thinks that an objective reality, besides being true, will carry with it the psychological state of certainty: "Certainty is nothing else than the objective essence of a thing: in other words, the mode in which we perceive a formal essence is certainty itself." (*TdIE*, Gutmann, 12) Certainty is a state of mind or consciousness, but it is not *just* a psychological state; not the mere absence of doubt. (*E* II, P49, S) A Cartesian representation that simply happened to be true would not produce a state of certainty for Spinoza, nor does the mere psychological state of being without doubt guarantee truth. To apprehend something directly, as it is in itself, combines, for Spinoza, both truth and certainty; certainty is identified with such apprehension.

But the most important instance of this sort of psychologizing is found in the concept of truth itself. The entities that are true for Spinoza are certain mental acts or apprehensions; apprehension of a certain sort of content and possession of truth are the same. An apprehension is true when it is the apprehension of what is; such an apprehension is said to "agree with" its object. Nowadays, "true" is a predicate that applies to linguistic entities, such as sentences or propositions, and "truth" is taken to name a relation that may obtain between such entities and the world. There are, of course, many views, but in none of them is truth taken to pertain primarily to the *mind*.[17] It was remarked above that to liken Spinozistic ideas to propositions leaves out the notion of mind, and we can now see the importance of the omission. To liken ideas to propositions has the consequence of likening Spinoza's concept of truth to our own also; we "de-psychologize" it, which gives us a view of truth closer to present-day opinions than to Spinoza, a view whose very closeness to our own makes it easy to forget what has been left out. Spinoza's position is not anomalous historically; to make truth reside primarily in the mind, not in linguistic entities, is quite common in some of the philosophical traditions with which Spinoza was familiar and on which he has often been taken to have drawn. Aquinas, for example, writes that "truth resides primarily in the intellect"; words, he says, "are said to be true [only] in so far as they are signs of truth in the intellect." Aquinas endorses the account of truth as "the equation of intellect and thing," and this formula was for centuries a standard definition.[18]

IV.

To say that a true idea is an apprehension of what is does not explain how one can recognize when an apprehension is of this sort. This problem must be distinguished from the analogous Cartesian problem; we are not asking how a representation directly before the mind can be known to correspond to something other than itself, which is not before the mind. Spinoza insists that no external criterion of truth is required: "The truth needs no sign, it is sufficient to possess the objective essences of things, or, what is the same thing, ideas, in order to remove all doubts." (*TdIE*, Gutmann, 13) Equivalent claims can be found in the *Ethics*. (*E* II, P43, S) But these claims about the criterion of truth do not seem especially illuminating; on the contrary, they suggest that Spinoza offers *no* answer to the question of how we recognize a true idea, except to say "we just *do*." His remarks on the criterion of truth are sometimes glossed by saying that he grounds truth on self-evidence; indeed, it is claimed, he *must* appeal to self-evidence as the only way of avoiding an infinite regress.[19] I am willing enough to concede that Spinoza appeals to self-evidence in some form or other, but that does not explain what self-evidence means, or tell us why it can be relied upon, and I think it is possible to say a bit more about what is involved. It is here that the concept of adequacy enters the picture, especially Spinoza's use of it in the central propositions of Part II, Propositions 14–30. He is there concerned to show that the human mind does not possess adequate ideas of various sorts of objects, and his discussion reveals quite clearly what possession of an adequate idea would consist in, thereby giving more content to the concept of adequacy than is supplied by the official definition.

Every finite mode, for Spinoza, is causally dependent on other finite modes, and they on others, *ad infinitum*. (*E* I, P28) But this means that every finite mode is an effect, and because the knowledge of an effect depends upon and involves knowledge of the cause (*E* I, A4), the knowledge of any finite thing must reflect or include all of its causal connections with other things; that is, such knowledge requires "the ideas of all things." (*E* II, P30, Dm.) Conversely, to show that an idea is inadequate, it is sufficient to show that it does not include ideas of all the things to which its object is causally related (*E* II, P 24, 25), and propositions derived from them. Thus, the adequate idea of some object is an idea which presents that object as it stands in the self-sustaining context of Nature, which is to say that possession of an adequate idea is awareness of a content exhibiting the logical feature of self-completeness. But self-completeness is the essence of substance; to exhibit the self-contained and self-explanatory character of substance is precisely what it means to *be*; this character, we might say, defines the necessary and sufficient conditions for existence. Nothing that is complete in itself could (by the ontological argument, or, equivalently, by the very concepts of being and reality) fail to exist and to be real. An adequate idea thus is the apprehension of a content that is self-contained and self-explanatory; from the two-term analysis of knowledge it follows that the content of the idea and the object of the idea are not distinct, and so an adequate idea amounts to a direct grasp of what is. Because its object must exist as apprehended, we can say that the idea agrees with its object, or that the idea is true. The analysis leaves no room for doubt; one could not apprehend in this way and yet wonder whether what was apprehended might fail to exist. To do so would be to confuse being with nonbeing, for a true idea is related to a false idea "as being to nonbeing." (*E* II, P43, S) It is important to notice here that although an adequate idea is a direct or unmediated apprehension, its certainty does not rest on its immediacy. (We perceive the modifications of our bodies immediately, although inadequately.) For Spinoza, certainty rests not on immediacy but on the intrinsic character of what is apprehended.

The preceding discussion makes clear that despite the definition of truth as a form of agreement, Spinoza's concept of truth is not the Cartesian one in which truth is external to the idea in the strong sense that the idea might be just as it is in itself and yet false. In the note to *E* II, P43, Spinoza explicitly denies that from the fact that a true idea differs from a false one by agreeing with its object one can infer either that the two are distinguished by an external sign alone or that the true idea has "no greater reality or perfection."

I have elsewhere claimed that there is a connection between the concepts of truth and substance in Spinoza.[20] The point is an important one, but it is not quite accurately expressed because conceptually truth and substance are *not* the same: "substance" has to do with self-completeness and "truth" with agreement. The connection between the two concepts comes about because a true idea is the apprehension of an object that has the property of self-completeness: "thought is said to be true if it involves objectively the essence of any principle which has no cause, and is known through itself and in itself." (*TdIE*, Gutmann, 24)

In addition, this explanation of a true idea as the apprehension of a thing as instantiating the essence of substance (or God) is close to Spinoza's own definition of the third kind of knowledge: "This kind of knowing advances from an adequate idea of the formal essence of certain attributes of God to the adequate knowledge of the essence of things." (*E* II, P40, S2)

V.

Before moving on to a general statement of the relationship between the concepts of truth and adequacy, it will perhaps be helpful to comment briefly on some of the more obvious interpretive problems raised by the discussion of adequate ideas just offered.

What has been said about adequate ideas may seem to have the consequence that regarding finite modes there can be just one adequate idea, the one which is the complete apprehension of all finite modes taken together. In fact, there is no need to say this; there is a difference between the adequate idea of a finite mode, x, and the adequate idea of any other finite mode, y. Granted, the adequate idea of x must include ideas of all other finite modes, because of the causal interconnectedness of things and because knowledge of an effect requires knowledge of the cause. But this means that in the adequate idea of x, x is regarded as *effect*, and all other things as (ultimate or mediate) *causes*. The idea of x is the *only* idea in which x figures solely as an effect or logical consequence. In the idea of y, the idea of x occurs with x regarded as causally and logically prior to y; in the idea of x the reverse is true.[21] Thus, although the idea of any finite thing includes ideas of all other things, the idea of each finite thing is a unique permutation of the ideas in the infinite intellect. In this way, it can be said even of ideas in the infinite intellect that they are ideas of one thing rather than another, and there is no need to say that there can be only one adequate idea.

Nevertheless, the adequate idea of any finite mode, because it would have to include the infinitely complicated causal relations of that mode with other modes, is clearly something that could occur only in an infinite intellect. As Spinoza puts it: "about the duration of individual things which are outside us we can have but a very inadequate knowledge" (*E* II, P31), and this proposition is not restricted as to the attribute under which the individual things are conceived. Whether humans are capable of *any* adequate ideas at all is clearly a problem, to which Spinoza turns in the propositions immediately following the one just quoted. Our concern in this paper being the concepts of truth and adequacy, not the precise extent of human knowledge, I shall not discuss his argument, except to say that he finds a way to claim that we do have *some* adequate ideas, although none with actually existing finite modes as their objects.

Having touched on the relation between human and divine cognition, let me mention another problem that is frequently raised about Spinoza's theory of adequacy: How can one and the same idea be inadequate in a finite intellect and yet adequate in the infinite intellect? The problem is gratuitous; Spinoza does not claim that this happens. If I have an inadequate idea of something, then an inadequate idea occurs in God's intellect also, for my intellect is a part of God's. (E II, P11, C) If we say that God has an adequate idea of the same thing, we are saying that God's intellect includes my inadequate idea, together with the ideas of all the other things which go to make the thing what it is, and whose ideas combine with mine to form an adequate idea. My idea is inadequate, though in God, and God's idea is adequate, though it includes mine. Whatever adequate ideas I have are adequate also in God (with no equivocation on "adequate"), although it is not the case that everything which can be understood from the standpoint of the infinite intellect can be understood by me. Thus, there is no reason to say that my idea is, somehow, both adequate and inadequate, and consequently no need to explain such a possibility.[22]

The connection pointed out earlier between adequate ideas as interpreted here and Spinoza's definition of the third kind of knowledge will no doubt raise questions about the status of the second kind of knowledge. Taking ideas as apprehensions, and noting that the second kind of knowledge is universal, whereas the third is of individuals (E V, P36), it would appear that the difference between them ought to be that the third is the apprehension of individuals, the second of universals. But that is certainly wrong; Spinoza does not grant real being to universals. A complete discussion of this topic would be lengthy, but I believe that the solution lies in taking literally Spinoza's definition of the second kind of knowledge; this sort of knowledge proceeds "from our possessing common notions and adequate ideas of the properties of things." (E II, P40, S2) Briefly, I think that the second kind of knowledge *is* to be thought of as apprehension, but what is apprehended is not a thing, say an individual triangle; instead, we apprehend certain of its properties which, together with relevant axioms or "common notions" (known by the third kind of knowledge), make it necessary that (say) each triangle have angles equalling 180°. Equivalently, we could say that space itself is such that we can see that anything which is a triangle must have its angles equal to 180°.[23]

VI.

We are now in a position to describe in a general way the relationship between the concepts of adequacy and truth. Truth is defined as agreement; adequacy, we have seen, has to do with self-completeness. Furthermore, truth is "external," adequacy "internal" or "intrinsic" to ideas. To call adequacy "intrinsic" is to relate it to the formal essence of the idea, the idea as it is in itself. But it was earlier asserted that Spinozistic ideas also retain what can be called a "referential" dimension, an element, we might say, of "pointing outward," and it is this element that is singled out when Spinoza describes an idea as objective essence. Objective essence, we have seen, is linked with truth (*TdIE*, Gutmann, 13, quoted above), whereas the formal characteristic of adequacy is specifically *not* the same as truth. (*E* II, Df. 4, quoted above) What all this comes to is that the self-completeness of an idea, when we take it as a formal characteristic, is the adequacy of the idea, but if we think of this characteristic as referred to an object, then we are thinking of it as a relational property of the idea; we are thinking of it pertaining to the idea insofar as the idea is an objective essence. That is to say, we are thinking of the *external* denomination of the idea, its agreement or truth.

There remains a problem. We have seen that truth cannot be external in the strong sense that the idea might be just as it is in itself and yet false. In that case, what can it mean to say that agreement with its object is "external" to the idea? I believe that it is simply objective essence, the element of "pointing outward," which Spinoza has in mind in calling agreement "external"; that is, he is *not* to be taken as saying that agreement is a case of what *we* would call an external relation whose presence or absence leaves the related things essentially unaltered. Nor, in fact, is it clear that he thinks of agreement or truth as a relation at all, according to the modern view of relation which explains it as a two- (or more-) place predicate holding of two (or more) entities jointly. We must remind ourselves that Spinoza inherited a concept of relation derived ultimately from the Greeks, and still dominant in the seventeenth century, in which relations are accidents of substance. There were, of course, various concepts, but the one particularly relevant here is the one according to which a relation is a real accident of one of its terms, and not of the other. The relational accident is said to *exist* in one term, although *with reference* to the other term. Such a view can be found in different writers throughout the history of philosophy, notably in Aristotle, Avicenna, and Aquinas, and it was thought to be particularly persuasive as an explanation of the relation that obtains between knower and known. Now, we have seen that in Spinoza the relation between a true idea and its object is the same as the relation between knower and known. I submit that truth in Spinoza should be understood as a relational accident, whose nature consists in *being toward* its object, that this is what Spinoza intends in the places where he talks of ideas as objective essences and equates objective essence with truth. Consistent with this, "agreement" in Spinoza is to be taken as a relational property; it is not to be interpreted in the present-day sense of satisfaction.

The concept of relations as accidents of substance was normally associated with certain fundamental metaphysical doctrines. In his study of the history of the concept of relation, Julius Weinberg writes:

> The insistence that the basic reality is primary substance, that basic existence has essential unity which can only be achieved by form, and that relation is the least real of accidents—all these propositions lead to the view of relation that was to dominate the reflections on this subject until very recent times.[24]

Of the two principal philosophical doctrines which, in Weinberg's view, prevented the development of the modern conception, the first, namely, the insistence on convertibility of *being* and *unity*, is a conspicuous feature of Spinoza's philosophy, and the second, namely the claim that relations are not real entities is, as Weinberg points out, explicitly stated by Spinoza in his early works.[25] Remembering his concept of relation is vital to understanding Spinoza's conception of truth.

The above remarks may seem to suggest a position of total unintelligibility. For we began, apparently, with an idea on the one hand, and its object on the other, the two of them linked by a relation called "truth." What we seem now to be saying is that truth is not really a relation after all, it is a property which inheres in the idea. Thus, it does not *connect* the idea with the object. Instead, by inhering in the idea and not the object, it leaves the object stranded, as it were, in complete isolation. And this is unintelligible because this very object is supposed to be what makes the idea true. But to interpret the situation this way is to forget the arguments presented earlier showing that knowledge is an affair of two, not three, elements. For the interpretation just suggested would, in effect, put us back in the Cartesian position by reintroducing the content of the idea as something distinct from its object, whereas in fact the content of the idea and the object of the idea are *not* separate for Spinoza. Ideas are direct apprehensions, and they are true when they are apprehensions of a content that exhibits the defining features of being or substance.

Despite the conceptual differences between adequacy and truth, the two are extensionally equivalent. Their equivalence has the consequence that falsity, which is defined in terms of inadequacy (*E* II, P35) is the contradictory both of adequacy and of truth. It is sometimes alleged that Spinoza's theory of ideas leaves no room for false ideas. Now, it *is* the case that for Spinoza everything is such that there can be an adequate idea of it, although in the case of finite modes that idea can occur only in an infinite intellect. But from this it does not follow that all ideas are adequate or true.

Nevertheless, the interpretation offered here of ideas as direct apprehensions of their objects may seem to support the claim that all ideas must be true. For how can the immediate object of apprehension fail to have the nature apprehended? And if it has that nature, then isn't that just to say that the apprehension is true? Now, it was pointed out earlier that Spinoza does not found certainty (or truth) on immediacy. Take a case in which we apprehend a finite mode. Such apprehension may carry with it complete psychological assurance; in Spinoza's phrase, we "do not doubt" it. But this is not the same as certainty, for certainty includes truth. The finite mode is something which, by hypothesis, is dependent on other things; its dependence is part of its *nature*, and in apprehending it I apprehend something that does not possess the internal characteristics which would establish it as a real thing. What I apprehend has being as part of a more comprehensive system, but as long as I do not apprehend it within that context I do not apprehend its real nature, despite my lack of doubt. My apprehension is false, not in the sense of being the apprehension of something which, while really possessing the features I apprehend, fails to agree with some reality beyond my apprehension (the Cartesian picture), but in the sense that what I apprehend is deficient ontologically; it is fragmentary, and so even though my apprehension is direct it does not contain the elements which would show the object to be real. This discussion of falsity will perhaps help to emphasize the way Spinoza's conception of truth departs from the Cartesian one, and from other versions of the correspondence theory.

Various commentators have asserted that adequacy is for Spinoza the criterion of truth.[26] From what has been said it is clear that adequacy is not a criterion of the Cartesian sort; it is not an internal characteristic of ideas which can be used (thanks to some external, transcendental argument) to justify claims about the relation between ideas and the "external world." Nevertheless, adequacy might serve in some other way as the characteristic by which we come to recognize true ideas, and the discussion of adequate ideas in Propositions 14–30 might seem initially to suggest this. Spinoza there talks about how the various ideas we have of finite things are not adequate, and we are perhaps supposed to infer that if our ideas *were* adequate we would thereby know them to be true. But the structure of argument in these propositions seems in fact to have a slightly different thrust: the argument is that a true idea (one that really agreed with its object) would have to be adequate because its object in its complete nature is part of something self-sufficient. From this it follows that if our ideas of finite things are not true, i.e., if they do not agree with the complete nature of their objects (which they do not because we are finite), then they are not adequate either.[27] Conclusion: we have inadequate ideas of finite modes. If my interpretation is correct, it would have as a consequence that if one *did* have an adequate idea, one could conclude from its adequacy that it was also true and claim in this way that it is by adequacy that we recognize truth. But *Spinoza* does not say this. What *he* says on the question of "how a man can know that he has an idea which agrees with that of what it is the idea" is: "I have shown almost more times than enough that he knows it simply because he has an idea which agrees with that of which it is the idea, that is to say, because truth is its own standard." (*E* II, P43, S) Thus, as far as Spinoza's words go, adequacy is not the criterion of truth, *truth* is the criterion of truth. To be sure, what one recognizes in a true idea is an instantiation of being or substance, which is to say that one recognizes the self-completeness that we have linked with adequacy. Nevertheless, recognition that our idea is true comes about not because adequacy is an indicator of truth, but because *reality* is self-complete and self-explanatory.

VII.

I wish to stress once more that what has been said in this paper applies to adequate or true ideas, not to images. Images *are* representational, and about them it *can* be asked whether they "correspond" to the "external world." But if we give the name "truth" to this sort of correspondence, we should remember that Spinoza normally reserves the word for ideas, not images, and to give the name "truth" to the correspondence of an image with an external thing is in no way to show that images can be true in the sense of truth that applies to ideas—to the second and third kinds of knowledge. I have used the word "true" in this paper exclusively to refer to the agreement between an idea and its object, but the word does have other uses, in Spinoza's writing as well as in the history of philosophy generally. It can be used to mean "real," or "correct," or "good," or other things but if we are once clear about the central conceptions of "true" and "adequate" as they occur in the contexts we have been considering, there need be no confusion when we encounter passages where the terms are used with other, or additional connotations.[28]

The presentation of Spinoza's views in this paper has been as affirmative as possible, but it should be obvious that on the interpretation offered here there are deep internal problems in Spinoza's position, the most important of which may be suggested by pointing out that if ideas are acts of apprehension they must nevertheless, as acts, have some structure; in Spinoza's terminology, they must possess some formal essence. But it is difficult to separate the properties an idea has as an act from those it has only insofar as it is the apprehension *of* something, and, again, from those which pertain to its object. Is adequacy, in particular, a property of the act as such or a property of the object of the act? In the preceeding discussion I have spoken both ways, and I even allowed myself to speak in one place of the adequacy of an idea being "referred to" its object. Such ambiguity cries out for resolution, and I have, unfortunately, no completely satisfying resolution to offer. But I do not believe that the problems are created by my interpretation; the different formulations have textual support, so that the same or an analogous difficulty will arise even if one rejects the interpretation offered here. Piecing together the relation between what can be recalled the intrinsic and the intentional properties of ideas, especially when an attempt is made to include Spinoza's theory of the attributes, is to my mind the most difficult problem in Spinoza interpretation. I do not pretend to have solved it in this paper, nor am I certain that it has a solution.

VIII.

The interpretation of truth and adequacy offered here has bearing on many parts of Spinoza's philosophy and to explore them all would be a major undertaking. But in conclusion I would like to discuss briefly the relevance of what has been said to a feature of Spinoza's view of language which has been a focus of controversy between some writers on Spinoza. I refer to the exchange between David Savan and G. H. R. Parkinson, in which the principal point at issue is whether language, on Spinoza's account, is "a suitable medium in which to express philosophical truths."[29] Professor Parkinson says that it is, and his arguments have been regarded as decisive by other commentators.[30] Now, I quite agree with Professor Parkinson concerning those issues he discusses, which is to say that Savan's contention that language is not a suitable medium in which to express philosophical truth is not established by the arguments that he offers. But there is a prior question not pursued by either participant in this controversy, but which should be addressed if the debate is to be settled, namely: what does "true" mean for Spinoza, and to what sorts of entities does the predicate apply?[31] The answer that has been proposed in this paper makes clear that there is a sense, at least, in which Savan's contention is right, although I am not sure whether the sense in which I accept Savan's view is one he would recognize.

We have seen that the entities in Spinoza's system which can literally be true are not linguistic entities such as sentences, they are ideas. Ideas are modifications of thought, and as such they are like direct apprehensions of what is. Sentences, on the other hand, do not bear the direct relation to reality that ideas do for Spinoza; a sentence, on internal grounds, could be taken as either true or false, which is to say that it operates on the level of representational entities or images and shares their undesirable features. In this sense, Savan is right.

Nevertheless, it is *also* the case that language is a suitable medium for Spinoza in which to express philosophical truth; to "express truth" is not the same as to "be true." A sentence may be the occasion of the formation of adequate ideas: a person may acquire insight because of having understood a sentence. But it is the insight—the vision of reality—which is the idea and which is true, not the sentence. A person may equally read and even understand a sentence (after a fashion) without gaining any increased insight, even though the sentence is one in which a more acute mind could have brought about true ideas. Thus, that sentences are not ideas and only ideas are true does not have the consequence that writing the *Ethics* is somehow pointless or that Spinoza cannot have been serious in his apparent hope that people would understand things better for having read his book. It is true that language, for some of the reasons pointed out by Savan, is a second best; finite beings put together a language using general terms based on images because as finite beings they are incapable of operating with ideas alone. But there are better and worse ways of using language; it can to some extent be used so that it reflects the order of ideas, and when this occurs it can provide (or be the occasion of) knowledge and understanding. Language thus offers a medium, but not an instance, of philosophic truth.

That linguistic entities are not the bearers of truth in Spinoza ought not to surprise us; on the contrary it is just what we ought to expect in a rationalist philosopher. For rationalism is based on the notion that unaided thought can provide genuine insight into the nature of things, that reality is intelligible, and certainty about it possible. Philosophical rationalism may include other elements as well: the goal of comprehensive understanding, the inclination toward system building, belief in the uniformity of nature; but I wish to focus on the central claim that knowledge of reality can be derived from pure rational understanding.

If such a program is to be successful, it must find some way of ruling out the possibility that thought might yield something less than truth, that it might give mere seeming instead of reality, and this demand helps to explain why rationalism may very well invoke special entities—ideas—instead of ordinary natural language for expressing its conclusions. For language has built into its descriptive uses the possibility of truth or falsity; it is an immensely important fact about language that it can be used to make statements that are false as well as statements that are true. This is the feature of language which makes it, first, learnable by humans, and second, capable of describing whatever facts we like. If there were a word for every separate entity no one would know the language, and if this problem is overcome by permitting words to refer to more than one entity—by making of them universals instead of logically proper names—then a finite vocabulary can be used to describe an indefinitely large number of cases. But it thereby becomes possible to make mistakes—to misapply the words. For the characteristics of language mentioned above have the effect that any linguistic statement with descriptive content can perfectly well be false, meaning that its truth or falsity is a separate question which remains even after the statement has been understood. This, however, is exactly the predicament that the rationalists wished to avoid. Therefore, if the properties mentioned are indeed essential to language, a successful rationalism would have to base its claims not on language but on something else without these undesirable features. Hence, the appeal to ideas.[32] The rationalists themselves were aware of the point, although they did not express it in the sort of terms in which I have stated it. Their works are filled with admonitions to their readers not to be misled by words but to look instead to ideas and the understanding for truth, and such passages are numerous in Spinoza.

But Spinoza pushes the point farther than the others. In both Descartes and Leibniz the link between ideas and the nature of things is less intimate and necessary than in Spinoza. Descartes' view leaves room for an external relation (a relation of truth or falsity) between reason and reality, the gap between the two being bridged by some argument (such as a theological one) that shows them to coincide. In Leibniz the doctrine of preestablished harmony acts as the same sort of external guarantee that "perceptions" correspond to some external reality.[33] But what this means is that Cartesian ideas and Leibnizean "perceptions" have become representational entities in their own right, or at least they have come to share their relevant features, and to

29

share thereby the defects, for a rationalist program, of language. In his rejection of the three-element analysis of cognition, Spinoza gives a more consistent attempt at a viable rationalism; he seems to have recognized—implicitly, perhaps, but nevertheless decisively—that representative entities could not supply the certainty in metaphysics that the rationalists wanted. He attempts to supply that certainty, and the attempt leads to the rejection of representative or linguistic entities as bearers of truth and to a view of knowledge that makes it more nearly analogous to simple acquaintance than to what we normally understand it to be. Furthermore, as we have seen, it involves rejection of the concept of truth as an external relation of agreement. That Spinoza nevertheless defines truth as agreement between an idea and its object comes about, as we have also seen, partly because he retains the traditional concept of relation which likens relations to accidents of substance. One might wish to say, therefore, that although Spinoza was more thorough and consistent in his attempt to work out a satisfactory rationalism that either Leibniz or Descartes (with respect, that is, to the particular issues under discussion here), such consistency as he achieves in this direction is possible only because he lacks a satisfactory concept of relation, and in consequence a satisfactory concept of truth. Nevertheless, however unacceptable to present-day thinkers in some of its doctrines, Spinoza's system stands as an example of an extraordinarily single-minded and thorough articulation of a particular philosophical program, which is enough, even apart from its other claims on our attention, to assure its continued philosophical interest.

NOTES

1. I have discussed Descartes' use of this terminology and the role of representationalism in his Third Meditation proof of God's existence in "Descartes' Proof in Meditation III," *International Studies in Philosophy*, VII (Fall, 1975), pp. 69–88.

2. The various concepts of "idea" found in different philosophers of the seventeenth century are related by Robert McRae to this ambiguity in Descartes' use of the term. " 'Idea' as a Philosophical Term in the Seventeenth Century," *Journal of the History of Ideas*, XXVI, 2 (April-June, 1965), pp. 175–90.

3. The first thesis, that ideas, and not judgments or acts of will, are bearers of truth, will seem dubious to many. Nevertheless, Descartes does talk of ideas being true, and he defines truth as conformity of thought with object (letter to Mersenne, 16 October, 1639). For a discussion of ideas versus judgments as bearers of truth, see Section 4 of Alan Gewirth's essay, "Clearness and Distinctness in Descartes," *Philosophy*, XVII, 69 (April, 1943). Reprinted in Willis Doney, ed., *Descartes: A Collection of Critical Essays* (Garden City, N.Y.: Doubleday, 1967).

4. Spinoza's later use of this axiom shows that he regarded agreement as a sufficient, as well as a necessary condition of truth. Cf. my *Spinoza's Theory of Truth* (New York: Columbia University Press, 1972), p. 56.

5. An essentially equivalent account of adequacy and truth appears in Ep. 60, Wolf(a), 300.

6. In quotations from this edition I have occasionally modified the Elwes translation.

7. E.M. Curley, *Spinoza's Metaphysics* (Cambridge, Mass.: Harvard University Press, 1969), pp. 121ff. Curley's proposal is introduced as a means of explaining the doctrine that a mode of extension and the idea of that mode are one and the same thing, expressed in different ways, and in that context his interpretation is quite suggestive. I have discussed the doctrine also, along different but somewhat related lines, in "The Spinozistic Attributes," *Philosophia*, Vol. 7, No. 1 (March, 1977).

8. A more literal translation of the last words, *nempe ipsum intelligere*, would be "understanding itself." But there is no doubt that the free version given in the text expresses the sense of the Latin.

9. My contention that ideas should be thought of as acts of apprehension would be misleading if it were taken to provide, without further elaboration, an explanation of Spinoza's theory of mind. The argument in the text is in part, of course, a rejection of the view expressed by Parkinson, that "to say that the mind forms ideas is no different from saying that there are ideas which are constituent parts of a certain complex idea" (*Spinoza's Theory of Knowledge*, Oxford: Oxford University Press, 1954, p. 103), insofar as *that* view is taken as giving the whole story. But, of course, Parkinson is right that the mind is a complex idea. Some of the necessary qualifications are persuasively presented by Douglas Odegard, "The Body Identical with the Human Mind: A Problem in Spinoza's Philosophy," in Maurice Mandelbaum and Eugene Freeman, eds., *Spinoza: Essays in Interpretation* (La Salle: Open Court, 1975), pp. 61–83.

10. The point seems evident, but it has eluded some commentators, to the deteriment of their interpretations. In a discussion that also contains some acute observations, Daisie Radner writes that Spinoza agrees with Descartes "that we are directly aware only of things in the mental realm," although she offers neither argument nor textual support for this assertion. "Spinoza's Theory of Ideas," *Philosophical Review*, LXXX, 3 (July, 1971), p. 346.

11. Spinoza's assertion in *E* II, P19, that the mind does not know "the body itself" does not have the consequence that what it *does* know must be mental. In this and subsequent propositions Spinoza is determining which objects are epistemologically primitive in such knowledge as we can have of the "external world," and considering whether this knowledge can be adequate. He is not saying that the mind cannot perceive the physical.

12. The contention that ideas are acts of apprehension is a claim about what ideas *are*—about their formal nature. And when there occurs an idea of an idea, it is the formal nature of the original idea which is the object of the new idea: "the idea, in its formal essence, can be the object of another objective essence." (*TdIE*, Gutmann, 11–12) Thus, the idea of the idea of Peter is the idea of an act of apprehension, it is not another idea of Peter, once removed, as it were. This is borne out in the *Ethics*: "the idea of the idea is nothing but the form of the idea in so far as this is considered as a mode of thought without relation to the object." (*E* II, P21, S).

13. I did not recognize this point when I wrote *Spinoza's Theory of Truth*, and some of what I said there, particularly toward the end of Chapter III, now seems to

me to be wrong. I thought, in effect, that it was sufficient to reject only the sixth of the Cartesian theses listed above, arriving at a view whereby the objects of ideas, as well as the ideas, could be objects of awareness. The result differs from the Cartesian view in that the mind is not insulated by its ideas from any direct access to the world, but the concept of ideas as objects of awareness is retained along with a three-element analysis of knowledge. Most (but not all) of what I said in Chapters IV and V still seems right to me, and most of it fits (or can rather easily be modified to fit) the interpretation of truth and adequacy presented in this paper.

14. The word "representation" (*repraesento*) is rare in Spinoza; it occurs in connection with the definition of images (*E* II, P17, S) and passages dependent on that definition (*E* III, P27) It also occurs in the definition of the first kind of knowledge. (*E* II, P40, S2)

15. Spinoza draws this consequence explicitly: "Knowledge of the first kind is the only cause of falsity; knowledge of the second and third kinds is necessarily true." (*E* II, P41) Some commentators have made much of the fact that Spinoza here says that knowledge of the first kind is the *cause* of falsity, not that it is false. But no adequate idea can cause an inadequate idea (*E* II, P40), so the cause of an inadequate idea must be inadequate also. Because inadequacy is sufficient for falsity (*E* II, P35), it follows that the first kind of knowledge is necessarily false. Admittedly, it sounds odd to our ears to speak of a form of *knowledge* being false (Spinoza's word is *cognitio*). E. M. Curley comments on this point, saying that the term "knowledge" is apparently not taken by Spinoza as an "honorific one" ("Experience in Spinoza's Theory of Knowledge," in Marjorie Grene, ed., *Spinoza: A Collection of Critical Essays*, Garden City, N.Y.: Doubleday, 1973, p. 31). But I think we get a better sense of Spinoza's intent if we associate the term with the view, argued in the text, of ideas as apprehensions. *Cognitio* does have the sense of "acquaintance" or "apprehension;" thus, the "kinds of knowledge" are like ways of apprehending or ways of being acquainted.

16. E.g., Parkinson, *op. cit.*, p. 105. This objection is a principal theme of Henry Barker's three-part article, "Notes on the Second Part of Spinoza's *Ethics*," *Mind*, XLVII (1938); reprinted in S. Paul Kashap, ed., *Studies in Spinoza* (Berkeley: University of California Press, 1972), pp. 101–67.

17. E.g., " ' True' is a predicate properly and primarily applicable to statements in language, rather than to thoughts or judgments or objective 'intensional entities'." P.T. Geach, *Mental Acts* (London: Routledge, 1957), p. 98.

18. *Summa Theologica*, Pt. I, Q. 16, Art. 1.

19. Stuart Hampshire, *Spinoza* (London: Faber and Faber, 1956), pp. 78–80. Also Frederick Pollock, *Spinoza: His Life and Philosophy* (New York: American Scholar, 1966. Reprint of the edition of 1899), p. 121.

20. See *Spinoza's Theory of Truth*, *op. cit.*, Chapter IV.

21. It is suggestive in this connection that Spinoza says that inadequate ideas are "like conclusions without premises." (*E* II, P28, Dm.)

22. The reply to Baker's arguments ("Notes on the Second Part of Spinoza's *Ethics*," *op. cit.*, p. 166 in Kashap's collection) about ideas adequate in God and in humans, rests on noticing that Spinoza does *not* talk of a single idea which is adequate in one context and inadequate in another. Instead, he identifies ideas by mentioning their objects, and describes the conditions under which an idea with *x* as its object will be adequate or inadequate. Thus, the idea with *x* as its object which occurs in God insofar as He constitutes the essence of the human mind is

inadequate; the idea with x as its object which occurs in God and is referred to the infinite intellect is adequate. But from the fact that the two ideas have the same object, it does not follow that they are the *same idea*; the adequate idea includes much more than the inadequate idea. The doctrine of one-to-one correspondence between ideas and objects holds for adequate ideas only; of a given object there can be *many in*adequate ideas.

23. We could say this, clearly, even at times when we were not confronting an individual triangle actually existing as a physical object; even if, indeed, we *never* had confronted such an individual triangle. Recognizing this provides the basis for explaining Spinoza's otherwise cryptic phrase "true ideas of non-existent modifications." (*E* I, P8, S; *Cf. also E* II, P8, and *TdIE*, Gutmann, 23–4)

24. J. Weinberg, *Abstraction, Relation, and Induction* (Madison: University of Wisconsin Press, 1965), p. 71. Throughout this paragraph and the second half of the one preceding, I rely heavily on Weinberg's study.

25. *Ibid.*, p. 112. Weinberg provides references also to Descartes, Gassendi, and Hobbes, and offers a brief discussion of Leibniz' views on the concept of relation.

26. E.g., Henry E. Allison, *Benedict de Spinoza* (Boston: Twayne, 1975), p. 99. This seems also to be the view of H.H. Joachim, *A Study of the Ethics of Spinoza* (New York: Russell and Russell, 1964. Reprint of the edition published in 1901), p. 148–49. An extremely interesting discussion of the criterion of truth, along rather different lines, is given by Martial Gueroult, *Spinoza II* (Hildesheim: Olms, 1974), Ch. XII.

27. The argument depends on the stipulation that truth and adequacy are materially equivalent; otherwise the argument sketched in the text would be an instance of the fallacy of inferring from "p implies q" that "not-p implies not-q."

28. Nevertheless, Spinoza himself sometimes invites confusion by using as examples objects of which the human mind could not, on his theory, have anything but images.

29. David Savan, "Spinoza and Language," *Philosophical Review*, LXVII (1958), pp. 212–25; G.H.R. Parkinson, "Language and Knowledge in Spinoza," *Inquiry*, 12 (1969), pp. 15–40. Both essays are reprinted in Marjorie Grene, ed., *Spinoza: A Collection of Critical Essays, op. cit.* The phrase quoted is Parkinson's, p. 92 in Grene.

30. For example, by E.M. Curley, "Experience in Spinoza's Theory of Knowledge," *op. cit.*, p. 33.

31. Professor Parkinson has, of course, discussed some of these questions elsewhere; see *Spinoza's Theory of Knowledge, op. cit.*, Chapter VI; also his contribution to this symposium.

32. In saying this I am not making a general claim about "ideas" in the seventeenth and eighteenth centuries, but a quite specific point relating to rationalism in the particular construal that I have given it. The term "idea" was put to a variety of uses, by many different philosophers. In an interesting discussion of the use of "idea" by some philosophers of the time, Ian Hacking points out that ideas could function *analogously* to certain ways in which language functions for twentieth-century philosophers, and that ideas could be appealed to precisely *because* of what I have called their "undesirable features" from a rationalist point of view. (*Why Does Language Matter to Philosophy?*, Cambridge, England: Cambridge U.P., 1975, Ch. 2–5, esp. p. 29).

33. This point depends on a nonphenomenalist reading of Leibniz, which is not

the only, or, perhaps, the most interesting way of reading him. For a discussion of the phenomenalistic strain in Leibniz, see Montgomery Furth, "Monadology," *Philosophical Review*, LXXVI (1967), pp. 169–200. Reprinted in Harry G. Frankfurt, ed., *Leibniz: A Collection of Critical Essays* (Garden City, N.Y.: Doubleday, 1972), pp. 99–135.

"Truth Is Its Own Standard": Aspects of Spinoza's Theory of Truth

G. H. R. PARKINSON
The University of Reading

I.

In the course of his philosophical works, Spinoza says a number of things about 'true ideas' that have a strange ring to modern ears. He says, for example, that a man who has a true idea knows that he has a true idea, and cannot doubt of its truth. (*E* II, P43) Commenting on this, he remarks (*E* II, P43, 5): "What can be clearer and more certain, as a standard of truth, than a true idea? Just as light manifests both itself and the dark, so truth is the standard both of itself (*veritas norma sui*) and of falsity."[1] All this may seem very puzzling.

(i) In what sense is Spinoza using the term "idea" here? Many philosophers would say that what are true or false are 'statements' or 'propositions', and that in the sense in which a proposition is true or false an idea is not. An idea may indeed be called 'true' or 'false' in the sense of 'genuine' or 'spurious'; but this sort of truth or falsity is not that which attaches to propositions. In what sense, then, are we to understand the term "idea" in Spinoza?

(ii) Even if it is granted that the word "idea" may have a sense which allows ideas to be true or false in the sense in which propositions are, how can it be seriously supposed that a man who has a true idea knows that it is true? If "know" and "true" have their usual senses, then it must be admitted that there are many cases in which we say or think things that happen to be true, but do not know that they are true. From the time of Plato (*Meno*, 97a), philosophers have seen this and accordingly they have distinguished between 'true belief' and 'knowledge'; it might seem, however, that Spinoza does not recognize this distinction. Is he, then, simply in error, or is it the case that, just as he may give a special sense to the term "idea," so also he gives a special sense to the term "true idea"?

This paper is devoted to an examination of these questions. In examining them, we shall not be discussing matters which are only of marginal importance in the philosophy of Spinoza; on the contrary, they take us to the very heart of his theory of knowledge.

Clearly, the first task must be an investigation of what Spinoza means by the term "idea." In doing this, it will be useful to begin with a short consideration of what Descartes means by the term; not because Spinoza's use of the term is the same as Descartes', but because the contrast will make Spinoza's views stand out more clearly. In the third of his *Meditations*,[2] Descartes declares that ideas are "as it were the images of things" (*tanquam rerum imagines*)—"as when I think of a man, a chimaera, the sky, an angel, or God." An idea, Descartes continues, is not true or false if it is considered purely in itself, and not referred to anything else; what are true or false are judgments. He means that the idea of a chimera, for example, is neither true nor false as long as that idea is considered merely in itself; but if I judge that the idea of a chimera, which is within me, is 'similar to or in conformity with' things outside me, then I do something that can be assessed in terms of truth or falsity. We need not go further into Descartes' views about judgment;[3] it is sufficient to note that for him, to judge *involves* having an idea, but is not *the same as* having an idea. Spinoza's use of the term "idea" is quite different. He defines an idea (*E* II, Df. 3) as a "conception" (*conceptus*) of the mind. The explanation that he gives of this term shows that he does not use it in the sense that is normally given to the word "concept": that is, as (roughly) the meaning of a word or phrase.[4] He says that he uses the word *conceptus* in preference to the word *perceptio* because the latter suggests that the mind is in a passive relation to an object, whereas *conceptus* seems to express an action of the mind. Ideas, he says more than once, are not like dumb pictures on a tablet. (*E* II, P43 S; *E* II, P49, S)

What action, then, does Spinoza have in mind? He says that an idea, insofar as it is an idea, involves affirmation or denial. (*E* II, P49, *E* II, P49, S; *cf. E* III, P2, S) By this he means (*cf E* II, P49) that an idea *cannot be conceived* without affirmation or denial. He also asserts in the same proposition that an affirmation or denial involves, i.e., cannot be conceived without, a corresponding idea. He gives as an example the affirmation that the three angles of a triangle equal two right angles; this, he says, involves the idea of a triangle. Conversely, this idea of a triangle involves the affirmation that its three angles equal two right angles.

It is vital not to be misled here by a common sense of the phrase "idea of," namely the sense in which it means "concept of." An idea in Spinoza's sense of the term, it will be recollected, is not a concept in the usual sense,[5] but is an action. Spinoza, then, does not mean that what we would call the concept of a triangle involves an affirmation, and conversely. What he does mean is perhaps best approached gradually. As a first approximation, we may suggest that he is saying that the term "idea of a triangle" and "affirmation that the three angles of a triangle equal two right angles" can be substituted for each other. However, this can hardly be an exact account of what he means. We make many affirmations about triangles, and there is no indication that Spinoza would want to include all these under the head of "the idea of a triangle." His meaning would probably be rendered better if he were taken as saying that the terms "idea of a triangle having its three angles equal to two right angles" and "affirmation that the three angles of a triangle equal two right angles" can be substituted for each other. This interpretation is supported by a remark in *E* II, P49, S, to the effect that to perceive (sc. have an idea of) a winged horse is "to affirm wings of a horse." In sum: although Spinoza regularly uses phrases of the form "the idea of *S*," his meaning would be expressed more clearly by the phrase "the idea of *S* as having a certain predicate, *P*," "the idea of *S*'s being *P*." But it can be expressed still more clearly. Let us take the word "judgment" to mean an act of affirmation or denial. Then we may say that for the phrase "the idea of *S*" we may substitute the phrase "a judgment about *S*"—it being taken for granted that in the act of judging one ascribes a predicate, *P*, to a subject, *S*.[6]

There will be occasion in the next section to say more about Spinoza's use of the term "idea of." For the moment, it will be useful to consider another respect in which what Spinoza says about "ideas" may cause confusion. In *E* II, P17, S, he refers to ideas that "represent external bodies as present to us (*velut nobis praesentia*)." Spinoza calls this way of "contemplating bodies" by the name of "imagination"; an example of it is the "perceiving a winged horse" that was mentioned above. Now, it is clear from what has already been said that we are not to regard these ideas as mental pictures; rather, they must be affirmations or denials of a certain sort.[7] That is, Spinoza's "ideas that represent external bodies as present to us" are not representative ideas, in the sense in which Descartes and Locke may be said to have believed in such ideas; they are actions, rather than entities.

II.

We can now consider what Spinoza says about a true idea. It may be surmised that his views on this topic will be to some extent unusual. An idea, as we saw, is for Spinoza an act; but one does not normally say that an *act* is true. Rather, one ascribes truth to *what* is said or thought, i.e., to a proposition. This surmise, as will be seen later, is justified; but when Spinoza introduces the term "true" in the *Ethics*, he does not give any indication that he is employing it in an unusual sense. He does not define the term, but introduces it in an axiom (*E* I, A6), stating that "A true idea must agree (*convenire*) with that of which it is the idea (*cum suo ideato*)."[8] Spinoza does not, in the *Ethics*, explain the status of his axioms, but it may be assumed that he would have agreed with his friend Lodewijk Meyer, who said in his preface to Spinoza's geometrical version of Descartes' *Principles* (Gebhardt I, 127) that "Postulates and axioms, i.e. the mind's common notions, are statements so clear and evident that all who simply understand correctly the words contained can in no way refuse their assent to them." What Spinoza says in *E* I, A6 would doubtless have reminded the seventeenth-century reader of similar-sounding definitions of truth, both in the medieval scholastics and in the logic manuals of his own day,[9] and he would probably have accepted the axiom without question. But whether he would have "understood correctly the words contained" is, as will be seen, another matter.

When one reads in Spinoza that a true idea must agree with that of which it is the idea, its 'ideatum', it is natural to see in this a form of that theory of truth which is commonly called the "correspondence theory." According to this, truth consists in an agreement, or correspondence, of proposition with fact. But, as has already been seen, an 'idea' in Spinoza is an activity and not a proposition; it is the activity of affirming or denying, of *judging that* such and such is or is not the case. What of the other term of the relation of correspondence, 'ideatum'? To see what this means, it is necessary to investigate a term that Spinoza often uses in its place, namely the phrase "the object of the idea" (*objectum ideae*).[10] In discussing this topic, we will concentrate on finite ideas,[11] and more specifically on the human mind, which according to Spinoza, is a complex idea, composed of very many ideas. (*E* II, P15)[12] Now, Spinoza asserts (*E* II, P13) that "the object of the idea that constitutes the human mind is a body, i.e. a certain mode of extension that actually exists, and nothing else." The question is, how the term "object" is to be taken in this context. We know that for Spinoza an idea is a judgment, i.e., an affirmation or denial, and it would be natural to assume that the object of a judgment is either (1) *what* is affirmed or denied, or (2) that *about which* the judgment is made. So, for example, if I judge that the sun is setting (or, as Spinoza would say, if I have the idea of the setting sun), then the object of my idea would either be (1) the setting of the sun, or (2) the sun. But it is clear that Spinoza cannot mean this by "the object of an idea." He has said that the object of the idea that constitutes a human mind is always a certain body and nothing else; but it would be absurd to suppose that a man is always making judgments about his body or its states.

38

What Spinoza means by an 'ideatum', or "object of an idea," seems rather to be linked with his metaphysical views about the substance-attribute relation. His reasoning may be expressed as follows. Consider the idea that constitutes the mind of a human being, X. This idea is the expression in the attribute of thought of that state of substance of which X's body is the expression in the attribute of extension. (E II, P17, S) Spinoza puts this (see especially E II, P13, S, and E II, P21, S) by saying that the idea in question has for its object the body of X; or, that it is the *idea of* the body of X.[13] This has concerned the idea that *constitutes* the mind of X, an idea that is complex, composed of many ideas. (See above, reference to E II, P15) Spinoza appears to think that the same is true of any one of these component ideas, the ideas which (we say) X 'has'; each is an idea of X's body, or at any rate of a state of that body.[14] Obviously, all this is highly metaphysical, but it may be that Spinoza is making a point that can be detached from his metaphysics. Suppose, for example, that I think that a chimera exists; in Spinoza's terms, I have an idea of a chimera as existing. Now, for me to do so it is not necessary that a chimera should exist—indeed, there are no such creatures. But what has to exist (Spinoza says) is a body, a body in a certain state. So we could roughly paraphrase Spinoza's views about the object of an idea as follows: the object of an idea is what there has to be (other than the idea itself) if there is to be an idea, i.e., if a judgment is to be made.[15]

It will be obvious that the term "idea of" has been used by Spinoza in two very different contexts, and indeed in two very different ways. In Section I, when E II, P49 was discussed, the term was used in such phrases as "the idea of a triangle," where the context was that of someone judging that a triangle has such and such a nature. In the present section, on the other hand, "idea of" has been used in the context of the phrase "the idea of the human body," where it is not meant that anyone is necessarily judging that the human body has such and such a nature; instead, "idea of" means the expression in the attribute of thought of that of which the body is the expression in the attribute of extension. In this sense, "the idea of the body of X" means either the mind of X, or a judgment that X makes.

Spinoza was aware of the fact that the phrase "idea of" was used by him in these different contexts, as E II, P17, S makes clear. Here, he takes as an example "the idea of Peter." He points out that there is one idea of Peter that constitutes the essence of the mind of Peter; this, as explained earlier, is the idea which is the thought-expression of that of which Peter's body is the expression in extension. On the other hand, there is also an idea of Peter that some other man—say, Paul—has. This idea, says Spinoza, "indicates the constitution of the body of Paul rather than the nature of Peter." Such an idea, we may say, is in a sense an idea of Paul's body; yet it is also an idea of Peter, in that it is a judgment made *by* Paul *about* Peter. So much, Spinoza recognizes clearly, but he gives no hint of recognizing that the term "idea of" has different meanings in these different contexts. He speaks of the "difference between" the two ideas of Peter; but he seems to regard these as different members of the same class of ideas of Peter, the one being Peter's and the other Paul's, instead of being ideas of Peter in different senses of "idea of."[16]

We began this inquiry into the phrase "object of an idea," together with the corresponding phrase "idea of," in order to see what Spinoza might mean in saying that a true idea "agrees with" its ideatum, i.e., with its object. We can now give an answer to this question. Let us for the moment disregard the adjective "true," and concentrate simply on the relation between an idea and its object. Now there is indeed a sense in which (in Spinoza's sense of the terms "idea" and "object") an idea may be said to correspond with its object. In E II, P7, S Spinoza says that a mode of extension[17] and the idea of that mode is "one and the same thing, expressed in two ways"; later in the same Scholium, he speaks of one and the same thing being "explained through" different attributes. Now, whatever the obscurities of the subject-attribute relation in Spinoza's philosophy, it is surely clear that a finite mode of extension, i.e., a body, and the idea of that mode may be said to correspond, in that they are different expressions or explanations of the same thing. They correspond somewhat as (say) two different ways of expressing the same thought, or two different ways of explaining the same state of affairs may be said to correspond.[18]

This raises two problems. (1) In explaining the sense of 'correspondence', we have not referred specifically to *true* ideas. It appears, then, that every idea must be true because (apparently) every idea agrees with its object.[19] Yet Spinoza certainly has a use for the term "false idea" (e.g., E II, P35); is he consistent in this?

We shall touch on this problem later; our main concern here, however, is with another problem: (2) Given that not all ideas are true, how are we to tell *when* an idea agrees with its object?

III.

When upholders of the traditional correspondence theory of truth are asked, "How is it known whether a given proposition corresponds with the facts?" they are apt to reply that the theory in question is about the nature, not about the criteria of truth. In *E* II, P43, S, Spinoza poses a similar problem when he asks how a man knows that he has an idea that agrees with its ideatum. His reply is that truth is its own standard; in other words (*E* II, P43), simply by having a true idea, we know that we have such an idea, and cannot doubt of its truth. At the beginning of this paper we mentioned the paradoxical nature of this assertion; it is now time to see whether the paradox can be removed.

Let us suppose that someone (say, Paul) has a "true idea" of Peter. According to Spinoza, Paul must know that he has a true idea of Peter. He must do so, Spinoza says, because (*E* II, P43, S), "To have a true idea simply means (*nihil aliud significat quam*) to know a thing completely (*perfecte*), i.e. in the best way (*optime*)." This is quite clear: to say that has *X* has a true idea of *S means that X* has a complete knowledge of S. We saw earlier (Section I, at p. 37) that when Spinoza speaks of "the idea of S" he means a judgment of the form 'S is P', i.e., of the form "S has such and such a property." A "true idea" of Peter, then, is a judgment that Peter is *P* (i.e., has such and such a property) made *in the complete knowledge that* Peter is *P*. It is now obvious why Spinoza should say that the man who has a true idea knows that he has a true idea. His line of reasoning is that if a man knows a thing completely, he must know *that* he knows it.

Spinoza says of such a person (*E* II, P43, Dm., at end) that he is 'certain' (*certus*). It is hardly necessary to stress that in calling someone "certain," Spinoza does not simply mean that this individual has a *feeling* of certainty; one can have such a feeling without having knowledge. Spinoza returns to this point later in the *Ethics*, when he says (*E* II, P49, S), "When we say that a man assents to what is false, and does not doubt it, we are not thereby saying that he is certain, but only that he does not doubt." Certainty, for Spinoza, does not involve the mere absence of doubt, it involves the logical inability to doubt. The man who has a true idea, he says in the Enunciation of *E* II, P43, *cannot doubt* of its truth.

Let us explore further the consequences of what Spinoza has said. Suppose that someone, *X*, makes the judgment that *S* is *P*, and that *S is P*. It must follow that unless *X* also knows—and knows "in the best way"—that *S* is *P*, then he does not have a true idea of *S*. Spinoza accepts this consequence. In the *Tractatus de Intellectus Emendatione* (*TdIE*, Gebhardt II, 26), he writes:

If someone says that (for example) Peter exists, but does not know that Peter exists, that thought is false—or, if you prefer, is not true—as far as he is concerned, even though Peter really does exist. The proposition (*enunciatio*) "Peter exists" is true only with respect to the man who knows with certainty (*qui certo scit*) that Peter exists.

Spinoza speaks of a "true thought" rather than of a "true idea," but it is clear from the context that the two terms are equivalent here.[20] We may also take it that to "know with certainty" is the same as what is termed in the *Ethics* knowing a thing completely or in the best way. We shall have to ask later (Section IV-V) what this involves; what is of particular interest in this passage, however, is Spinoza's use of the phrase "or, if you prefer, is not true." If I understand him correctly, J. J. McIntosh would say that Spinoza is here anticipating J. L. Austin's view that a speech act may on occasion be neither true nor false, nor meaningless, but "void." In his stimulating paper, "Spinoza's Epistemological Views,"[21] MacIntosh writes: "For Spinoza ideas had, and could not but have, illocutionary forces attached to them. They are, in fact, in this respect at least, on all fours with our 'speech acts'." It will be noticed that MacIntosh does not say that Spinoza's ideas are *the same as* what are now called "speech acts"; and indeed, Spinoza would probably say that these belong to different attributes—the former to the attribute of thought, the latter to the attribute of extension.[22] But he might perhaps say that idea and speech act are expressions in different attributes of the same state of substance, and in this respect ideas would (if MacIntosh is correct) be "on all fours with" what is now called a speech act. Let us now see if this interpretation is correct.

Austin's theory of speech acts is a complex one; for our purposes, however, all that is required is a very rough sketch. Austin is concerned with what is involved in saying something, "in the full sense of 'say.' "[23] To say something, Austin argued, is to do something: it is to utter certain *noises*, to utter certain *words* in a certain construction, and to utter them with a certain *meaning*.[24] Austin calls this the "locutionary act." Now, to perform such an act is in general also to perform an "illocutionary act"[25]; that is, *in* saying something we do something, e.g., we promise, warn, advise, etc. Austin also refers to this as an "illocutionary force," in that our words *have the force* of a promise, warning, etc.[26] Besides this, it often happens that *by* saying something we do something, e.g., we persuade, convince, annoy. Austin calls this a "perlocutionary act."[27] What concerns us here is the illocutionary act. One such act, Austin argues, is the act of stating; that this is so is indicated by such remarks as, "In saying that it was leading to unemployment, I was not warning or protesting: I was simply stating the facts."[28] All this may seem a rather routine matter of classification, but there is more to be said. One assesses an illocutionary act, Austin

42

argued, in terms of its "happiness" or "unhappiness." Suppose, for example, that there is a certain legal transaction in which a certain formula has to be spoken, but that what is actually said on a certain occasion is (although perfectly meaningful) not this formula. In this case, the act would be void, and the utterance would display one form of what Austin calls "unhappiness." Or again, suppose that the correct words are uttered, but that the person who utters them does not have the right to do so, for example, the words that would be correctly used to bequeath a certain object are used by someone who has no right to make such a bequest. Once again, this would be a case of an utterance that is "unhappy," a case of "infelicity." Now let us consider stating, and more specifically, the example given by Spinoza. Let us suppose that someone says, "Peter exists," but that he does not know that Peter exists; he is just hazarding a guess. Let us suppose, further, that Peter does exist. Now, there are many cases in which, when X says that p, and p is the case, we would assert that what X says is true. But not (Austin would argue) in this case. It is, he says, "important to take the speech-situation as a whole,"[29] and taking it as a whole, we would say that the person in question *cannot* state that Peter exists—meaning by this that he is not *in a position* to state it, has no *right* to state it. What he says is neither true nor false; but neither, on the other hand, is it meaningless. Rather, it should be called "void," just as the putative bequest that was mentioned just now would be called "null and void."[30]

Now, is this the point that Spinoza is making when he says that this utterance (or rather, the idea that goes with it) is "false—or, if you prefer, is not true"? Certainly, he would have us consider what Austin calls "the speech-situation as a whole"; the proposition[31] that Peter exists is true only in respect of *a certain type of person. Further*, a person of this type *has the right* to state that Peter exists in that he *knows* that Peter exists. Despite these similarities, there are great differences between Austin and Spinoza here. Spinoza's "idea" which "is not true" is not, after all, to be compared with Austin's "void" utterance. For Austin, the falsity of an utterance does not make it void; a person may have the right to make a statement, and yet be wrong, just as, in a corresponding way, someone may have the right to give an order to another, but may give an order which in the circumstances (a battle, say) is the wrong order.[32] For Spinoza, on the other hand, the only question is, "Is the assertion that S is P made by X in the complete knowledge that S is P?" If the answer is no, then X's judgment is not a true idea. The distinction suggested between a false idea and a not-true idea is not between a genuine and a void utterance, but between two types of the judgment that S is P made by people who do not have complete knowledge that S is P, the difference between the two types being that in one case S is P and in the other it is not.[33]

What, then, is behind Spinoza's theory of the true idea? What problems does it try to solve? In saying that the man who has a true idea knows that he has a true idea, Spinoza is expressly (E II, P43, S) opposing one theory of the nature of ideas to another—the theory that says that an idea is an act of thought, and the theory that says that it is a kind of picture. Spinoza's argument for the superiority of his theory seems to be that only by the theory of the idea as act can we account for the fact that we have knowledge. If (Spinoza argues)[34] it is said that truth consists in the agreement of idea with reality, much as a faithful picture of something resembles its subject, then there is no answer to the question, "How can we know that this agreement holds?" For clearly, we cannot get outside thought, to compare a thought-picture with its subject. The solution is to abandon the picture-view of the idea, and to say that a judgment that S is P, made in the complete knowledge that S is P, is *its own* standard.

It may perhaps be asked why Spinoza should say that a true *idea* (that is, a judgment of a certain sort) is its own standard, instead of saying that knowledge is its own standard. In fact, he does make the latter assertion, saying in Chapter 3 of the *Tractatus Theologico-Politicus* (TTP, Gebhardt III, 30) that knowledge (*cognitio*) needs no sign. However, it seems fair to suppose that he would have regarded the formulation contained in the *Ethics* as more precise, and for the following reason. In his treatise on method, he warns against thinking in terms of abstractions. (*TdIE*, Gebhardt II, 28–9, 34–5) Now, it may well be his view that to speak of someone's knowledge just *is* to speak of his ideas; X's knowledge, in other words, has no existence outside X's ideas.

We can now add a few remarks about falsity, as Spinoza understands it. As we have seen, to have a true idea of S is to judge that S is P when S is P, and in the complete knowledge that S is P. In the *De Intellectus Emendatione*, Spinoza seems to consider having separate terms for two types of judgment that S is P, made without the complete knowledge that S is P. If S *is* P, then he seems prepared to call the idea of S 'not-true'; if S is not P, then he seems to suggest that the idea of S should be called 'false'. In the *Ethics*, however, there is no trace of this. If an idea is not true, then it is false. Falsity is defined in the *Ethics* in terms of a lack of knowledge; more exactly, it is said to consist in "the privation of knowledge, which inadequate—that is, mutilated and confused—ideas involve." (E II, P35) The full meaning of this assertion will not yet be clear, in that the terms "inadequate" and "mutilated and confused" have still to be discussed. However, it is at any rate clear that to have a false idea of S is to judge that S is P without the complete knowledge that S is P—whether S really is P or not. This means that, in Spinoza's sense of the term "false idea," (1) to judge that S is P when S is not P is to have a false idea of S, for in such a case we cannot be said to know that S is P. But (2) to judge that S is P when S is P may *sometimes* be to have a false idea of S, namely, when the judgment is made without the complete knowledge that S is P. In sum: to judge that S is P, when S is P, is for Spinoza a necessary but not a sufficient condition of having a true idea of S. The relations between what Spinoza would call a "false idea" and what would normally be called falsity are easily seen. By virtue of (1) above, Spinoza would not count as a true idea what would in ordinary usage be called the assertion of a false proposition. But by virtue of (2), he would say that what would in ordinary usage be called the assertion of a true proposition may be a false idea.³⁵

Early in Section II, reference was made to one respect in which Spinoza's theory of the true idea differs from traditional correspondence theories of truth. Such theories see truth as an agreement of proposition with fact; Spinoza speaks of the agreement of an idea (namely, an act of judgment) with its object, where (as explained later in Section II) the object of an idea is what there must be, apart from the idea itself, if there is to be an idea. It can now be seen that there is another important difference. Some philosophers have seen the kernel of the traditional correspondence theory of truth in Aristotle's remark³⁶ that "To say of what is that it is, and of what is not that it is not, is true." But it has now become clear that one can judge that S is P, when S is P, and yet one's idea may be what Spinoza calls "false," namely, when the judgment is not made in the complete knowledge that S is P.

IV.

What has been said so far leaves one important question unanswered. We have said that, for Spinoza, to have a true idea means "to know a thing completely i.e. in the best way." (*E* II, P43, S) But what *is* it to know a thing in this way? Spinoza's reply can be given briefly, although a full explanation of it would be far from brief. To have a true idea is to know a thing either by what Spinoza calls the second kind of knowledge ("reason") or the third kind ("intuitive knowledge"); to have a false idea is to know a thing by the first kind of knowledge ("imagination"). This is shown by *E* II, P41 and 42. As has been seen, Spinoza holds that a true idea is the standard of both truth and falsity. (*E* II,

P43, S) In *E* II, P42, he says that it is knowledge of the second and third kinds that teaches us to distinguish the true from the false, from which it follows that to have a true idea is to have knowledge of the second or third kind. It is knowledge of the first kind that (as Spinoza puts it in *E* II, P41) is the sole cause of falsity, by which he seems to mean that it is the *formal* cause of falsity, i.e., that the first kind of knowledge *consists* of false ideas.[37]

A full discussion of all this is beyond the scope of the present paper; however, perhaps enough can be said to outline what Spinoza means, and also to throw light on the problem (problem (2) of those mentioned at the end of Section II) of how, in the light of what he says about correspondence, Spinoza can account for the existence of false ideas.

In order to follow Spinoza's account, it is necessary first to say something about two terms that he uses constantly in expounding his theory of knowledge: these are the terms "inadequate idea," of which mention was made at the end of the last section, and its opposite, "adequate idea." Spinoza says in *E* II, Df. 4 that "By an 'adequate idea' I understand an idea which, insofar as it is considered in itself without relation to the object, has all the properties or intrinsic denominations of a true idea." He adds: "I say intrinsic to exclude that denomination of a true idea which is extrinsic, namely the agreement of the idea with its ideatum." In other words: a true idea has both intrinsic and extrinsic denominations, that is, it has both what would now be called one-place (i.e., nonrelational) and many-place (i.e., relational) predicates. An adequate idea simply is a true idea, shorn of its relational predicates, of which the only one that Spinoza mentions is that of agreeing with its object.[38] Similarly, an inadequate idea simply is a false idea, without the relational predicate of nonagreement with its object. Clearly, a fuller understanding of adequate and inadequate ideas will give us a fuller understanding of what it is to have a true or a false idea.

As may be expected, Spinoza says (*E* II, P41) that all inadequate ideas belong to the first kind of knowledge, whereas adequate ideas belong to knowledge of the second and third kinds. Our main concern here is with adequacy and truth; however, Spinoza's views about these are made clearer, by way of contrast, by what he says about inadequate ideas. Let us being, then, by asking what it is to call an idea "inadequate." We have seen already that an inadequate idea is "mutilated and confused" (*E* II, P35, quoted in Section III);[39] Spinoza also speaks simply of "confused ideas." (*E* II, P28) What is meant by this is perhaps most easily seen from *E* II, P25–8, where Spinoza discusses that type of the first kind of knowledge that would now be called "sense-perception."[40] To simplify the issue, and also relate it to an example given previously, let us consider a case in which Paul sees Peter; let us suppose that he really does see Peter, i.e., that Peter exists in the place where and at the time at which Paul judges him to exist. Spinoza would view the situation in the following way. Paul has an idea of Peter, in that he makes a judgment about Peter; but this idea is also the idea of Paul's body, in that it is the thought-expression of that of which Paul's body is the extensional expression. More precisely, it is the idea of Paul's body *as determined by* an external body (*E* II, P25), that of Peter; that is, it is the idea of a body whose sense-organs are affected in a certain way by Peter's body. Now, Peter's body is not Paul's body, and Peter's body has an idea in just the same sence that Paul's body has, i.e., both Paul and Peter are thinking beings. But this idea of Peter's body is not in God insofar as God constitutes the mind of Paul (*cf. E* II, P25), and, "When we say that God has this or that idea, not only in so far as he constitutes the nature of the human mind, but also insofar as he has the idea of another thing at the same time as the human mind, then we say that the human mind perceives the thing partially (*exparte*), i.e. inadequately." (*E* II, P11, C) Paul's idea of Peter, then, must be inadequate.

There is much here that is obscure, but it is at any rate clear that Paul's idea of Peter would be called inadequate because it is only partial, i.e., incomplete; it is not the infinite idea (*cf. E* I, P21) that God has. But what exactly does Paul's idea lack? In what precise way is it "mutilated and confused"? A phrase in *E* II, P28 gives us a valuable clue. Here, Spinoza says that confused ideas are "like consequences without premises." Applying this to our example, we may interpret the inadequacy of Paul's idea of Peter in the following way. Paul sees Peter: that is, there occurs in Paul's body a physical process which cannot be explained without reference to Peter's body, which affects the body of Paul,[41] and corresponding to which Paul has a certain idea, namely the judgment that Peter exists. Now, Spinoza would say that although Peter really does exist, Paul (insofar as he merely perceives Peter) knows nothing about the physical processes involved, still less does he know anything about the metaphysical basis of perception, i.e., Spinoza's theory of substance and its attributes. It is in this sense that Paul does not "know a thing completely, i.e. in the best way," and so does not have a true idea.[42] Summing up, one could say that a man who has inadequate ideas of the type discussed does not *understand* what he perceives. In this connection, it is significant that when Spinoza describes the active nature of an idea (he seems to mean, a *true* idea) in *E* II, P43, S, he says that it is a "mode of thinking (*cogitandi*), namely, understanding (*ipsum intelligere*)."

In the example just considered, the inadequate idea was the assertion of a proposition that would normally be called "true"; what made it inadequate was the fact that the person making the judgment lacked a full understanding of what is involved. Sometimes, however, an inadequate idea involves the assertion of what would normally be called a false proposition. An example of this is to be found in E II, P35, S, in which Spinoza discusses falsity. Men, he says, are wrong in thinking themselves free. Now, Spinoza thinks that men are *not* free, but he still says that the falsity of the judgment in question consists in a lack of knowledge. What he means is that men are indeed conscious of their actions; a man judges, on the basis of his self-awareness, that he performs various actions, and he does indeed perform various actions. To this extent, then, the man judges that S is P, when S is P. It is because he is ignorant of the *causes* of his actions—i.e., does not know that, or how, they can be explained—that his judgment, "My actions are free," is an inadequate idea. In other words: what makes the judgment "My actions are free" an inadequate idea is not so much the fact that my actions are not free (although indeed they are not free), as the fact that the judgment issues from a lack of understanding of the nature of human actions.

To conclude this account of inadequate ideas, let us return to an earlier problem. In Section II it was asked: if a true idea must agree with its ideatum, while at the same time *every* idea agrees with its ideatum, how can any idea be false? The answer is provided by what we have just seen about inadequate ideas. When Spinoza says things that imply that every idea agrees with its ideatum, we are to understand by 'idea' one that is *not* mutilated and confused, i.e., an idea that he calls "complete (*perfecta*) or (less helpfully) "clear and distinct."[43] In this way, he leaves room for false ideas, because not every idea is complete.[44]

V.

We are now faced with the question, "In what sense is an adequate idea *not* mutilated and confused; i.e., in what sense is it 'complete'?" Let us consider briefly one possible answer, and then suggest another. There is a strong temptation to see Spinoza as holding, or at any rate as tending toward, a coherence theory of truth of the idealist type. For the coherence theorist, "The true" (in Hegel's famous phrase[45]) "is the whole"; similarly, it may seem that a complete idea in Spinoza must be only *one* idea, namely the knowledge of the whole of reality. What is more, Spinoza's account of the three kinds of knowledge seems to follow the general pattern of Hegelian dialectics. The first kind of knowledge, 'imagination', gives us some kind of knowledge of particulars, but is knowledge of a low grade, in that it does not involve any grasp of the universality and necessity that must attach to knowledge. Knowledge of the second kind, 'reason', does indeed provide knowledge of what is universal and necessary (*cf. E* V, P36, S), but it is defective by virtue of its abstractness; what it grasps "constitutes," in Spinoza's phrase, "the essence of no particular thing." (*E* II, P37) Only the third kind of knowledge, 'intuitive knowledge', proceeding "from the adequate idea of the formal essence of some of the attributes of God to the adequate knowledge of the essence of thing" (*E* II, P40, S2) has the concreteness of the first kind (without its lack of universality) and the universality of the second (without its abstractness).

I have argued elsewhere against this interpretation;[46] here, I shall concentrate on just one aspect of the issue that is relevant to this paper. A true idea, as has been seen, is its own standard. It follows that if the coherence interpretation of Spinoza is correct, then only the third kind of knowledge—the only kind which provides us with a genuinely true idea—can teach us to distinguish the true from the false. But, as has also been seen, this is not what Spinoza says; in his view, both the second and the third kinds of knowledge teach us how to do this.[47]

What, then, is a complete idea? Since inadequate ideas are said to be "like consequences without premises," complete ideas may be thought to be consequences *with* premises. So, sometimes, they are; but it will be seen shortly that one needs a wider concept of completeness than this.

(1) If the knowledge is of the second kind, 'reason', one has a complete idea if:

(a) One's idea is a judgment that one makes on the grounds that it is a self-evident axiom. (On the self-evidence of axioms, compare Section II, p. 38). These axioms will either be what Spinoza calls "common notions" or they will be "adequate ideas of the properties of things." (*E* II, P40, S2) The former, which are said to be "the bases of our reasoning" (*E* II, P40, S1), appear to be axioms of absolutely universal application (*E* II, P38), whereas the latter seem to be of only limited application, holding, e.g., only of bodies of a certain degree of complexity. This latter sort will be true, say, of all *human* bodies, but not of all *bodies*, in the sense of physical objects of whatever kind.[48]

(b) One also has a complete idea if one derives one's judgment from another whose axiomatic nature one grasps—if, in other words, one's idea is a consequence *with* its premises. This is shown by *E* II, P40, which states that the ideas that follow from adequate ideas are them-

49

selves adequate,[49] and also by the example of 'reason' given in *E* II, P40, S2. Here, Spinoza refers to someone who derives the truth that 1 is to 2 as 3 is to 6 from a theorem of Euclid (Book 7, Prop. 19); we are doubtless to understand that that idea in turn is true insofar as the proposition is derived from Euclid's axioms, which will be examples of what Spinoza calls "common notions."

(2) Let us now briefly consider knowledge of the third kind, 'intuitive knowledge'. As mentioned already, such knowledge "proceeds from the adequate idea of the formal essence of some of the attributes of God to the adequate knowledge of the essence of things." (*E* II, P40, S2) An example of what is meant here is contained in *E* V, P36, S, where Spinoza refers to the way in which it is known that the human mind depends on God. The problem is that in *E* II, P40, S2 Spinoza seems to say that in the third kind of knowledge, no process of inference is involved; it is, he says, like *seeing* the answer to the problem, "What is to 3 as 2 is to 1?" Yet he also says that in this kind of knowledge, something "proceeds" *from* something *to* something. Perhaps the answer to the problem is that Spinoza is drawing a distinction between *inferring* something, "performing an operation" as he says in the *De Intellectus Emendatione* (*TdIE*, Gebhardt II, 12), and *seeing* the essence of a concrete thing *as following from* God.[50]

A 'complete idea', then, may be of any one of these three types. What is it, then, that these ideas have in common, such that it may be called 'completeness'? Perhaps we may say that anyone who has an idea belonging to any one of these types has *sufficient reason* for asserting what he does assert. His idea is complete in that nothing that is relevant to its justification is left out. But, as already indicated, this does not mean that absolutely nothing is left out, i.e., that the complete idea is all-inclusive.

Let us, in conclusion, consider briefly the relation of Spinoza's theory of the true idea to his philosophy as a whole. It has been seen that in speaking of the nature of the true idea, Spinoza is not discussing what philosophers have commonly regarded as the problem of truth; his concern is with understanding, rather than with truth as such (*cf.* Section IV above). The reason for this concern is, without doubt, to be found in the predominantly ethical tendency of his work—a tendency that is displayed, not only in the *Ethics* (where it may be expected), but also in his treatise on method, the *Tractatus de Intellectus Emendatione*. The *Ethics*, as is well known, culminates in a discussion of the nature of human freedom; and the free man, for Spinoza, is not one who can merely recite a string of true propositions, but is a man who *understands* nature, and in understanding nature, understands himself.

It is also well known that the *Tractatus de Intellectus Emendatione* begins with an expression of what may be called a moral concern; Spinoza says that he has found that everyday life is vain and futile, and asks if there is a true good, which will bring eternal joy. Although the *Tractatus* is incomplete, it is clear that the 'true good' does not lie in the mere accumulation of new truths; it lies in seeing things in relation to God (*cf. TdIE*, Gebhardt II, 16–7), i.e., in what may be called the acquisition of understanding. In examining Spinoza's account of the true idea, then, we have examined a key idea, not only of his theory of knowledge, but of his philosophy in general.

NOTES

1. The English translations of Spinoza's works cited here are my own.

2. Descartes, *Oeuvres*, ed. Adam and Tannery, Vol. VII, p. 37; *Philosophical Works*, trans. Haldane and Ross (2nd ed., Cambridge, 1934), Vol. I, p. 159.

3. One may ask what, according to Descartes, it is to judge that an idea is "in conformity with" reality. In Princ. Phil. I 34, Descartes says that judgment presupposes both intellect and will: intellect, because we cannot judge about an object that we do not perceive, and will, so that we may assent to what has been in some manner perceived. This is confused. If we take the object perceived to be an idea in the sense just mentioned—e.g., the idea or mental image of a chimera—then it does not seem true to say that we assent to, or dissent from, the idea of a chimera. Perhaps, however, Descartes thinks of the intellect as entertaining a *proposition* (e.g., the proposition that chimeras exist) which it presents, as it were, to the will for its acceptance or rejection.

4. *Cf., e.g.*, Leibniz, *Introductio ad Encyclopaediam Arcanam* (c. 1679): in *Opuscules et fragments inédits*, ed. L. Couturat, Paris, 1903, p. 512.

5. In *E* II, P49, Spinoza does speak of a "conceptus sive idea," but it will be recalled that in his usage, the term "conceptus" refers to an *action*. (*E* II, Df. 3)

6. As is well known, the term "judgment" is often used to refer to *what* is asserted or denied, i.e., to what is commonly called a proposition or statement. It must be emphasized that here it is used solely to refer to a certain *act*. For the connection between the 'idea' and the subject-predicate form of judgment, compare *TdIE*, Gebhardt II, 24: "a conception; that is, an idea, i.e. (*sive*) the coherence of subject and predicate in the mind."

It must be added that there are passages in the *TdIE* where 'idea' seems most naturally rendered by our term "concept": e.g., the account of the idea of the globe in Gebhardt II, 27 or of the idea of quantity in Gebhardt II, 39. It may be conjectured that this uncertainty about the term "idea" was one reason why Spinoza abandoned the *TdIE*.

7. We say "of a certain sort," because there are also affirmations and denials that are the work of pure thought. In such cases we exercise, not the imagination, but what Spinoza calls the "intellect" (e.g., *E* I, P15, S).

8. The term "ideatum" was used by some Scholastics to refer to something produced by God as a copy of the idea that he had. E.g., Chauvin, *Lexicon Rationale* (1690) says that, "An idea is an exemplar, to which the agent looks by its intellect in producing an ideatum." (Quoted by L. Robinson, *Kommentar zu*

Spinozas Ethik, Leipzig, 1928, p. 90 n.) It will be noted that the term "idea" here has its Platonic sense of an exemplar or pattern, which is very different from Spinoza's sense of the term. As often, Spinoza employs old terminology, but gives it a new meaning.

9. See, e.g., Aquinas, Sum. Theol. I, Qu 16, Art. 1; Art 2, Obj. 2. Similar remarks may be found in the seventeenth-century logic manuals of Burgersdijck and Clauberg (*see* Robinson, *op. cit.*, p. 90; also M. Gueroult, *Spinoza*, Vol. I (Paris, 1968), p. 101, n. 84).

10. For this equivalence, compare *E* II, P13 ("objectum ideae . . . est corpus") with Ep. 64 (Gebhardt IV, 277), "ejus ideatum, nempe corpus." See also the Dutch version of *E* II, P43 S, which was based on an early draft of the *Ethics*. Here, Spinoza probably wrote originally "quae cum suo objecto sive cum suo ideato convenit."

11. Ignoring, that is to say, the "infinite idea of God." *E* II, P8 and C; *cf. E* I, P21; *E* II, P3–4; *E* V, P14) There will be occasion to touch on this topic in the discussion of inadequate ideas in Section IV. (See the references there to *E* II, P25.)

12. For Spinoza, then, the mind is not a substance that has ideas; the mind is a (complex) idea. This throws some additional light on his definition of "idea" in *E* II, Df. 3. He says there that an idea is "a concept of the mind, that the mind forms on account of the fact that it is a thinking thing." We spoke in Section I of the term "concept" in Spinoza; we may add now that as the mind is really nothing other than its ideas, the word "forms" (*format*) should be taken in the sense of a formal cause.

13. For this phrase, see, e.g., *E* II, P13, S; *E* II, P17; *E* II, P21, S.

14. Because there is an infinity of attributes, it seems to follow that each idea will have an infinity of objects. However, Spinoza's view is that the object of that idea that is the human mind just is the human body. Each thing, he writes to Tschirnhaus (Ep. 66), is expressed in infinite ways in the infinite intellect of God; but these ideas do not constitute one and the same mind.

15. It should be added that it appears from *E* II, P21 that not every object of our ideas is a body. The human mind, Spinoza says here, can also think of itself, and in this case the idea that is the mind has the mind as its object. It is not the idea of a body, but is the "idea of an idea." But Spinoza seems doubtful as to whether an idea is an object of an idea in the same sense that a body is. In the Scholium to *E* II, P21 he says that the idea of the mind (i.e., the idea of an idea) is nothing but the "form of an idea," insofar as it is considered "without relation to an object." Here, "object" must surely refer to the human body. Perhaps Spinoza was conscious of having said earlier (*E* II, P13) that the object of the idea constituting the human mind is a body, *and nothing else.*

16. This point has often been made: see, e.g., F. Pollock, *Spinoza, his life and philosophy*, 2nd ed., London, 1899, pp. 123–26; H. Barker, "Notes on the second part of Spinoza's *Ethics*," *Mind*, 47 (1938), p. 295. (*Cf.* S. P. Kashap (ed.), *Studies in Spinoza*, Berkeley, 1972, pp. 137, 168.) Spinoza could of course say (*cf. E* II, P17) that for Paul to have an idea of Peter is for there to be an idea which is the correlate in thought of Paul's body as modified by Peter. This appears to be the point made by H. F. Hallett, in his article "On a Reputed Equivoque in the Philosophy of Spinoza"; Kashap, *op. cit.*, pp. 168ff., esp. p. 182. But this (as Hallett fails to see) does not affect the fact that when Spinoza speaks of "Paul's idea of Peter" he uses the term "idea of" in a sense different from that

which it has when he speaks of the idea of Paul's body which is the essence of Paul's mind. To put this in another way: suppose that Paul's idea of Peter is the judgment that Peter is a fisherman. In this case, Paul does not judge that his body is modified by Peter's, although (according to Spinoza) it is *because* his body is modified by Peter's that he judges as he does.

17. It will be recalled that a body is a mode of extension: *cf*. *E* II, P13, cited earlier in this section (p. 38), and *E* II, Df. 1. But not every mode of extension is a finite mode, and so not every mode of extension is a body.

18. This has concerned those cases in which the object of an idea is a body. As mentioned in note 15, an idea may also be said to correspond with its object when that object is another idea. In such cases, "one and the same thing" is expressed, not through different attributes, but through the one attribute of thought.

19. In my *Spinoza's Theory of Knowledge* (Oxford, 1954, p. 113; also in Kashap, *op. cit.*, p. 213), I argued for this conclusion on the basis of the premise that "When Spinoza speaks of a true idea as 'agreeing with' its *ideatum*, he means that it *is* its *ideatum* expressed through the attribute of thought." I now think that this is not quite accurate. It presupposes that the *ideatum* is substance; and so, in the last analysis, it is. But what Spinoza means is rather that the *ideatum* is substance *as expressed through an attribute*.

20. Later, in this same paragraph, he goes on to speak of a "true idea" without any indication of a change in sense. *Cf. TdIE*, Gebhardt II, 28: "cogitationes, sive ideas."

21. See G.N.A. Vesey (ed.), *Reason and Reality* (Royal Institute of Philosophy Lectures, 1970–71, London, 1972), p. 38.

22. On the relation between thought and language in Spinoza, see my "Language and Knowledge in Spinoza," *Inquiry*, 12 (1969), p. 21; also in Marjorie Grene (ed), *Spinoza* (New York, 1973), p. 79.

23. J. L. Austin, *How to Do Things with Words*, (Oxford, 1962), p. 92 (hereafter, *HTD*).

24. *HTD*, p. 94.

25. *HTD*, p. 98.

26. *HTD*, p. 99.

27. *HTD*, p. 101.

28. *HTD*, p. 133.

29. *HTD*, p. 137.

30. In Austin's technical terminology, it is a "misapplication," which is a special type of "misinvocation." In the case of a misapplication, there exists a certain accepted type of procedure, which involves the utterance of certain words; however, although the words uttered are the right ones, the person or the circumstances involved are not right (*HTD*, pp. 14ff.).

31. I translate *enunciatio* as "proposition" because the term has a certain generality. An 'idea' in Spinoza is always an idea possessed by (or constituting) this or that mind; but *the same* "enunciatio" may be uttered by various people, just as (in modern usage) various people can assert the same proposition.

32. *HTD*, p. 137.

33. It is interesting that, in the *Ethics*, Spinoza gives another example of what Austin would call the "infelicity" of an utterance. Mention was made in note 24 of "misinvocation"; this is a sub-form of that type of infelicity that Austin calls a "misfire." The other sub-form consists of "misexecutions" (*HTD*, p. 18), e.g.,

the use of a wrong formula in law (*HTD*, 35–36), or of saying something that one does not really mean by using the wrong sentence. (*HTD*, 137) In *E* II, P47, S Spinoza mentions such a case, when he refers to a man whom he had heard exclaiming that his yard had flown into his neighbor's hen. He observes that we do not believe that such a man was in error; but he does not say that the man's utterance was void. What he says is that the man's intention (*ipsius mens*) was clear enough.

34. See especially *E* II, P43 S, "Quod denique ultimum attinet . . . ."

35. In *Spinoza's Theory of Knowledge*, p. 124 (Kashap, *op. cit.*, p. 223), I assumed that a false idea of *S* must always involve the judgment that *S* is *P*, when *S* is not *P*; consequently, I argued that a true idea must not only supply what a false idea lacks, but must also negate it. This overlooks the fact that an idea of *S* can be false when it is judged that *S* is *P*, and *S* is *P*, but the judgment is not made in the complete knowledge that *S* is *P*. In such a case, a true idea of *S* would not negate the judgment that *S* is *P*.

36. *Metaphysics*, 1011b 27, trans. W. D. Ross. *Cf.* A. Tarski, "The Semantic Conception of Truth," in H. Feigl and W. Sellars (eds.), *Readings in Philosophical Analysis* (New York, 1949), p. 54.

37. This is why it is important to stress that to have a true idea involves *complete* knowledge. Imagination is a kind of knowledge, but it comprises nothing but false ideas.

38. *Cf.* Ep. 60 (to Tschirnhaus, Jan. 1675), in which Spinoza observes that there is no difference between a true and an adequate idea, except for what he calls the "extrinsic relation" of correspondence.

39. *Cf. E* V, P28; also *E* II, P29, C ("confused and mutilated knowledge"), and *TdIE* (Gebhardt II, 28) ("mutilated and truncated thoughts").

40. On sense-perception as a type of imagination, see also *E* II, P17, S.

41. There seems to be a reference to this in *E* II, P25. When Spinoza explains there why the idea of an external body is inadequate, he says that this idea is in God "in so far as God is considered as affected by the idea of another thing, which is prior in nature to the external body." He appeals here to Eth. II 9, which is stated in causal terms.

42. Compare *TdIE*, Gebhardt, 30, in which Spinoza cites the case of a man who "knows that the senses have at some time deceived him, but knows this only confusedly—for he does not know *how* the senses deceive." This is a good example of what Spinoza would call a "conclusion without a premiss." (On the topic of "confusion," compare *TdIE*, Gebhardt, 24).

43. "Complete," *E* II, P34, 46; "Clear and distinct," *E* II, P28; *TdIE*, Gebhardt, 24. In *E* II, Df. 6, Spinoza says that he understands by "perfection," "reality." But in the present context, the word "complete" (a standard sense of the word "perfectus") seems to give his meaning more adequately. In calling the term "clear and distinct" "less helpful," what is meant is that it is not explained by Spinoza exactly what this term means; in particular, how (if at all) it differs from "complete."

44. When Spinoza speaks of a "true" idea, does he perhaps mean a *genuine* idea? Again, is a "false" idea merely a pseudo-idea? Certainly, "verus" can mean "genuine," but there is no hint in the *Ethics* of a distinction between genuine ideas and pseudo-ideas. False ideas are *ideas*, but ideas which are incomplete. It is also worth noting that in *Cogitata Metaphysica*, I, 6 (Gebhardt I, 246), Spinoza rejects as illegitimate the use of such phrases as "true" or "false" gold. For him, an

54

idea is true if it "shows us a thing as it is objectively (*utin se est*)" and false if it "shows us a thing as other than it really is (*quam revera est*)." The *CM* is an early work, but Spinoza did not reject it completely in his later years. (Cf. *Spinoza's Theory of Knowledge*, p. 6.)

45. *Phänomenologie des Geistes*, ed. J. Hoffmeister (6th ed. Hamburg 1952), p. 21. For a Hegelian interpretation of Spinoza's views on truth, see e.g. H. H. Joachim, *A Study of the Ethics of Spinoza* (Oxford, 1901), pp. 146–52.

46. *Spinoza's Theory of Knowledge*, pp. 114ff.; Kashap, *op. cit.*, pp. 214ff.

47. Section IV, p. 46, quoting *E* II, P42.

48. *Spinoza's Theory of Knowledge*, pp. 164–66; see also my "Being and Knowledge in Spinoza," in J. G. van der Bend (ed.), *Spinoza on Knowing, Being and Fredom* (Assen, 1974), p. 36. "Common notions" and "adequate ideas of the properties of things" are what correspond (in Spinoza's sense of the term) in the attribute of thought to certain features of the attribute of extension, which he calls respectively "what is common to all" (*E* II, P38) and "what is common and proper to the human body and certain external bodies by which it is often affected." (*E* II, P39) Roughly, Spinoza's view is that although the finite human mind can never be identical with God's infinite mind, any more than the finite human body can be identical with the attribute of extension, yet there are certain respects in which the fact of this finitude is irrelevant to our knowledge. If, for example, the human body has motion and rest in common with all bodies (as it has), then the idea that the human being has of motion and rest will not differ from God's, i.e., must be adequate (*E* II, P38, and Lemma 2 after *E* II, P13)

49. See also *E* V, P12: "The things that we clearly and distinctly understand are either the common properties of things, or what are deduced from them."

50. In my *Spinoza's Theory of Knowledge*, pp. 183ff., I argued that because intuitive knowledge proceeds from God to the individual, it must be a kind of inference. I now think that this does not do justice to the difference between the second and third kinds of knowledge. It is hardly necessary to stress the difficulty of explaining the nature of the third kind of knowledge, or the tentative nature of the interpretation that is offered here. In support of this interpretation, it may be pointed out that it relates intuitive knowledge to a view put forward by a philosopher whom we know Spinoza to have studied, namely, Descartes. Descartes insists that "Cogito, ergo sum" is not an inference—more specifically, it is not a syllogistic inference—but it something known by a simple mental intuition (*simplici mentis intuitu*) ('Reply to Second Objections': *Oeuvres*, ed. Adam and Tannery, Vol. VII, p. 140; *Philosophical Works*, trans. Haldane and Ross, Vol. II, p. 38). It is not suggested that Spinoza would count "Cogito, ergo sum" as an example of the third kind of knowledge; for example it is not obvious how, in Descartes' proposition, one proceeds from a knowledge of God to a knowledge of the essence of things. Nevertheless, there are striking similarities. As has been seen, "Cogito, ergo sum" is for Descartes an intuition and not an inference; further, in asserting the proposition one "proceeds" (as Spinoza might say) *from* something *to* something. These similarities may not be very deep; the exact nature of the "intuition" in "Cogito, ergo sum" is still a matter of controversy, but it seems unlikely that it is the same as Spinoza's "intuitive knowledge," which Spinoza seems to regard, not as proving the existence of anything, but rather as saying something about the *nature* of what exists. Nevertheless, the similarities exist, and they seem enough to enable us to place Spinoza's views about intuitive knowledge within a wider philosophical context.

Spinoza's Use of "Idea"

S. PAUL KASHAP
University of California, Santa Cruz

The word "idea" is used by Spinoza in so many different ways that an attempt to understand it literally in terms of his definition of an idea as "a conception of the mind which the mind forms because it is a thinking thing" (*E* II, Df. 3) leads to nothing but confusion. Such confusion can be and needs to be avoided by making some crucial distinctions to which I wish to draw attention in this paper.

Consider, for instance, Spinoza's statement, "In God there necessarily exists the idea of His essence, and of all things which necessarily follow from His essence." (*E* II, P3) Here, by "idea" he does not and cannot mean straightforwardly, "conception of the mind which the mind forms because it is a thinking thing." Spinoza's God is not a thing that thinks in the sense in which a human being is a thing that thinks. When Spinoza says, "God is a thinking thing," this means no more than what he says in the same proposition, namely, "Thought is an attribute of God." (*E* II, P1) Thought constitutes the *essence* of God, but it is *not a property* ascribable to God. It would be senseless to expect Thought, an attribute, to form conceptions. What sense is to be made, then, of his statement in E II, P3? It can only mean that to say 'The essence of God consists in the attribute of thought,' is the same thing as to say 'In God there necessarily exists the idea of His essence.' And this latter must not be understood in such a way as to render God as an anthropomorphic entity believed, therefore, to have ideas which are conceptions of His mind. All it means is that Thought forms a necessary part of the nature of reality that is being referred to by the term 'substance' or 'God'.

The word "idea" as it occurs in *E* II, P3 is to be understood, in fact, in the sense in which Spinoza uses it in *E* II, P4, in saying, "The idea of God, from which infinite numbers of things follow in infinite ways, can be one only." 'The idea of God' is the same thing, that is to say, as His essence or "the necessity of the divine nature" (*E* I, P16), from which infinite numbers of things are said to follow in infinite ways. As the essence of God is identical with the Attributes, Spinoza wishes to specify, by the use of the word "idea" in respect to God, reference to *one* of the attributes which constitute the nature of Substance—namely to Thought, and to no other.

'Idea' also refers to that of which the idea in an individual mind is an idea, that is to say, to a particular object of thnking, which is a concept or (in the terminology of the period) an objective idea, and which I prefer to call a 'thought-object'. An 'idea' in this sense is quite independent of being thought *of* by any finite individual mind. This is the sense in which the word "idea" occurs in, for example, *E* II, P49, Dm., where Spinoza says that when the mind affirms that the three angles of a triangle are equal to two right angles, "This affirmation involves the concept or idea (*conceptum sine ideam*) of the triangle. . . .[W]ithout it the affirmation cannot be conceived." The distinction between ideas that are 'ideas in the human mind' and ideas that are 'thought-objects' is extremely important. For Spinoza, an idea is not merely something subjective, or an idea in an individual mind, but also something objective. An objective idea is that of which the idea in any finite mind is an idea. It is the objective idea that it is the *object* of the idea in an individual mind. This may seem obscure but it is not really incomprehensible. When a man thinks of anything, what he thinks of is an object of thought in a rather special sense. We normally say, "I am thinking of so and so," when "so and so" is a person or some spatio-temporal entity. But Spinoza wants to say that this is misleading. For when I think of "so and so," for example, a person, what I think of is the *idea* of a person, which is the *object of thought*, rather than an entity in space. Of course, the object of thought, in this instance, is itself logically related to the person. But it is not the physical entity that is directly the object of thought. The object of thought is something thinkable. It is a mode of Thought, and hence a thought-object. *It* does not have the characteristics of a physical body, such as weight or extension.

Furthermore, because there is no such objective idea or thought-object as a square circle, a finite mind (or, for that matter, an infinite mind) cannot ever form an idea of a square circle. Contradictions cannot be thought-objects. It is the thought-objects or objective ideas which Spinoza describes as "ideas related to God." One can see why he should say "all ideas, in so far as they are related to God, are true." (*E* II, P32)

If I say I am thinking (or trying to think) of a Euclidean triangle whose internal angles are *not* equal to two right angles, I am thinking of something, and whatever constitutes my idea is a mode of Thought. But the idea in my mind, whatever else it may be, cannot be the idea

58

of a Euclidean triangle as a thought-object. Hence, the idea in my mind is bound to be inadequate. Spinoza expresses this in his terms by saying:

> When we say that God has this or that idea, not merely in so far as He forms the nature of the human mind, but in so far as He has at the same time with the human mind the idea also of another thing, then we say that the human mind perceives the thing partially or inadequately. (*E* II, P11, C)

A true idea in a human mind then, being the idea of the objective idea or thought-object, is a manifestation of the nature of God through the nature of the human mind. It is of such thought-objects again that Spinoza speaks when he says, "The knowledge of everything which happens in *the object of any idea* necessarily exists in God in so far as He is considered as affected with the *idea* of that object." (*E* II, P12, Dm., my italics)

The word "knowledge," when used by Spinoza with reference to God, is not to be construed in the sense in which it is used with reference to human beings. Why then did Spinoza use it? What is the analogy, if any, between the two which might explain Spinoza's use of "knowledge" with reference to God? This is not an easy question, but one plausible answer to it may be as follows. When I say that I have a true idea or that I possess a true idea, this is the same as saying that a true idea is in my mind or the knowledge of this idea exists in me. A true idea in my mind must be the idea of the thought-object, which is related to God insofar as the thought-object itself is a mode of the attribute of Thought. But since saying that a true idea is in my mind is the same thing as saying that the *knowledge* of that idea exists in me, then the thought-object which, for Spinoza, is also an 'idea' may, by analogy, be said to be the idea 'known' to God. However, the knowledge which we may thus ascribe to God is not the *idea* (i.e., consciousness) of the thought-object as it is ascribed to the human mind, but the thought-object itself.

There is a much more complex use of the word "idea" in *E* II, P7. This proposition says, "The order and connection of ideas is the same as the order and connection of things." This is indeed one of the most important propositions in the *Ethics*, and a correct interpretation and understanding of it can have crucial consequences for gaining an insight into Spinoza's philosophy of mind and action.

Initially, this proposition seems to point out that logically related modes of Thought have correlative modes of Extension that are causally related to each other. The term 'idea' in the proposition itself does not appear to refer to 'conceptions' of any particular mind, or to ideas in any human mind, but to modes of Thought as thought-objects. Spinoza might as well have expressed the proposition by saying, "The order and connection of modes of Thought is the same as the order and connection of modes of Extension." But this is not all that he has in mind. What he means to say further is that whether we human beings conceive the world as a thought-object or as a part of the spatio-temporal order, we shall discover, if our conception is true, one and the same order of explanation, and sequence of things.

Take the example of a circle. It will be agreed that in order to entertain a true *conception* of the circle, one must understand *why* a figure is a circle rather than anything else. One must, in other words, have a grasp of the conditions that determine the conception one has, to be the conception of a circle. It will also be agreed that if a circle exists in nature, say a circle drawn on paper, it must necessarily embody all the conditions which go to make it a circle. The conditions for the existence of a circle in nature are also those which must be comprehended in the conception we form of a circle if it is to be a true conception. These conditions are numerically identical (although qualitatively distinct). They must, that is to say, exist in nature, and our thinking (ideas) must involve ideas (thought-objects) *of* those very conditions, in order for us to have a true idea or concept of a circle. These are not two different sets of conditions. Spinoza expresses this by saying that a mode of extension (a circle existing in nature) and the idea of that mode (the thought-object correlative to it), are one and the same thing expressed in two different ways. "The order and connection of ideas is the same as the order and connection of things." The very conditions which would explain the existence of things in the spatio-temporal order are the conditions that will have to be incorporated in the thought-objects of those things in order for *our* thoughts to be true thoughts of those particular things. Therefore, to put it in Spinoza's terms, whether we view the world under the attribute of extension, or under the attribute of thought, or under any other attributes whatever, we shall discover one and the same order, one and the same connection of causal relations, one and the same set of explanatory conditions. (E II, P7, S)

The term 'idea' is used by Spinoza also to refer to what we normally describe as fictions of the mind or imaginations, which would include dreams. These are what he calls "ideas of non-existent individual things." (E II, P8) The notion of 'non-existent individual things' would also include things that may be said to be *possible* and/or in the future as well as those that existed in the past.[1]

'Idea' is also sometimes used as "the idea of individual things actually existing." (E II, P9) In this sense 'idea' refers to (1) sense perception of objects as part of the common order of nature; (2) memories of such objects; and (3) conceptions (as distinct from perceptions) of things, either as part of the common order of nature, or as part of the order of intellect, without the aid of direct perception or memory of them. This last use of the word 'idea' is significant in Spinoza, for it is ideas taken in this sense that Spinoza seems to regard as 'adequate' as well as 'true'.

If we remember Spinoza's example, in E II, P7, S, for instance, of a circle existing in nature and the idea that is in God of an existing circle which, he says, are one and the same thing manifested through different attributes; and if one takes the phrase "idea that is in God" to refer to the thought-object or the objective idea, then one can perhaps follow what Spinoza means by the following statement:

Whatever happens in the object of the idea constituting the human mind must be perceived by the human mind; or in other words, an idea of that thing will necessarily exist in the human mind. That is to say, if the object of the idea constituting the human mind be a body, nothing can happen in that body which is not perceived by the mind. (E II, P12)

Spinoza seems to be saying that whatever constitutes the thought-object of, for instance, a circle, must be included in the conception that I form of a circle in order for the idea of a circle in my mind to be true. Because the thought-object corresponding to the idea in my mind is the thought-object correlative to the mode of extension, namely a circle existing in nature (which is a body), it is inconceivable that there be anything which constitutes the nature of that body but is not included in my true idea of it. The order and connecton of ideas being the same as the order and connection of things, it is in principle impossible that the idea of a thing in my mind be true and yet fail to reflect the connectons constituting the thought-object correlated with the nature of the thing as it is.

The word "object" in phrases such as "the object of the idea" (E II, P12 and 13), has two senses, which are correlative but distinct. In one sense, as noted above, it means the 'objective idea' or 'thought-object,' which is also said to be an idea 'existing in God' or 'in the infinite intellect of God." In another sense, it refers not to the mode of Thought but to the mode of Extension correlated with the thought-object. To *conceive* a thought-object is to have an idea in one's mind.

But to have an idea is also at times to *perceive* the mode of Extension of which the objective idea is an idea.

Suppose a primitive man or a child looks at a circle drawn on paper, but does not know the conditions that explain its nature. He does not know, in Spinoza's terms, the 'definition' of a circle. Assuming normal eyesight, he would see the figure of a circle as would another man who understands the nature or definition of a circle. The visual object in both cases is the same, but the conceptual object differs. In both cases, however, the sense perception of the circle consists of the ideas (of sense perception) of the way in which their respective bodies (eyes and brain) are affected by an object in space and time (the circle drawn on paper). Spinoza's view seems to be that the objective idea or thought-object of the circle, as it is in nature, remains unchanged. For the thought-object is, in a sense, nothing but that which *can* be (although in fact may not be) an object of an idea in an individual mind. When an individual mind does conceive this object, his idea of the circle is a true idea.

A man may, of course, have a false idea of the circle. A false idea is an idea in a mind which is not the idea of the thought-object correlated with the actual circle, but the idea of a thought-object correlated with the circle as merely perceived by the senses—the circle as it exists in 'imagination', as Spinoza would say. A false idea, therefore, being the idea of a thought-object of a superficial aspect of the circle, would fail to be the idea of the thought-object correlated with the circle as it is. A false idea is, therefore, an inadequate idea by failing to be the idea of the thought-object of a thing as it is in its nature. This is what Spinoza tries to convey when he says, "Falsity consists in the privation of knowledge which inadequate ideas involve." (E II, P35) To be in error is not the same thing, to Spinoza, as to be ignorant. For in the case of ignorance, there clearly can be no thought-object involved whatsoever. The primitive man in our example does not suffer from absolute ignorance, for he does perceive the circle, but he does not conceive the thought-object correlated with the nature of the circle. Spinoza might want to add that what the primitive man fails to conceive is not something which depends for its existence upon *his* nature. For even if there were no human beings to form an idea of the thought-object correlated with a circle existing in nature, it would still remain a mode of Thought —something conceivable in itself—"an idea in God's mind."

We have observed that Spinoza uses the word "idea" to refer to the "thought-object" as distinct from the "idea in the human mind." There are, furthermore, two kinds of thought-objects: (1) those which are correlated with the modifications of my body as affected by external bodies (the ideas of these thought-objects constitute my perceptual consciousness of the external world); and (2) thought-objects which are correlated with the nature of external bodies as they are, without affecting my body. Spinoza's contention seems to be that it is only when ideas in an individual mind are ideas of thought-objects correlated with the nature of external bodes as they are, that an individual can be said to have true ideas.

The expression 'true idea' also refers to two different things. It can refer (1) to the *thought-object* correlated with the nature of an external body independently of being an idea in any finite mind; and (2) to the *idea in a finite mind*, which is the idea of the thought-object correlated with the nature of the external body. When Spinoza says in his essay *On the Improvement of the Understanding* (*TdIE*, Boyle, VI. 33), "A true idea is something different from its correlate; thus a circle is different from the idea of a circle," the word "idea," it seems to me, refers to the thought-object rather than to the idea in a human mind. He explains that "the idea of a circle is not something having a circumference and a centre, as a circle has; nor is the idea of a body that body itself." (*TdIE*, Boyle, VI. 33) Because the thought-object is something different from its correlative body, it is capable of being understood through itself. Spinoza explains himself further with an example. The man Peter is something real. The true idea of Peter is the reality of Peter represented as an objective mode of thought and is itself something real and quite distinct from the spatio-temporal Peter. "Now as this true idea of Peter is in itself something real, and has its own individual existence, it will also be capable of being understood—that is, of being the subject of another idea (idea in a human mind) which will contain by representation all that the idea (the thought-object) of Peter contains actually." (*TdIE*, Boyle, VI. 33, parenthetical inserts mine)

From this it would seem to follow that since my perception of my body (as existing) consists of ideas of the thought-objects correlated with my body as a spatio-temporal entity, it is in principle impossible that my idea of its existence not be a true idea. Consequently, as Spinoza says, "The human body exists as we perceive it." (*E* II, P13, C) Furthermore, if my perception of objects in the external world consists of ideas in my mind of thought-objects, correlated with affections of my body causally connected with the external body, then, it is impossible for any idea in my mind which constitutes veridical perception to be an instance of false knowledge.

An account of Spinoza's view of 'error' would further clarify his conception of 'true idea'. There is a distinction between the idea a man, say Peter, has of his own existence (consisting of ideas of thought-objects correlated with the affections of his own body), and the idea of Peter's existence that another man, say Paul, has (which are ideas of the thought-objects correlated with Paul's body). It is possible for Paul to have ideas of thought-objects correlated with the nature of his own body, and believe Peter to exist even if Peter in fact does not exist. In other words, Paul can have ideas representing Peter as an externally existing entity, even when Peter does not exist. But it is in principle impossible for *Peter* to have ideas of the affections of his own body, unless there is a body whose affections are correlated with thought-objects whose ideas constitute Peter's mind. So that, although Paul can perceive Peter when Peter exists, and can also imagine that he exists when he does not, it is impossible for Peter to perceive or imagine his own body when it does not exist.

So long as Paul *merely imagines* Peter to exist (when he does not or no longer does), Paul is not making any error. But he will be in error if on the basis of his idea, he *believes* that Peter not only exists as an idea of his imagination, but also exists as a spatio-temporal entity. For then Paul's mind, in not having an idea of the thought-object correlated with the nonexistence of Peter's body, entertains a false idea of Peter's existence. This is what Spinoza means, I believe, when he refers to Paul in the above example and observes, "These imaginations of the mind regarded by themselves contain no error, and . . . the mind is not in error because it imagines, but only in so far as it is considered as wanting in an idea which excludes the existence of those things which it imagines as present." (*E* II, P17, S) "There is something real in the ideas themselves," Spinoza says, "whereby the true are distinguished from the false." (*TdIE*, Boyle, IX. 70) This 'reality' must belong, clearly, to ideas as thought-objects rather than to ideas as constituting the human mind. For, as Spinoza points out, "If an architect conceives a building properly constructed, even if such a building may never have existed, and may never exist, nevertheless the idea is true; and the idea remains the same whether it be put into execution or not." (*TdIE*, Boyle, IX. 69) If one considers the above two statements together, then not only is the architect's idea true whether the building is built or not, but the idea is also true, whether he continues to think it or not. What makes the architect's idea true is the nature of the idea as a thought-object, and not the fact that it exists as a thought in his mind.

A man's perception, then, of external bodies can only occur *through* ideas correlated with the affections of his body. To perceive an external body as actually existing is not the same as imagining it to exist, in the sense in which Paul imagined Peter's body to exist when in fact it did not. It is only insofar as the mind *imagines* external bodies in the above sense, that it does not possess a true idea of them. (*E* II, P26, Dm) It is important to remember that Spinoza is not rejecting all knowledge derived from sense perception as false. The demonstration of *E* II, P26 says, "When the human mind through the ideas of the affections of its body contemplates external bodies, we say that it then imagines." Spinoza refers here to *E* II, P17, S, where, in explaining his use of the term 'imagine', he says:

> We will give to those affections of the human body, the ideas of of which represent to us external bodies as if they were present, the name of *images of things*, although they do not actually reproduce the forms of the things. When the mind contemplates bodies in this way, we will say that it imagines.

And if this is what 'imagining' means, then he is, of course, correct in saying that, "So far as the mind imagines external bodies it does not possess an adequate knowledge of them." (*E* II, P26, Dm)

There is one other point Spinoza discusses in *TdIE* that is of interest here. We may all agree that if on the basis of the ideas of his imagination Paul believes Peter to exist (when in fact Peter does not), then he is entertaining a false belief. Spinoza, however, goes further; he suggests that if Paul made a statement asserting the existence of Peter, without knowing whether Peter in fact did or did not exist, then Paul's statement, so far as Paul himself is concerned, is false, even if Peter did exist. For, Spinoza says, "The assertion that Peter exists is true only with regard to him who knows for certain that Peter does exist." (*TdIE*, Boyle, IX. 69) Does Spinoza mean that Paul's statement is false because Paul does not have the evidence required for his statement to be true? If this is what he means, then he may be implying a distinction between merely asserting or making a statement, and believing something, or entertaining or having an idea. Perhaps Spinoza has in mind that just as one may entertain an idea or believe a proposition without stating it, one may also state or assert a proposition without believing it.[2] The grounds for the falsity of belief then may not be the grounds for the falsity of the statement. Another example he gives would tend to support this reading. "When I heard a man lately complaining that his court had flown into one of his neighbors's fowls," says Spinoza, "I understood what he meant and therefore did not imagine him to be in error." (*E* II, P47, S) He is suggesting that although the man's statement was false, there was no error in his belief.

There is little doubt that he does have this distinction in mind, but it is not likely that this is all that he means. I think that he further means that the grounds which make a belief true (or a true idea) are also the grounds which make the statement of those beliefs true statements. For if Spinoza were asked, "What does it mean for someone to know for certain that an idea is true?", he would have to say that an idea of Peter in *my* mind is true if it is the idea of the thought-object correlated with the actual existence or non-existence of Peter. The man who asserts that Peter exists without knowing it for certain, makes a statement which is not evidentially but only accidentally related to (the thought-object of) Peter's actual existence. So that although what is asserted or stated (namely a proposition) taken in itself is true, yet the man who asserted it did not have in his mind the idea of the appropriate correlative thought-object. It is the lack or absence of any evidentially appropriate relation between the idea in the man's mind and the thought-object correlated with Peter's existence which explains the falsity of his statement. It is also the lack of an evidentially appropriate relation between what Paul imagines and the thought-object correlated with Peter's nonexistence that makes Paul's belief a false belief.

It is not generally understood that there is a difference in Spinoza's thought between the inadequacy, or uncertainty of an idea and its falsity, and likewise between its adequacy and its truth. In *E* II, P29, C, Spinoza states that the human mind, when it perceives things in the common order of nature, has no adequate knowledge of external bodies, but only a confused and mutilated (or inadequate) knowledge. He holds, furthermore, that the human mind perceives external bodies as actually existing only through the ideas of the affections of its body. (*E* II, P26) This, however, does not amount to saying that whenever we perceive external bodies as actually existing we are involved in making an error. Error or false knowledge consists in the absence of that certainty which is the defining characteristic of an adequate idea, and this certainty is more than a mere psychological certainty. For it is quite common for a person to feel psychologically certain and yet entertain a false idea. The criterion for the adequacy of an idea given by Spinoza is that it be one which, considered in itself, without reference to an external object, has all the properties or internal signs of a true idea. (*E* II, Df. 4) The notion of the adequacy of an idea in Spinoza's thought seems to exclude all reference to the agreement of the idea with an object, so that the certainty that is involved in having an adequate idea is not based upon the negative criterion of absence of doubt, or grounds for doubt (*E* II, P49, S), but on the positive criterion of 'seeing' its truth to be undeniable on any grounds. (*E* II, P43 and S) Therefore, on the grounds of its internal self-consistency, an adequate idea must be a true idea. It is this kind of adequate idea or knowledge, which is necessarily true, that belongs to what Spinoza describes as Reason and Intuition. Indeed, he also says (as noted earlier), that the human body exists as we perceive it (E II, P13, C), in spite of the fact that our perception of it from the common order of nature is inadequate. Spinoza could not, and does not, however, mean by this that his knowledge of the existence of the human body derived from sense perception is false. It may, of course, be a case of inadequate knowledge. For while he does say (E II, P41) that falsity or error occurs only at the level of the first kind of knowledge, namely 'opinion or imagination'— which must include sense perception—it does not follow that *all* knowledge at this level is necessarily false. Imagination and perception by themselves, he tells us, contain no error or falsity (E II, P17, S), but rather falsity or error arises when one assents to, asserts, or believes in the existence of what one merely imagines or perceives to be the case, without having excluded all those ideas which might lead one to believe something on inadequate and inappropriate evidence. Spinoza's thought may perhaps be expressed as follows. From the fact that one has an adequate idea, it follows that one must also have a feeling of certainty about its truth. From the fact, howeevr, that one feels certain, it does not follow that the idea which is entertained is an adequate idea. In every case of a person's entertaining a true idea, he must also feel certain about its truth. Yet this certainty may be a consequence of having the evidence required for the idea to be true, and this evidence may involve reference to something other than or external to the idea itself. But a true idea is an adequate idea only if its certainty does *not* require any reference to an object other than the idea itself. Perhaps this was the distinction Spinoza wished to draw when he wrote to Tschirnhaus (Ep. 60), "I recognize no other difference between a true and an adequate idea than that the word true refers to the agreement of the idea with its ideatum, while the word adequate refers to the nature of the idea itself." If this *is* the distinction he is making, then Spinoza would appear to hold that an idea may be true even though it may not be adequate. This would explain the assertion that the human body does exist as we perceive it. Nothing in Spinoza's discussion of inadequate knowledge gives the reader any grounds for believing that Spinoza was dismissing the external world, or our veridical perception of it, as a mere illusion.

To perceive things truly, that is to say, to have ideas which are ideas of thought-objects correlated with the nature and constitution of things as they are in themselves, is to have rational knowledge. Rational knowledge, or 'knowledge in accordance with reason,' consists precisely in 'seeing,' grasping, or understanding the necessary relation between ideas in one's own mind and thought-objects correlated with the nature of things as they are. This is what Spinoza means, when he says, "It is of the nature of reason to consider things as necessary and not as contingent. This necessity of things it perceives truly; that is to say, as it is in itself." (E II, P44, Dm) And to perceive things truly, he points out, is to have an idea which *agrees* with that of which it is an idea. (E I, A6) The necessity of this relation between a true idea in a mind and the thought-object is the same as the necessity of the divine nature of God, referred to earlier in E I, P16, Dm. It is, he is suggesting, the nature of the universe, and of the nature of the principle of its origin, that to know things truly is to know the necessary relation between ideas in one's mind and the thought-objects correlative to things in the world.

The foundation of rational knowledge is that a human being knows with certainty that he has a body and that he has ideas, or is conscious. As all ideas in the human mind are ideas of the affections of the body (that is, ideas of thought-objects correlated with changes occurring in the body), it is in principle impossible that a man be conscious of these ideas (or have ideas of ideas), without the correlative changes occurring in his body. Hence, in being conscious of having ideas, or in being self-conscious, he is necessarily affirming not merely the existence of ideas, but also the existence of his body. His body is only one mode of extension among infinite others, all of which are equally extended objects. The fact that we know objects as extended logically implies that Extension is an attribute forming a necessary part of the nature of our knowledge of the universe. It is not merely a category under which we *perceive* bodies; it must also form part of the nature of the principle of origin of the universe, by reference to which alone it can be explained why certain things are bodies, rather than anything else.

The knowledge a human mind has of bodies, not as this or that particular body, but as modes of Extension, and of ideas as modes of Thought, is knowledge that cannot be false and hence is adequate knowledge. It belongs to the category of 'common notions' in the sense that I, in having a body, also know those common properties (of Extension) which form the essential character of other bodies. It is by having this common nature that my body is both capable of being, and in fact is, affected by other bodies, the ideas of whose thought-objects constitute my mind. What makes 'common notions' true, however, is not just the fact that their ideas are present in a human mind. Common notions refer to "things which are common to everything" (E II, P38), as well as to their correlated thought-objects. It is the ideas of these thought-objects which constitute adequate ideas in a man's mind.

Because the nature of *natura naturans*, the 'source' or 'origin', the primal reality, is such that the universe as its manifestation, *natura naturata*, is constituted the way it is, *therefore*, the intellect perceives the nature of that reality by experiencing the world under two distinct categories of Thought and Extension. My knowledge of the world, as consisting of physical objects and thought-objects, constitutes ideas which cannot but be adequate and true; for these ideas are logically related to the thought-objects of which they are ideas. Because it is impossible that an effect can follow if there be no determinate condition or explanation for it (*E* I, A3), the ideas we have in our minds are effects whose nature can be understood only in terms of the conditions that explain them. When we know these conditions as they are, and the necessity of their relation to the ideas in our mind, it is logically impossible that our knowledge of these universal conditions be inadequate or false. Once we have an initial idea that is adequate and true, then other ideas logically related to them will have to be ideas of thought-objects reflecting the causal relations between correlated modes of extension. These common notions, and other ideas logically related to them, are thought-objects of things as they are in themselves. They do not pertain to the nature of any one given individual, but to the nature of all things considered under a given category. In this sense, common notions, being thought-objects correlated with the actual nature of the universe, and to actual properties of things in the universe without reference to any time or place, are universally true notions.[3]

If someone were to ask now, "How can one be certain that the ideas one has are not merely true but also adequate?", Spinoza would answer: if one is asking for a *criterion* to determine the adequacy of ideas, which is separate from the ideas in question, then there can be no other criteria to establish it except these ideas themselves. They are adequate and true for the simple reason that, being ideas of thought-objects correlated with the actual nature of things, they could not (logically) be false or inadequate. They are their own criteria of truth. Their logical certainty is also the ground for their psychological certainty. Hence, "He who has a true idea knows at the same time that he has a true idea, nor can he doubt the truth of the thing." (*E* II, P43) By 'true idea' here, Spinoza must mean an idea which is at once adequate *and* true.

Thus I have tried to show how a much more coherent picture of Spinoza's theory of knowledge begins to emerge in light of the recognition of the distinctions drawn in this paper, as to Spinoza's use of 'idea' than would be possible if they were ignored.

NOTES

1. I am indebted to Bruce Kermott for the contents of this last sentence. Kermott pointed out that ideas of things that do not yet exist, are not the same as ideas of things that do; and an idea of a thing that once existed but does not any longer, is not the same as an idea of a thing that is still existent. An idea of a person who is alive is one thing; an idea of him when he is no longer alive, quite another. Although both may be described as 'rememberings', to confuse one with the other would lead to false knowledge. Spinoza's examples of Peter and Paul (see pp. 65–66) would appear to suggest this distinction.

2. I might, for instance, entertain various thoughts, beliefs (i.e., ideas) about, say, immortality or life after death without stating (uttering or writing) them. I might also utter the sentence and thereby state that "the chair I am sitting on is on fire," without believing that the chair is in fact on fire. Or, I might simply make a verbal mistake in the course of making a statement of my belief.

3. A corollary of this would be that two individual minds entertaining such universal ideas cannot but agree with each other. The question of difference of opinion among them about the truth of these ideas cannot (logically) arise.

The Physics of Spinoza's ETHICS

DAVID R. LACHTERMAN
Swarthmore College

I.

Since my title might appear to announce a somewhat narrow theme, I want to begin by locating the inquiry to be undertaken here within a broader setting. The supreme problem for the interpreters of Spinoza, in my judgment, is set by the first word in the title of his most noted work: *Ethica ordine geometrico demonstrata*.[1] Why did Spinoza give his work this title? Hampshire's remark,[2] that the title "Ethics" is "just and essential" must have struck most readers as itself just; but whence does the title derive its justice? Surely, so all must feel, it is not simply an instance of synecdoche, masking an irreducible heterogeneity of content. If, then, the work has some sort of unity, both in its content and its unfolding development, what is responsible for this unity? What draws together into a manifest whole the seeming diversity of themes to which the book is addressed?[3] To employ a Kantian distinction, the question of fact seems sufficiently and finally answered by Spinoza's own decision to give his work this name, but the *quaestio juris* still remains: what are the conditions of possibility that make this decision adequately conceivable?

Spinoza himself provides a valuable initial clue in a clause in his letter to Blyenbergh of June 3, 1665: "Ethics, which, as everyone knows, ought to be based on metaphysics and physics. . . ." (*Ep.* 38, Land, III) At first blush, this clue seems obvious enough. The text of the *Ethics*, completed and circulated in the following decade, would now appear to be the straightforward carrying through of the promise implicitly made to his correspondent of 1665. However, this foundational program will come to look stranger and stranger as we attempt to grasp the peculiar gestures of its conception and its realization.

Conditions of possibility or grounds of intelligibility are, I would want to argue, among other things, *historical* conditions: a text situates itself along a "continuum" of other texts and within a constellation of claims and prescriptions, performances and anticipations traced out by an author's predecessors and contemporaries (and, in some instances,

71

his successors). This notion of the historicity of a philosophical text must be distinguished rather sharply from some similar-sounding notions associated with vulgar historicism, principally that a text is in some sense the unself-conscious and inevitable product of its historical circumstances. To the contrary, the picture I am crudely sketching here requires that the authors of the most significant texts are piercingly aware of the historical conditions within which they work; in other words, that they are self-conscious of their relations to old and new *traditions,* that it is indeed this self-consciousness that makes possible the discursive structures by which their texts are articulated.

But what bearing does this alleged historicity have on the matter of Spinoza's foundational program for *ethics?* After all, most of us are probably inclined to believe (*pace Nietzsche*) that the questions of ethics remain reasonably invariant over diverse European cultures and intellectual traditions, that is, that the differences show up in the *answers* to what, at bottom, are the same *question.* (E.g., the moral issue of free will is a perennial one, although open to the most discrepant resolutions.) Moreover, the goal of founding an ethics on metaphysical principles, that is, minimally bringing one's claims about human action and character into consonance with theses concerning what is real (or what is knowably the case) sounds familiar and unexceptionable enough.

(The addition of *physics* in the clause cited from the letter to Blyenbergh will perhaps have given longer pause; I shall return to this point quote soon.) Spinoza's proposal is apparently in keeping with the professed or implicit aims of systematic philosophy generally and thus does not seem exposed to any historically specific or peculiar factors, whether of a philosophical or extra-philosophical sort.

Appearances, here as elsewhere, may be deceiving. Consider, to start with, the relationship between Spinoza's foundational program and certain key features of Aristotle's thought with which Spinoza was undoubtedly familiar (even if only *via* Aristotle's late scholastic expositors).[4]

When Spinoza announces that, as everyone knows, ethics must be founded on metaphysics and physics, he is not only embracing the minimal claim that one's understanding of human things should be consistent with one's theory of entities in general, he is putting forward, as the text of the *Ethics* testifies, the much stronger theses that (1) ethical conclusions are strictly derivable from metaphysical and physical principles, and (2) ethical conclusions inherit the exact degree of certainty and precision to which the latter principles attain. The *ordo geometricus* by which the *Ethics* is exhibited dramatizes the identical epistemic status all of its contents, *in principle,* enjoy. That is, the discursive structure of metaphysics, physics, and ethics remains homogeneous, even though this sameness is not always or immediately visible to every (finite) intelligence alike. Moreover, the *ordo geometricus* is not merely a methodological scaffolding that remains external to the completed structure or to the nature of the entities it embraces; instead, it brings under its epistemic and ontological influence the very nature of the items upon which it is turned, so that Spinoza can say, in the Preface to *Ethics* III: "To these it will doubtless seem strange that I should undertake to treat human vices and follies *more Geometrico.* . . .But such is my plan *(ratio)* . . . . I shall consider human actions and appetites in exactly the same way as if it were a question of lines, planes or of solid bodies. . . ."

The unicity of method seems to force us to the inference that there is, in the end, only one philosophical science, capturing within its scope classes of entities that might otherwise have seemed generically and irreducibly diverse in respect to their scientific knowability. It is certainly in harmony with this inference that when Spinoza does speak in the plural of "all sciences" he is quick to add that they all are directed upon a single end and target (*viz.,* the greatest human perfection).

How would an Aristotelian of fairly strict observance react to the picture I have just sketched? It would seem to him, I think, to be conspicuously in violation of three basic interrelated tenets: first, the distinction between theoretical and practical sciences; second, the differentiation between the capacity for science in the strict sense (*episteme*) and the capacity for prudential truth in actions performed (*phronesis*); finally, the restrictions imposed on precision or exactitude (*akribeia*) by differences in the subject matter of various kinds of inquiry.[5] The procedural lessons Aristotle draws from these tenets (although he does not always faithfully observe them), give his way of philosophy an ineliminable multiplicity, a regionality, so to speak, that must do justice to the locale where each of its topics is found. This means, especially, that principles of the being, and thus, of the knowledge of entities in *one* locale are not generally transferable to another locale (when a transfer is made, nonetheless, Aristotle calls this a *metabasis eis allo genos*). So, for example, the principles of geometry, a theoretical science, cannot be invoked in ethics, a practical science because the former have to do with beings that never change, the latter with being open to variation. "Some people," Aristotle says chidingly in *Metaphysics* II (995a 6–7), "won't accept someone's statements unless he speaks mathematically."

Consequently, if it would be premature to describe Spinoza's position as that of an *ontological* reductionist, his concept of a uniform method of philosophical science, his "methodological monism," in Wartofsky's phrase,[6] is decisively at odds with the most influential pre-Modern tradition of the division of the sciences. In particular, his ambition to give an *apodeictic* account of ethical and political truths raises in quite a pointed way the question of historical or contextual grounds of possibility. How does this ambition come to appear sensible? Why does its fulfillment look likely to one who has it?

The contours of Spinoza's project stand out more sharply when set alongside those works of his most prominent contemporaries or near-predecessors in which a radical break with pre-Modern or Aristotelian tradition ushers in new style and new initiatives for philosophy. Seen in this perspective, Spinoza's enterprise might come to look like a redemption of the promissory notes issued, for example, by Descartes and Hobbes, the first, in the famous image of the "Tree of Philosophy" set out in the preface to the French translation of his *Principles*,[7] the latter, in his plans for the three-part *Elementa Philosophiae*, which would tie together, with synthetico-deductive chains, his theory of bodies in general, man and citizens.[8]

And yet, the energy of these initiatives, when directed upon the domain of ethics, would seem to be held in check by obstacles which are themselves products of the radical revolt against pre-Modern thought. The rejection of that tradition, in other words, seemingly threatens to demolish the very basis on which a rationally coherent ethical *teaching* could be erected, and to demolish it, not for any "abstract" epistemological reason, but rather, because the pretheoretical phenomena of ethical experience incorporated into that basis are eliminated in the name of a systematic theory of such experience. What I have in mind is not, principally, the simple repudiation of Platonic and Aristotelian discourse about the virtues (for Descartes, their moral writings are to be compared to "very proud and very magnificent palaces built on sand and mud");[9] rather, it is a critique of two intertwined principles by which that discourse is sustained, *viz.*, the teleological principle, that action is always for the sake of an intelligible end or goal, and the principle of the objective or genuine distinction between real and apparent goods. The two principles mesh in such a way as to allow the pursuit of those ends which are real goods and to discriminate, within the latter class, between sub- and superordinate goods.

This is obviously not the place for a thorough discussion of the arguments put forward in defense of these principles; it must suffice to remark that they are at the heart of the Ancients' claim that reason

74

can establish hegemony over appetite, or, alternatively, that in the end desires can be satisfied only by good apprehended and endorsed by reason. Thus in a genuinely flourishing human life we desire what we judge and know to be good.

It is one of the hallmarks of early Modern thought that both of these principles are explicitly rejected. The first is a victim of the critique of final causes of all sorts;[10] the second is overturned in favor of a relativistic and subjective concept of goods. These two negations fit together in their own right, because what each man desires is good (to him), while a man's desires are caused by efficient, not final, causes. The upshot seems to be that talk of reasons for human action gives way to a science of the deterministic causes of human action.

Whatever substantive ethical teachings arise out of the ruins of the Ancient tradition will therefore have to overcome or eliminate *both* the pretheoretical "evidence" on which teleological explanations of conduct allegedly rest, *and* the pretheoretical basis for discriminations between apparent and real goods. This elimination of the preanalytical phenomena of moral conduct becomes persuasive just to the extent that its results are in harmony with a new model of what it is to explain other sorts of preanalytical phenomena, e.g., the "conduct" of material bodies generally. Thus, the distinctively modern enterprise within the field of ethics comes to be carried out in tandem with the distinctively modern project of physics. To borrow a phrase from Robert Musil, early Modern thinking is engaged in a "collateral campaign," the yoking together of a radically new physics of bodies and their motions and a new "anthropology."[11] While the aims pursued by individual participants in this campaign may vary in clarity and in kind, although the order of discovery may shift from thinker to thinker, with respect to its essential form, this collateral campaign joins its two elements within a relation of reciprocal effectuation.[12]

II.

In the sections to follow I shall sketch a reading of a Spinoza who belongs squarely and self-consciously to the tradition inaugurated by the promoters of this collateral campaign. In particular, I shall argue that the new, mechanistic physics, suitably interpreted and modulated, plays as essential a part in Spinoza's *Ethics* as it does in, say, Hobbes's *Leviathan* or Descartes' *Passions of the Soul*.[13] Accordingly, the miniature treatise on the nature of bodies inserted between Propositions 13 and 14 of Part II, the "Physical Digression," as I shall call it, will turn out to be the fulcrum that sets in motion the weightiest ethical arguments.

Of course, to set Spinoza in this tradition does not presuppose that his physical theories are identical with those of Descartes or Hobbes; moreover, this tradition itself does not impose a uniform outcome on the meshing of physics and moral philosophy. This is brought out forcefully by comparing, in advance of detailed arguments, Hobbes with Spinoza. Hobbes derives from his mechanistic views the conclusion that men cannot be happy in any final or complete way; the endlessness of the sequence of desires shows the Ancients' *summum bonum* to be a chimera. Spinoza, to the contrary, will marshal the arguments of physics to prove that and how human beings can achieve perfect felicity.

In any case, the portrait of Spinoza to be drawn in this paper will differ signally from that limned by the German Romantics and Idealists in the first flush of the revival of Spinozism occasioned by Jacobi's *Über die Lehre des Spinoza in Briefen an den Herrn Moses Mendelssohn.*[14] Novalis epitomizes this current of interpretation in his famous aphorism: "Spinoza is a God-intoxicated man."[15] And Hegel, who once wrote that "when one begins to philosophize, one must first be a Spinozist,"[16] takes it to its extreme limits in an account of Spinoza's *Ethics* in his *Lectures on the History of Philosophy*, marked by the most curious assertion that in Part II, "Spinoza does not treat of the subject of natural philosophy, extension and motion at all, for he passes *immediately* from God to the philosophy of mind, to the ethical point of view" (my emphasis).[17] This lapse, if it was that, is certainly in accord with Hegel's view that for Spinoza all individual differences and determinations vanish into the "abyss of annihilation," another name for the one, absolute Substance. This thesis is at the root of Spinoza's so-called "Acosmism."

Hegel's exegesis is far from being merely willful distortion, indeed, it might be argued that he supplies the most cogent criticism of Spinoza's failure to come to grips with the modern (i.e., Christian) principle of subjectivity, "the moment of self-consciousness in Being," *if* this principle has the status of Hegel assigns it.[18] Be this as it may, the *Spinoza redividus* of the late eighteenth and early-nineteenth centuries has undergone profound transformations, due, in the main, to the occlusion of historically specific conditions of possibility by an alien context.

III.

Thus far I have offered little more than a peremptory, although not wholly implausible, postulate, namely, that Spinoza's speculative intention can only be gauged when set into relation with the parallel enterprise of Descartes and Hobbes, both of whom take the new science of motion and matter to be both the point of departure, and the court of evidentiary appeal, for a new understanding of human affairs. But, is it the case that Spinoza, as well, assigns physical science, *stricto sensu*, an equivalently pivotal role? If he was not *ignorant* of developments in this realm, still, might he not have held them at arm's length, only admitting them offhandedly and from time to time into his more preoccupying metaphysical or onto-theological design?

To judge by the main directions of scholarly comment on Spinoza, such was, indeed, the case. Not only does Spinoza's name rarely, if ever, figure in histories of seventeenth-century science; most philosophical commentators pay little, if any, heed to his physical principles and speculations;[19] when they do, it is with an air of duty, since, in their judgment, physics occupies only a marginal place in Spinoza's thought.[20] Correlatively, the sources inspiring that thought are sought elsewhere, in medieval Jewish philosophy and/or Cabbalistic speculation, in the revived scholastic metaphysics of the Counter-Reformation or in the pantheistic "naturalism" of Late Renaissance authors, such as Bruno and Telesio.[21] (It is, needless to say, not my point that such "sources" do *not* enter into the stream of Spinoza's thinking; it is only a matter of relative proportions and of the difference between the central flow and the peripheral eddies.)

Accordingly, it makes little sense to push ahead with an account of Spinoza's *Ethics* in terms of his physics until a minimal basis of documentary fact has been laid. Ultimately, the scheme of Spinoza's own arguments in the *Ethics* can yield a substantive confirmation of this interpretive strategy.

That Spinoza had more than a passing or amateurish interest in the new physics is rather quickly apparent from his correspondence. His letters to and from Henry Oldenburg, Christian Huyghens, and Leibniz show that he was treated as their equal in matters of scientific controversy; his range of expected expertise was not limited to lens-grinding. Leibniz, for example, sent him in 1671 a copy of his *Hypothesis Physica Nova*, presumably confident of a well-informed assessment. Moreover, elements of Spinoza's own work testify to an abiding interest in, if not preoccupation with, science. Significantly, it was the second and third books of Descartes' *Principles* that Spinoza chose to put into geometrical form when tutoring a young student; it was only at the urging of Louis Meyer that he added on his exposition of the First Book. Tschirnhaus asks in his letter of January 1675 (*Ep.* 59) "[when shall we procure your] Method of rightly directing the Reason towards the Acquisition of knowing of Unknown Truths," as well as the "Generalia in Physics? I know that you have already made great progress with

77

them." Both expressions seem to refer to (or to paraphrase) titles of works on which Spinoza was thought to be engaged.[22] In reply, Spinoza says that, "as for what concerns the other matters, namely, of motion and of Method, since these are not yet written up in an orderly manner, I shall reserve them for another occasion" (*Ep.* 60).[23] His opusculum, "Algebraic Calculation of the Rainbow," bears the revealing epigraph "serving the closer conjunction of physics (*Naturkunde*) with Mathematics (*Wiskonsten*)." (Land IV, 233)

I think this evidence suffices for the present, at least to the extent that it shows us a Spinoza quite involved in the elaboration of a "natural philosophy." Nonetheless, someone might question how germane the involvement is to the concerns Spinoza manifests in the *Ethics.* After all, this is the climactic expression of his philosophical thought, and it is here that his primary intentions must surely have been most strongly at work. This is, indeed, the case, but its truth is in no way in contradiction to the alleged preeminence of physics, as I shall try to argue in the next two sections. For the moment, one need only call to mind the following: in the *Ethics* Spinoza argues that the human mind is the idea whose unique object is the body (*E* II, P12); therefore, all of our knowledge, of whatever sort or variety, is at least mediated by the "affections"[24] of the body and by the features all bodies have in common. The false view that the mind can move the body is traced to a failure, up till now, to determine what a body can do. (*E* III, P2, S) If *all* that concerns bodies can and must be understood in terms of the quantities, relations, and causes that fall within the province of physics, then the latter's place in the fabric of the *Ethics* is secure.

It might also be pertinent to recall that the controversial thesis of the *Ethics* is not that God thinks, but that he is a *res extensa.*

Spinoza has no *complete* physical system, in the sense of the Cartesian, or later the Leibnizian system. To think and write otherwise is to build "castles in the air" (*Luftgebilde*), as von Dunin Borkowski rightly warned.[25] What Spinoza does introduce into seventeenth-century physics is a number of subtle and sophisticated readjustments, criticisms, and rearrangements of the underlying conceptual-explanatory format of science; moreover, he "solves," at least at one abstract level, some of the key dilemmas left as a scientific inheritance by the Cartesian program. With a thoroughness rivaled only by Hobbes, he draws from this format all of the consequences and projections—onto politics, ethics, epistemology, and psychology—required by a unified and conceptually homogeneous theory of the world.

To take the measure of Spinoza's endeavors, we need to avoid a purely system-immanent account in which the technical terms of Spinoza's philosophical art (extension, motion-and-rest, *corpora simplicissima*, etc.) are assembled and combined into an abstract pattern. This does make Spinozism seem like system-building for its own sake! We should try instead to identify the actual questions and perplexities to which Spinoza's physics is responding. This can only mean, in the present context, highlighting those features of Descartes' philosophy of physical nature that loomed most prominently and provokingly within Spinoza's intellectual vision, for it was with Descartes that he was unmistakably engaged in a dialogue of singular intensity.[26]

Accordingly, I shall begin by outlining, with scandalous brevity, the aims and *aporiai* of Descartes' physics. Then I shall return to Spinoza in order to show in some detail how his central physical notions make coherent sense when viewed as part of an effort to avoid those *aporiai* and thus to guarantee the continuing success of the original Cartesian project itself.

"My entire physics is nothing other than a geometry. . . ."[27] This is the epigraph, or better, the battle-cry that mobilizes the conceptual armory Descartes throws into his battle against Aristotelian-Scholastic physics (and metaphysics). Accustomed as we have become to the notion of a mathematical physics, the traces of the violence necessarily done to the pre-Modern tradition when this notion was first articulated have sedimented far below the surface of our attention. Here, too, it is to start with a matter of undercutting the Aristotelian distinction between two heterogeneous theoretical sciences, one which studies beings that move and change, the second, mathematics, which studies certain unchangeable beings. Similarly, the categorial difference between quantity and quality is abrogated, or rather, sensible qualities are reduced to mathematicized quanta.[28]

Descartes brings the two sciences together in his theory of pure mind and simple natures set out in the *Regulae*; perhaps the most consequential and familiar result of this coalescence of the two sciences is the identification of matter and body with three-dimensional extension, the proprietary object of geometry. Mathematical physics is to give a complete rational acount of the external world by means of those and only those properties or attributes of corporeal substance which can be reduced to, i.e., rendered intelligible in terms of, geometrically representable and measurable dimensions. This holds especially true of motion. "L'univers cartésien, on le sait bien, c'est la géométrie réalisée."[29] It is as though what Aristotle calls intelligible matter had been substituted for the cosmos.

A vast array of detail opens out at this point; I shall have to restrict myself to those consequences of greatest relevance to the present study.

There is one and only one *res extensa* in the true sense, because geometrical extension is itself everywhere homogeneous, divisible beyond limit, and invariant.[30] This is the *space*, as one might say, in which analytical geometry gets done, not Aristotelian *place*.[31] However, because this unique space is identical with body or matter, it is a *plenum*. Its continuity obviously excludes any void or vacuum; it also seems to militate against any genuine *individuation* of "bodies" in the familiar, molar sense or in the Atomists' sense.

Nonetheless, some kind of variation must still be possible, for without it the project of explaining all that "takes place" in the world by the new physics would be aborted. But exactly what kind of variation meets the requirement set by the theory of simple natures?[32] And, what "laws" does variation obey? What causes explain its nature and effects?[33]

The variation in question is, of course, motion, in particular *rectilinear* and uniform *local motion*, because Descartes refuses to recognize any of the other instances of Aristotelian *kinesis*.[34] This is, as he says, at least in *Le Monde*, the motion geometers have in mind when they explain a line by the movement of a point. To be sure, Cartesian motion is not as simple and intelligible as he asserts it to be—it is a state (not a passage or a process), it has a quantity and degrees, it can be transferred from one body to another, gained and lost—but we must leave these peculiarities behind,[35] for the sake of addressing the central issue: Is motion of the designated sort compatible with the geometrized matter that constitutes physical nature?

Descartes' procedure in Book II of the *Principles* shows us that the answer must be negative. There are two distinct kinds of explanation, in play.[36] One, a purely kinematic or phoronomic explanation takes account only of the *circulatory* movement of the "parts" of the geometrical plenum; the other concerns the forces that cause or are manifested in the rectilinear motion (and rest) of individual bodies and is, accordingly, a dynamical explanation. It is a straightforward conclusion from kinematic considerations that the situation envisaged by the laws of rectilinear motion can never be actualized because no one body or part of matter can be spatially separated from a set of contiguous parts themselves surrounded on every side by still other parts, and so on, throughout the indefinitely extended plenum. Thus, no motion in a straight line ever takes place; this casts a most curious light on the three laws of nature and seven laws of impact Descartes articulates in Book II, as all require perfectly hard (inelastic) bodies[37] *and* real separation among these bodies.

The geometrization of matter is, therefore, irreconcilable with the dynamics of rectilinear (inertial) movement. This has at least three disconcerting ramifications:

1. The laws of nature and of impact are derivable from God's *immutability*, supposed, therefore, to explain motions in terms of *causes*. However, the physical circumstances of the universe are such that these causes seem never to take effect. This paradox leads Descartes to introduce the idea of a body's tendency to move in a straight line, a tendency later named the body's *conatus*,[38] (as more than one of his readers quickly noted, this looks suspiciously like a reversion to the Scholastic notion of potentiality or virtuality), but this is of no help because *conatus* is itself derived from the "abstract" principle of inertia.

2. God creates the universe in such a way that the total quantity of motion (and of rest) is continuously conserved.[39] The principle of inertia is also a principle of (local) conservation of the quantity of motion (and rest) following upon God's immutable nature.[40] However, the conditions of realization of these two principles of conservation cannot be jointly satisfied. Moreover, in the *plenum* the relativistic concept of motion (either of two bodies can be regarded as at rest or in motion with respect to the other), violates the universal principle of conservation.[41]

3. Finally, what defines an individual body in Cartesian dynamics (i.e., its *conatus*) is an abstraction; conversely, an individual part or body has no independent definition. A body is defined as what is "transported together"; movement is defined as "the transport of a body from the neighborhood of those that touch it immediately. . . ." The conditions of movement and rest in the plenum rob parts of matter of any identifiable individuality. The plenum is the only individual body and *its* individuality is obviously not a function of local transport.[42]

Descartes' physical system thus confronts its partisans and opponents alike as a body of principles rent by tensions, incompatibilities, and discrepancies. A variety of responses to this situation are registered in the history of seventeenth-century physics, some resting on experimental "falsifications" of Cartesian claims (e.g., Huyghens on the laws of impact), others stemming more from a conceptual, even speculative, reassessment of their constitutive elements. Spinoza's undertakings in the realm of physics *stricto sensu* fall squarely within this second category. He sets out to achieve a comprehensive *unification* of exactly those uncoordinated levels and strategies of Cartesian explanation responsible for the gap dividing intent and performance in this strange new field of mathematical physics.

How, more partcularly, does Spinoza go about this task of unification? At the most general level, two key issues are at stake, *viz.*, the principle of corporeal individuation continuity, and the cause(s) of motion.[43] As we have seen, Descartes' answers to these two issues are mutually incompatible, that is, the basis of his kinematic theory is at odds with his dynamics. Spinoza eliminates this incompatibility by adopting a strategy yielding a single ground or principle both for genuine physical individuation and for genuine physical change and movement, namely, the principle of *conatus*. This will allow him (1) to save the Cartesian phenomenon of inertial motion, and, *at the same time*, (2) to bring the latter into harmony with the conditions imposed on local motion by the infinity and continuity of (geometrical) extension. For the transeunt or extrinsic causality exercised by God in the form of continuous creation/conservation, Spinoza substitutes what we may call the intrinsic or immanent causality of the modes of extension themselves; he replaces, so to speak, the Cartesian *Deus ex machina* with a *Deus intra machinas*.

These rather sweeping claims need patient analysis and defense.

Spinoza, as I have said before, nowhere furnishes a complete or systematic physics; he himself signals from time to time the lacunae that remain to be filled. These expressions of modesty, however, are not incompatible with his claim, as reported by Louis Meyer, that nothing in principle exceeds the grasp of the human intellect.[44] Although programmatic and elliptical, Spinoza's theses thus point ahead to a fully articulated and comprehensive theory of physical nature. It is in this same spirit that one must go about assembling the elements of his position from their sometimes sporadic appearance in various texts and letters. (I shall concentrate, in the main, on what I called above the "Physical Digression" set between Propositions 13 and 14 of *Ethics* II.)[45]

The set of these elements is something of a mélange, drawing, as it does, on Cartesian notions that Spinoza retains, and criticisms of other Cartesian notions that did lead, or would have lead him to new principles and formulations. However, a Cartesian spirit may be said to govern the membership-conditions of this set: all physical phenomena are to be explained *via* uniform "laws of motion and rest" that explicate nature as it is in itself and not as it makes itself seem to the human senses. Knowledge of such laws and their influence on bodies is to be obtained by "demonstration and computation," not by experimentation that is essentially arbitrary in its appeal to the deliverances of perception.[46] Thus a rational theory of bodily nature demands homogeneity both of explanatory principles *and* of the behavior of the corporeal phenomena to be explained. It is when Descartes himself violates this twofold requirement of homogeneity that he becomes the target of Spinoza's criticism, as we shall see shortly.

For Spinoza, this principle of homogeneity entails, among other things, that as we pass from simpler to more complex phenomena, the same factors remain in play; that is, that the increments caused by an increase in complexity are quantitative, not qualitative or "essential" in nature. It is this application of homogeneity that will furnish the underpinnings of the "Physical Digression" after the scholium to proposition 13, Part II, and will allow Spinoza to accommodate certain fundamental Cartesian themes without becoming trapped in Descartes' *cul-de-sac*. It is to this pivotal text, therefore, that we now should turn.[47]

The *Ethics* really has two beginnings or starting points and, correspondingly, follows two styles of exposition and argument. This duality is brought home by the place and function of the "Physical Digression," which, far from being arbitrarily intercalated into the main body of the work, is in fact a new beginning because (1) its contents are not *derived* from the theory of God as infinite substance set out in Part II and continued through Part II, Proposition 13, and (2) it is, as Spinoza notes, a necessary prologue to the account of the mind's union with the body and of the consequences of that union, the account, namely, that occupies the remainder of the *Ethics*. If Part I is the proper starting point in respect to the *ordo essendi*, because substance is prior to its modifications (*E* I, P1), the "Physical Digression" answers in turn to the *ordo intelligendi*, inasmuch as bodies and, in particular, our own bodies, are the objects of our thinking from the start, that is, even when our ideas are inadequate and our mental activity fails to rise above the first kind of cognition, imagination. (As I shall argue later in Section IV, what is established about bodies in the "Physical Digression" supplies the motive force by which we can pass from imagination to the second and third kinds of knowing.)

The corpus of the "Digression" has an easily discerned structure; it proceeds from so-called "most simple bodies" (*cf. E* II, A2*) to a sequence of "composite bodies" (*E* II, A2*, Df.; *E* II, L7,5), ending with a set of six postulates regarding the human body, a special case, as far as we are concerned, of a composite body. The simplicity of logical structure cannot long disguise the tangle of vexed questions that have arisen over almost every point of detail. I want to postpone consideration of these in order first to elicit the constitutive principles of this text. This procedure by no means guarantees that all obscurities can be removed; it at least stands a chance of illuminating the context and motives of their origin.

Two principles seem to be at work here: (1) the principle of motion-and-rest, and (2) the principle of aggregation and integration. When taken in concert with the infinity and indivisibility of the attribute Extension (*E* I, P15, S), that is, with the impossibility of a vacuum, these principles yield the result that all the properties and states, the entire career of bodies, of whatever level of complexity, can be explained as the consequences of motion-and-rest. As we progress along *scala naturae*, no *new* physical qualities or capacities appear which cannot be analyzed in terms of the qualites and capacities of bodies on the very first rung. Let us try to see more closely how Spinoza enacts this mechanistic scenario.

At the end of Axiom 2* after Lemma 3, Spinoza states retrospectively, "And these points concern the most simple bodies (*corpora simplicissima*) which distinguish themselves from one another only by motion and rest, quickness and slowness."[48] The rubric has, to be sure, occasioned enormous debate as to the precise physical character of these simplest bodies; are they atoms, or infinitesimally small particles, corpuscles of aetherial fluid or oscillating pendula, or what?[49] I shall not try to resolve this question as it seems to me that Spinoza is principally concerned to introduce certain "theoretical entities" whose main, if not unique, explanatory burden is to anchor subsequent complex systems to the most elementary features of entities devoid of complexity and exhibiting distinctiveness only *via* their immediately comprehensible relations of motion and rest. In other words, Spinoza's *corpora simplicissima* can be, for the purposes at hand, understood in functional terms; for example, they and they alone fulfill the Cartesian law of inertia. (*E* II, L3, C)[50] Later I shall return to other aspects of the matter; for the moment let me note that neither the term *"individuum"* nor the phrase *"unum corpus"* (*cf. E* II, A2*, Df.) is ever applied to any of the "simplest bodies"; indeed, *that* phrase occurs only in the plural.

The simplest bodies are distinguished from one another only by motion and rest, quickness and slowness; the plenary character of extension entails that every body is under the external constraint of circumambient bodies. Hence, if a number[51] of simplest bodies can be brought into contact with one another or be moved at the same or different velocities (moved, that is, by other bodies) in such a way that their motions share with one another a definite ratio, then "we say that these bodies are united with one another and that all together they form at the same time one body or individual, which is distinguished from other bodies through this union of bodies." (*E* II, A2*, Df.)

This criterion of individuation is caried over into Axiom 3*, where Spinoza defines hard, soft, and fluid bodies, and into Lemmata 4–7, each of which establishes formal conditions under which an individual can remain the same (keep its *natura* or *forma*) despite various changes (e.g., of size and direction) its component simple bodies or it itself can undergo. The thread that links together these further conditions of identity is the preservation of a certain ratio of motion-and-rest among the component parts (*cf.* Lemma 5: *ad invicem motus et quietis rationem servent*; Lemma 6: *invicem eadem qua antea ratione communicare*; Lemma 7: *[motum] uti antea [sc. eadem ratione] communicet*).[52]

Needless to say, the sense of this criterion does not leap to the eye. What does Spinoza *mean* when he says that an individual retains the same form or nature as long as its component parts (the original parts of those of the same nature that can be substituted for these) retain the same *ratio* of motion-and-rest? This seems, at the least, unintuitive; nonetheless, it is a doctrine central to Spinoza's thought here and elsewhere. For example, in the *Korte Verhandeling*, his formulations are even bolder: "Every particular corporeal thing *[lichaamelijk ding]* is *nothing other than* a certain ratio *[zeekere proportie]* of motion and rest." (*KV*, Land, 98; Wolf(b), 161)[53]

Spinoza unmistakably intends by this a numerical (or quantitative)[54] ratio; any doubt is removed by the sole example Spinoza gives, in the notes to the Preface: "As soon as a body has this same ratio as, e.g., the proportion of 1 to 3. . . ." To gain some purchase on the ideas involved here, we need to recall that for Spinoza, no less than for Descartes, motion and rest are not only states, they are quanta associated or identified with states. That is, at any given moment, a body has a certain measurable *amount* of motion (or of rest) which is not the same thing as its speed (or absence of speed) at that moment. Consequently, we can, in principle, calculate the ratio of these amounts for an individual body, in Spinoza's special sense of "individual," by reckoning up the relevant quantities of all its component parts. Thereby, we can rather quickly see that this total ratio remains impervious to the sorts of alteration considered in Lemmata 4–7, because an infinite number of pairs of different integers will satisfy any fixed ratio $m:n$;[55] thus, an individual can lose some of its constituent parts so long as these are replaced by other new ones having the same *natura* (which thus must mean here the same as *ratio*).

A change in the ratio, on the other hand, will mean that a "new" individual now exists, i.e., *that* an individual exists and *what* individual it is which exists both depend on the satisfaction of some fixed ratio holding between quantities of motion and rest "possessed" by the ingredient parts. This is why Spinoza can say in the passage cited above from *KV*, preface to Part II, that "the body is subject to change,

85

but never so great that it goes beyond the limits of 1 to 3." Matheron has usefully baptized such a ratio the "corporeal equation" of an individual.[56]

The one numerical example of a constitutive ratio makes matters appear simpler than they are, for not only is an individual *qua* individual a certain ratio of motion and rest, that is, a ratio between the sum of the quantities of motion and the sum of the quantities of rest of all its parts, the parts as well can, and indeed must, communicate their motions to the other according to fixed ratios if the individual to which they belong is to continue in existence. "Communicate," in this context, means that one part transfers some fraction of its quantity of motion to other parts, while receiving, in turn, fractions of motion from other parts of the same individual.[57] In other words, the internal economy of an individual should satisfy the Cartesian laws of impact in such a way that the ratio defining the individual is preserved.[58] This requirement is satisfied by individuals composed only of most simple bodies if the "communication" of motion takes place in a cyclical manner, undisturbed by external interventions. If the individual were abstracted from all other individuals, this condition could be met; but, the protasis here is contrary-to-fact, necessarily so, given the fact that *res extensa,* so to speak, is everywhere dense, with *corpora simplicissima* and their correlative *individuals.* Indeed, as we have seen, the coercion of environing bodies (*E* II, A2*, Df. *a reliquis ita coërcentur*) is a necessary, although not sufficient, condition for the union of simplest bodies by which an individual is defined. Consequently, still another level of explanatory complication will be ushered in when the "closed-system" previously defined *via* a fixed ratio of motion-and-rest is opened up, as it must be, to the influence of other individuals. Spinoza has already pointed to this interaction in Axiom I*: "All the modes in which one body is affected by another follow from the nature [*natura*] of the affected body and, at the same time, from the nature of the affecting body."

We shall have to return to this thesis later on, since it is reiterated in the Postulates concerning the human body (*E* II, Post. 2 and 6) and eventually forms the basis for the all-important distinction between actions and passions. (*E* III, Df. 3) In very provisory fashion we can say at this point that the conditions of individuation are under constant threat from without; satisfying them thus will turn out to be more effortful an affair than earlier premises may have suggested.

From the Definition of individual following Axiom 2 through Lemma 7, Spinoza tells us in the Scholium to Lemma 3, he has been considering only those individuals compounded of *corpora simplicis-*

sima, "individuals of level–1," as we might say. Clearly, the circumstances that led to the formation of level–1 individuals can and will be reiterated, so that individuals of level–2 will emerge composed of level–1 individuals. The gain in numerical and structural complexity will be reflected in the heightened probability for a level–2 individual, that its component parts can "communicate" their motions to one another in accordance with this new individual's "corporeal equation." Similarly, the same process can and will be repeated, until we "reach" an individual of level–ω, this is (extended) Nature as a whole, a single individual whose parts are all the bodies that there are. Because there is no other individual, nor, presumably, any residual simplest body, by which this level–ω individual could be coerced or compromised, its continued identity is *eo ipso* guaranteed because its status as an individual is compatible with every possible variety of affection, that is, with an infinite number of variations in the ratios of motion and rest among its ingredient parts. (*E* II, L7, S: *omnia corpora infinitis modis variant, absque ulla totius Individui mutatione*) In Letter 32 to Henry Oldenburg (20 November 1665), Spinoza fleshes out this notion by way of the famous example of a worm living in the blood stream, unable to apprehend the blood as a whole and thus forced to consider each particle of blood a whole in its own right. The analogy is with the situation of the human body in the universe at large; what is regarded as a genuine, independent, whole, *quoad nos,* turns out to be merely a part of the unique whole; it is only the artificial isolation of an individual of level–n (n < ω) that creates the perspectival illusions to which we, as well as the worm, are subject. In any case, Spinoza quite explicitly points to the principle of identity to which the Scholium alludes: "all bodies are surrounded by others and are mutually determined to exist and to operate in a fixed and determinate ratio, *while the same ratio of motion and rest is always conserved* in all of them at the same time, that is, in the universe as a whole." Elsewhere Spinoza gives to this universal individual the name *"facies totius Universi"* (*Ep.* 46, Land, 205; Elwes, II 399) and furnishes it to his correspondent as an infinite mediate mode in the Attribute Extension.

Between *corpora simplicissima* and the *facies totius Universi* lies the human body, the subject of the final postulates. It is an individual of level–k (2 < k < ω) (*cf.* Postulatum 1: *"valde compositum"*). Its behavior is to be explained by exactly the same principles that hold true for individuals at every other level.[59] No special privileges can be awarded to the human body over against inanimate or nonhuman bodies.

What are the primary results and ramifications of this "Physical

Digression" in which Spinoza claims not to be speaking *ex professo* about the body? How has he integrated Cartesian conclusions into his physics without falling prey to Cartesian paradoxes?

1. First of all, this text, studied together with the *KV* and Letter 32, makes plain what is involved in Spinoza's answer to the question of criteria or conditions of individuation. One and the same principle, *viz.*, conservation of the same ratio of motion and rest, bears responsibility for the existence of an individual of whatever level. In other words, a body, in the ordinary as well as in the Cartesian sense, preserves its physical integrity in just the same way the whole universe preserves its: they differ only with regard to the degree of probability that each can "survive" externally caused modifications. Only the unique individual of level–ω can be modified in infinite ways without giving up its identity. The homogeneity of the principle of conservation at every level therefore eliminates the tension between the Cartesian geometrical plenum, i.e., the unique *res extensa* identical with the *whole* of three-dimensional space, and those bodies that come about because of local motion and contiguity within this plenum (e.g., the small and large vortices). Both are "individuals" in precisely the same sense and in virtue of the same conditions.

2. Any instance of the state of motion or rest must be explicated by way of some antecedent instance of a body in the state of motion or rest; this second instance must, in its turn, have been determined by still another body and so on, *ad infinitum*. (*E* II, P13, L3) Only so will the principle of intrinsic causality argued in *E* I, P28 be preserved; that is, all causal efficacy among finite modes of one attribute must rest on an infinite sequence of finite modes determining one another in turn to assume the relevant effect. If we leave aside the "metaphysical" aspects of *E* I, P28 & L3 in the "Digression," we can more readily appreciate its significance *vis-à-vis* Descartes: any transeunt or extrinsic cause of motion and rest has vanished; if God under the attribute of extension is the cause of motion and rest in finite individuals, He is so *not* in virtue of this attribute taken absolutely, but, rather insofar as the attribute is modified by a finite modification. It no longer makes sense to speak of God's creating and then conserving the same quantity of motion and rest in the universe because such language presupposes a modality of action on God's part which cannot be explained in terms of an infinite sequence of his finite modifications. If no one finite motion is eternal, the sequence of finite motions is eternal; hence, a state of motion (or rest) can be accounted for only in terms of other states of motion (or rest).

3. Descartes' principle of inertia falls out as a special and very limited

case of the principles governing the states of bodies generally; "to persevere always in the same state" now takes on a broader scope when seen in the light of Spinoza's definition of individuality. The relevant points can be most simply put as follows:

a. Only *corpora simplicissima* satisfy the strict principle of rectilinear inertia (*E* II, P13, L3, C), for only they are distinguished from one another purely and simply by their singular states of motion and of rest (in contrast to the composite ratios defining true individuals).

b. This privilege is purchased at the cost of artificial abstractions from the "real world" of individuals. As Spinoza himself states, the notion that a body persists in its state supposes that we pay no attention to other bodies in motion. (*E* II, P13, L3, C) In other words, the causal conditions specified under (2) and the definition of *"unum corpus"* under (1) exclude any case in which a single body is totally free of outside influences (with the exception of the body of level–ω. Spinoza had already pointed to the artificiality of the contrary assumption in the *Principia Philosophiae Cartesianae*, Part II, Proposition 14, when he adds to Descartes' enunciation of the principle of inertia the two restrictive clauses *"quatenus simplex et indivisa est, et un se sola consideratur."* (PP, Land, 159; Hayes, 72)[60] (Compare, by way of anticipation, the formulation in *Ethics* III, P6 of the definition of *conatus*.)

d. Nothing in the phenomena is lost, however, because the *corpora simplicissima* that fulfills the principle of inertia *in the abstract* are concretely the constituent parts of true individual bodies which can maintain their identities even when no longer isolated from the plenum. Thus, the motion transmitted through a "ring of bodies" is not necessarily destructive of the integrity of any one individual body.

e. Furthermore, Spinoza can retain the Cartesian laws of impact (except for the Sixth) inasmuch as the communication of motion (and rest) among the parts of an individual is in conformity with these laws, so long as *that* individual persists. There is no longer any need to isolate the bodies that satisfy these laws from the rest of the plenary environment. So long as the total ratio of the motion and rest of parts is conserved under impact, the body that integrates these parts remains intact.

f. Spinoza lifts, by implication, still another restriction endemic to Descartes' dynamics, namely, that the bodies covered by the laws of impact are perfectly hard or inelastic. The point of Axiom 3* is to relativize the concepts of hardness, softness, and fluidity. This comes out clearly in his definition of hardness, which is no longer the absolute hardness postulated by Descartes and demanded by the *mise-en-scène* of the laws of impact, but a matter of degree, a function of area of surface-contact between component parts.[61] Absolute hardness or in-elasticity would therefore imply at least two infinite surface-areas in contact with one another and this, given the uniqueness of the infinite individual, is absurd. In his comments on Boyle's treatise, *Historia fluiditatis et firmitatis* in Letter 6, Spinoza goes even further in suggest-ing the interchangeability of hardness and fluidity when the large parts composing an individual move relatively to one another's bulk (*moles*) in the same ratio as do the small parts of what we would ordinarily call a fluid body.

g. The upshot of the six preceding paragraphs is that Spinoza is attempting to reduce, even to eliminate, that gulf between dynamics and kinematics which was the source of the "duplicity" in Descartes' physical science. For Spinoza, the restrictions imposed on bodies by Cartesian dynamics are unnecessary; what was for Descartes a purely kinematic situation of reciprocal displacement, lacking any reference to true causes (God and the three laws of Nature), is now to be seen as the ideal setting for the operancy of just those causes and the obtaining of just those dynamic conditions that safeguard the identity of individ-uals in the midst of a material continuum.

h. This last paragraph leaves hanging one last nagging question: Are these causes and conditions in fact "dynamic"? That is, is the con-servation of the same ratio of motion and rest in any sense an expression or manifestation of an individual's force or power? More briefly, is the concept of *conatus* applicable to Spinoza's physics?

Gueroult thinks not,[62] and, although the negative case he argues leads to an acknowledged equivocation, his authority is not lightly to be ignored. Nonetheless, I think one can make out a plausible case for bringing the thesis of the "Physical Digression" into close connection with the theory of *conatus* unfolded in Part III.

To be sure, Spinoza avoids using the term "*conatus*" in the "Physical Digression," although he makes a tantalizing allusion to one congeneric notion, i.e., *conservatio*, in the fourth Postulate concerning the human body. The more relevant clues lie elsewhere, in the notions of law and of a body's *nature*. In the present context, I can pursue these clues only a short distance.

In his letter to Oldenburg (*Ep.* 32) referred to above, Spinoza explains that the cohesion or coherence [*cohaerentia*] among parts of an individual (e.g., blood) means nothing other than the fact that "the laws of nature (*leges sive natura*) of one part accommodate themselves to the laws or nature of another part so that they are as little as possible contrary to one another." (*Ep.* 32, Land, 120; Elwes II, 290) ("*Sive*" here, as in the notorious phrase "*Deus sive Natura*," clearly signifies apposition, rather than exclusive alternation.) Later, in the same letter, it is the *universalis natura* of blood that "demands that its parts are forced to accommodate themselves to one another so that they accord with one another in a fixed ratio." (*Ep.* 32, Land, 120; Elwes II, 290) A whole of level–n imposes its nature or law on its constituent parts of level–(n–k); they obey by bringing their natures or laws in turns into accord with one another, that is, by preserving among themselves the characteristic ratio of motion and rest by which the essence of the whole is defined. (*cf.* KV, Appendix 2; Wolf(b), 157–62) Accordingly, a full account of the physical universe would require knowing all the laws of all its parts, so as to explain how and why each of them is in agreement with its whole and coheres with the remaining parts of that whole.

It is this same notion of law that Spinoza seems to have in mind in the *Tractatus de Intellectus Emendatione*, when he writes that, "The innermost (*intima*) essence of things . . . is to be sought from fixed and eternal things, and, at the same time, from the laws inscribed in these things as in their true volumes." (*TdIE*, Land, 31; Elwes II, 37)[63]

These texts establish a suggestive link between law, nature, essence, *and* the conservation of the same ratio of motion and rest. Can *conatus* be excluded from this series of mutually implicative concepts? Answering this requires that we look at least briefly at Spinoza's discussion immediately prior to the "Physical Digression" and cast at least a passing glance at much wider themes that this question inevitably evokes.

(1) In the Scholium to Proposition 13 preceding the "Physical Digression," Spinoza refers, proleptically, to the degree to which the actions of some one body depend on that body alone, a degree inversely proportional to the concurrence of other bodies in the action of the first. The theme of "action" points us ahead to the official discussion of action in Part III and, in particular, to the correlations between the *conatus* each thing has to preserve in its being (*esse*), the "*actual essence*" (*actualis essentia*)[64] of each thing *and* the potency through which a thing can act, or endeavor to act, alone or in concert with other things. (*E* III, P7, Dm.) It follows from the actual essence of anything that it cannot do anything other than what follows necessarily from its determinate nature. (*E* III, P7, Dm.; cp. *E* IV, P59, Dm.; *E* III, P37, Dm.) The conjunction of these claims, viewed synoptically with the account of law and nature above, apparently implies that the *conatus* of an individual body *is* its power of acting so as to preserve the characteristic ratio or "corporeal equation" by which its essence is defined.[65] Two "options" are open to these bodies: to preserve the

corporeal equation by their own actions alone, or to do so in concert with other bodies. In either case, it is the *conatus* of each body which is at work.

In any case, *conatus* will have to figure in any complete account of the nature of *res physicae* because it is common to all of these and thus falls within the domain of the second kind of cognition. (*E* II, P38 & 39)

Nevertheless, as Spinoza employs the notion, *conatus* looks more like an incorporeal force than a feature of bodies. Isn't this a case in which Spinoza can be said to strain against the limits of a mechanism that confines bodily episodes to instances of motion and rest? Doesn't Spinoza approach, with his concept of *conatus*, the Leibnizian theory of *vires vivae*, Leibniz's own opinion notwithstanding? To meet these objections fully it would be necessary to ventilate the complex question of the status of "forces" in Spinoza's physics and metaphysics, a task I cannot undertake here. The pathmarks toward an understanding of what is at issue will be found in Spinoza's use of terms for "force" both in the *Ethics* and in the *KV*. These, in turn, will lead one to the description of God as *"essentia actuosa,"* or, in the phrasing of the *Short Treatise*: "God's essence has an infinite activity [*een oneyndige doening*]." (*KV*, Land, 91; Wolf(b), 147)

These mysteries aside, I hope to have shown that Spinoza's physics, inchoate and incomplete though it may be, not only is an active response to dilemmas arising from Cartesian mechanics, but, further, is a sophisticated attempt to purge mechanism of alien elements. It would be a mistake, however, to judge this physics in narrow terms, for the presentation in the "Physical Digression," the second, elementary starting point of the *Ethics*, will prove to have been the philosophical Trojan Horse with which Spinoza invades the fortress of both Ancient and insufficiently modern conviction. Again, a line from the *Short Treatise* comes powerfully to mind: *"Want zoo't lichaam is, zo is de Ziel, Idea, Kennis, etc."* "For as the body is, so is the soul, idea, knowledge, etc." (*KV* II, Pf. 11, Land, 37; Wolf(b), 64) (See *Excursus, infra.*)

IV.

If my earlier claims about the pivotal role of these physical notions have merit, they should begin bearing interpretive fruit when we turn to Spinoza's theories of human behavior and of human knowledge. Moreover, it should be these same physical notions that explain the intimate linkage between Spinoza's moral psychology and his epistemology, a linkage made altogether evident in Part V of the *Ethics* where *scientia intuitiva* is identified as the source and form of man's beatitude. The challenge Spinoza sets himself in the Ethics as a whole is, therefore, to show how mechanistic determinism and *eudaimonism* are not merely compatible, but mutually entail one another. If I am right, then it is the mathematico-physical theory of the body that will permit man to enjoy that "continuous and supreme happiness" which Spinoza makes his goal in the *TdIE* (Par. 1).

A great many elements must ultimately be incorporated into the arguments for this thesis; indeed, I suspect that nothing less than an interpretation of the entire *Ethics* would be satisfactory. I am constrained, here, to setting out only a few of the most important elements and to suggesting, often in unavoidably elliptical fashion, how they are linked together.

Spinoza intends to teach us in the *Ethics* how we can negotiate the passage from bondage to liberty, that is, from the diminution of our power due to our passive emotions (*affectus*) to the liberation and heightening of our power brought about by the active emotions. Alternatively, the *Ethics* is an attempt to teach us what the Good is and how we may obtain it. This second formulation makes possible an extremely short "proof" of the claims I have been putting forward, thanks to a series of definitions or characterizations of "good" that runs through Parts IV and V:

1. The good is what we know for sure to be *useful* to us. (*E* IV, Df. 1)

2. We call *good* what contributes to preserving our being, that is, what increases or forwards our *power of acting*. (*E* IV, P8, Dm.)

3. The *useful* is "whatever disposes the human body so that it can be affected in very many ways or what renders the body apt for affecting external bodies in very many ways." (*E* IV, P38)

4. The more a man endeavors and is able to seek what is *useful* to him, the more he is endowed with *virtue*. (*E* IV, P20)

5. *Virtue*, by definition, is "the power of effecting certain things which can be understood solely through the laws of man's nature." (*E* IV, Df. 8)

6. We are *active* insofar as we are the adequate causes of what happens either within us or outside of us. (*E* III, Df. 2)

7. Those things which bring it about that the *ratio of motion and rest* which the parts of the human body have to one another is conserved, are *good*. (*E* IV, P39)

8. "A man who has a *body apt for very many activities* has a mind of which the greatest part is eternal." (*E* V, P39)

9. Thereby, such a man is affected by the love toward God (*E* V, P39, Dm.), from which arises (*E* V, P36, S) that emotion Spinoza

calls *acquiescientia in se ipso,* the pleasure or joy arising from man's contemplating himself and his power of acting. (*E* III, Df. 25)

I do not expect this "proof" to be convincing on its own; it does little more, in fact, than evoke a number of the important synonyms and conceptual affinities Spinoza employs throughout Parts III–V. Especially significant, nonetheless, are the connections between goodness, utility, virtue, the power of acting, the aptitude of the body for being an adequate cause of what occurs in it or in its external environment, and, lastly, the conservation of the ratio of motion and rest among the parts of the body, the conservation, that is, of what we earlier found to be the *essence* of the body. *Conatus* could also have been brought into this series, since it is the effort of each thing to persevere in its being and the being of the body *is* its nature as expressed in its "corporeal equation."[66] Because the human body is very complex and therefore both needs very many other bodies and can itself move and dispose external bodies in very many ways (*E* II, P13, Post 4 and 6), its perseverence will involve it in a complicated network of relationships with other bodies; the more it can *use* these other bodies in such a way as to preserve its own nature, the more its power of acting (hence, its virtue and its possession of good) will be liberated and allowed to flourish. This condition is what Spinoza refers to in the phrase *corpus ad plurima aptum* which figures so crucially in Part V, P39; if the body does not enjoy that condition, that is, if its power effecting useful occurrences in itself and in external bodies is diminished or lost, the mind stands no chance of conceiving its own eternal part and will thus fall far short of the eternal blessedness which is its very perfection.

To many readers, this way of looking at the matter will no doubt seem both incomplete and unpersuasive; after all, the liberty of the mind is said by Spinoza to be the power the *mind* has over the affects and this must mean that knowledge is essential to the process of achieving beatitude, whereas I have talked mostly of the body and only secondarily of the mind and its knowledge, especially the highest kind of knowledge, *scientia intuitiva.* A human being *is* both a mode of extension and a mode of thought, and no amount of emphasis on the first can succeed in obscuring the second!

To meet these objections in full would consume more space than I can here usurp; thus, I can do nothing more than project the course my argument would have to follow.

The familiar thesis of psycho-physical parallelisms attributed to Spinoza and regarded as his chief "advance" over Descartes fails to do justice to a point of capital importance subtly woven through the text of the *Ethics*: where the career of the body is autonomous, the life of the mind is heteronomous, in the sense that thinking has no objects all its own, no *noēta*; it has as its object the nature and affections of its own body and, derivatively, the nature and affections of the external bodies by which its own body is affected, i.e., forced to move or to come to rest. The advance from inadequate imagination to adequate conception is by means of the things which are common to all (*E* II, P38); the reference (in the Corollary) to Lemma 2 of the "Physical Digression" makes it plain that common notions are those of the physical characteristics of all bodies (e.g., motion, rest, quantity, etc.).

But, what of the idea of an idea, which might appear to demonstrate the autonomy of the mind, at least in respect to reflective knowledge?[67] Two things count against this. Spinoza's "strict definition" of an *idea ideae* (*E* II, P21, S) shows, as I would want to argue, that he is using "forma" (Nam *reveva* idea Mentis, hoc est idea ideae nihil aliud est quam forma ideae, etc.) in the same way Descartes had when attempting to meet one of Arnaud's objections: "ideas are forms" which *can* be considered, not "as representing something, but only insofar as they are operations of the intellect."[68] Second, the *ideas of ideas* are not the independent source or form of what we might think of self-consciousness, for Spinoza goes on to argue in P23 that the mind has knowledge of itself only by way of the ideas of the affections of the *body*. As Gueroult puts it: "The interior (sc. of the mind) is thus reduced to a pure mental translation of the exterior."[69]

(The only other possibility is the object answering to intuitive science, *viz.*, the unique essence of a singular thing. I shall pass over this at this point, reserving a brief comment until later.)

The heteronomy of mind, its lack of access to intelligible objects other than bodies (for *entia rationis*, for instance), universals, stem from that confusion of bodily images reflected in the mind's failure to form distinct ideas of singular bodies (*E* II, P40, S1), should not be confused with a causal dependence of the mind on the body. Spinoza is emphatic and unwavering on this point in the *Ethics*: "Body cannot determine mind to think, nor can mind determine body to motion or to rest, or to anything else (if there is such)." (*E* III, P2) His one direct reproof of Descartes is saved for this topic (*E* V, Preface); he can scarcely believe, so he says, that such an illustrious philosopher would put forth the hypothesis of the pineal gland, "more occult than any occult quality." (*E* V, Preface)[70] The infinite causal series responsible for ideas in the mind is altogether distinct from the infinite causal series producing an affection in the body. (*Cf. E* I, P28; *E* II, P6)

If this is the case, then it is no longer clear how the mind can *act* in any way to bring about its liberation or felicity; given this theory of causal independence, together with the thesis that the order of the mind's ideas is an exact replica of the order of bodily states and changes, it begins to look as though nothing I can think *qua* mind will influence the body to behave differently. This, in fact, is already implied in Spinoza's critique of the distinction between will and intellect. (*E* II, P49, C and S) If felicity is attained by passing from the first and second kinds of knowing to the third (*E* V, P24–28), and if all our ideas, inadequate as well as adequate, have as their objects states and changes of bodies completely determined within their own causal order, no meaning would apparently be left to the notion of "wanting" or "choosing" to pass from the pain or unhappiness of inadequate conception to the pleasure and self-satisfaction (*acquiescientia*) of adequate conception.[71]

This "paradox" is mitigated in two ways. First, Spinoza's enthusiastic reminder, placed significantly as the Scholium to Part II, P2, that "no one up till now has understood the 'fabric' of the human body so accurately that he could explain all of its functions" (*E* II, P2, S),[72] brings out how vast and artful the power of the body to change its "world" may prove to be. Mind is otiose or extraneous even when it is a question of constructing buildings, pictures, and temples; the causes of these may be deducible from the laws of corporeal nature alone. Second, the doctrine of the formation and concatenation of corporeal images will turn out to be all-important. Through it we can draw together a very large number of threads that might otherwise have seemed to be hanging loosely from the main fabric of the book, for instance, the curious inclusion of the law of reflection (*E* II, A2*),[73] and the Fifth Postulate concerning the soft parts of the human body in the "Physical Digression," for these, in fact, lay the groundwork for the accounts of imagination, memory, the laws of association and, eventually, the power of ordering and concatenating the affections of the body according to an order in conformity with the intellect (*secundum ordinem ad intellectum*). (*E* V, P10, Dm.; *E* II, P39, Dm.) This is the power at the root of the mind's remedies against passive affects; it can only be engaged if the *body* successfully combats affects contrary to its nature, that is, if it is apt for bringing about, on its own, a very great number of effects. (*E* V, P39, Dm.) In "practical" terms, this means that the body must find and put to use all those things that agree with its nature (*E* IV, P31 and C), in other words, are compatible with its essential ratio of motion and rest. Alternatively, the body must endeavor to unite its nature with the natures of other bodies so as to augment the total power of the resultant whole (*E* IV, P35 and C1), to become a functioning part of a more complex individual, e.g., a civil state. To perform those and only those actions that follow from the laws of its own corporeal nature is to associate the images occasioned by external bodies and retained in memory, thanks to the material properties of the *brain* (for it is certainly this that Spinoza means in *E* II, P17, C and Dm.), according to an order explicable by that nature itself. In other words, it is to leave behind what Spinoza calls the "common order of nature," i.e., "the fortuitous encounter of things" (*E* II, P29, S), for the order of strict necessity ingredient in the nature of each finite extended mode. If this seems a marvelous ability to ascribe to the body, Spinoza is on hand to remind us that "the body can do many things as a result solely of the laws of its nature at which the mind marvels." (*E* III, P1, S)[74]

One last link remains to be forged. The highest endeavor of the mind is to understand things by the third kind of knowledge, knowledge of the essence of a singular thing *via* primary causes of that thing. This is knowledge of the generation of all the properties and states of a singular thing from its defining essence. Spinoza gives us little to go on in the way of specifying examples. In both the *TdIE* and the *Ethics*, the model is that of intuitive, i.e., nondiscursive knowledge of the fourth proportional. In the *TdIE* also, genetic (essential) definition is exemplified in the construction of geometrical figures through the motion of lines and planes. (*TdIE*, Land, 33; Elwes II, 39)[75] Now, the intuitive science, hence blessedness, the mind is alleged to achieve in *Ethics*, Book Five, turns crucially on the mind's power to conceive something *sub specie aeternitatis*; it exercises this power, as Spinoza argues, only insofar as the essence of its own body is so concerned. (*E* V, P29; *E* V, P31, Dm.) It can know itself (and God) as eternal only if it knows its body's essence "under the form of eternity." This leads us to infer that the knowledge in question is knowledge of how from the corporeal equation of its own body (which *qua* equation or complex ratio has no reference to duration) all that body does and suffers is genetically derived.

This third kind of knowledge produces the highest possible self-satisfaction (*acquiescientia*) of the mind, for thanks to this knowledge, we know to the fullest extent the eternal essence of our own bodies, and thus take the greatest pleasure in what these bodies necessarily do in consequence of their respective eternal essences. (*E* V, P37 and Dm.)[76] In both the ordinary and the deepest sense, the mind's knowledge *changes* nothing; everything that the body actually and thus essentially does is affirmed by the mind without cavil or correction. My intellectual love toward God is the same as the love of my corporeal fate. And this is knowable because it is nothing more than the necessary sequence of states and relations of motion and rest in a certain mode of extension. There may, perhaps, be some question whether it is lovable just for that reason.

V.

Throughout this paper I have resolutely, not to say perversely, attempted to see the unity of Spinoza's *Ethics sub specie corporeitatis*. I would be quick to acknowledge the one-sidedness from which this account consequently suffers; many matters of prime importance (e.g., the immediately and mediately infinite modes of *cogitatio*) have not found their way into my discussion. Nonetheless, the "bias" of this account is, I think, valuable and justified if it allows one to see how much Spinoza, too, shares in the characteristically modern inversion of the relationship between mind or soul and body: the body, one might say, having usurped the place of the charioteer in Plato's myth of the soul, must now hold the mind in tight rein. "Reason is and ought to be the slave of the passions," even if we rename the passions Spinozistic actions.

Perhaps a speculative route leads forward out of Spinoza to the Hegelian principle of self-consciousness and the theory of Absolute *Geist*; perhaps a path may be traced backwards from him to the Platonic and Aristotelian theories of human excellence displaying itself in the "substantial ethical life" of the *polis*. Anyone who tries to steer a course between Hegel and the Ancients past the crashing rocks of seventeenth-century thought will greet with wonder Russell's epithet: Spinoza was the "ethically supreme" philosopher.

Excursus

My discussion in Section III of Spinoza's physical conceptions has inevitably left much of the technical detail still shrouded in obscurity. I am by no means sure that this can ever be wholly eliminated, not so much because of lack of clarity on Spinoza's part, as because of the "state of the art" such as Spinoza knew it, especially in regard to mathematically precise formulations of physical notions and relations.[77] Nevertheless, it remains a challenge to uncover the models that govern his physical concepts, models that will be referentially opaque just to the extent that he mixes together pretheoretical intuitions and theoretical commitments. By way of responding to this challenge, I shall offer a series of observations and conjectures.

1. It is quite wrong to suggest, as Pollock did, that Spinoza conjoins motion and rest only because he was misled by, or tended excessively to

imitate, Descartes' merely "rhetorical" addition of "rest" in his statement of the principle of conservation.[78] The suggestion distorts both Descartes' intentions and Spinoza's use of his Cartesian inheritance, as the following comments should make clear.

(a). Having made motion a state and not a process of change, Descartes rejects the Aristotelian view that rest is the privation of motion; he makes it, instead, the contrary of motion and places these two ontologically on a par with one another. This justifies, indeed, requires, the inclusion of rest in the formulation of conservation.[79]

(b). As I mentioned earlier, Descartes often speaks of a body's giving up or transferring some or all of its motion or of its rest. This must be understood in terms of quantities of rest or motion associated with the corresponding states. How Descartes proposes to measure these quantities is far from clear; in one key text he seems to suggest two alternative functions which are not mathematically equivalent.[80]

(c.) In any case, the split between kinematics and dynamics discussed above shows itself once again in the case of motion and rest. At the level of nature, motion and rest are reciprocal, to the point of being indistinguishable: we can just as well say that body A is transported from the vicinity of body B considered at rest, as vice versa.[81] Motion and rest are really distinguishable only by reference to the *forces* of motion and rest and these forces are extrinsic to the plenum on whose 'parts' they are causally exercised. Forces and their laws are manifestations of God's immutability and are not entailed by the extended subtance which is the subject of purely geometrical kinematics.[82]

(d). The force of rest is especially obscure because Descartes assigns to it at least three distinct physical roles, *viz.*, to explain (i) the perseverance of a body at rest in its state of rest, (ii) the capacity of a resting body to resist being set in motion by another moving body, and (iii) the cohesion between parts of a solid body.[83]

2. Spinoza elaborates his concept of motion and rest out of these ambiguous materials. It should first be pointed out that the pairing of motion and rest is a doctrinal and terminological constant in Spinoza's works. Indeed, he takes pains in his official exposition of Descartes to emphasize the inclusion of rest (and the force of rest) in his scheme of things.[84]

3. In KV Spinoza gives an extended argument for the necessary copresence of motion and rest in "substantial extension." (KV I, chap. 2; Land, 12n.; Wolf(b), 28n.) To the objection that motion is possible only in a part of infinite extension, because there is nowhere to which the whole can be moved, Spinoza replies that no part or finite mode can be prior to extension taken as a whole. Therefore, "there is not motion

alone, but motion and rest together; and this is (*deze is*) in the whole and must be in it, since there is no part in extension." This seems to mean that motion can only be assigned to some determinate quantity of rest which is just as eternal as motion is said to be. (*KV* I, chap. 9; Land, 34; Wolf(b), 37)[85]

4. This argument still leaves opaque just what it is that Spinoza means by rest and by motion here and elsewhere. Are these kinematic or dynamic concepts? Several of the subtle emendations and amendments Spinoza introduces into the *PP* display his intention to sublate this Cartesian distinction.[86] For instance, having reminded his pupil of Descartes' warning against confusing local transport and the moving force or action (*PP* II, Df. 8, N2; Land, 144; Hayes, 53–54), Spinoza goes on to use "motion" and "force of motion" synonymously in the body of his demonstrations. (*PP* II, P21 & 22) Similarly, in *CM* he argues the identity of reference of the following terms: *conatus, vis in suo statu perseverandi, motus ipse, natura motus* and *leges et natura motus*. (*CM* I, 6; Land, 201; Hayes, 124)[87] The pattern is the same as that observed in the main discussion above, namely, that Spinoza is eager to make the powers and properties of a body intrinsic to that body. The motion or rest a body exhibits should be the direct expression of the corresponding force immanent to that body.[88]

5. Some residual puzzles can now be partially untangled. Spinoza does not identify rest with inifinitesimally slow motion, despite what more than one commentator has claimed.[89] For him, as for Descartes, quickness (*celeritas*) and slowness (*tarditas*) are varieties of speed (*velocitas*); speed is *not* the same as motion, but is one of the components of the quantity of motion.[90] Nonetheless, both speak of slowness "participating in rest" and apply this locution in setting out the laws of impact.[91] The point is that distinction among *degrees* of speed should be rooted in the ontological contrariety of motion and rest themselves, so as to account for oppositions in kind (e.g., direction) consequent upon the interaction of moving bodies. (*PP* II, P27; Land, 169; Hayes, 84)

On the other hand, Spinoza does not reduce the effects of (the force of) rest to cohesion among parts or to equilibrium among individual bodies, as still other scholars have suggested.[92] Both of these phenomena are the result of the pressure of circumambient bodies on another individual. (*Cf.* "Physical Digression," A2*, Df. 1 and *PP* II, P32; Land, 174; Hayes, 91) Nor, finally, is rest for Spinoza a protoform of "potential energy," as Pollock, Wolf and Roth maintained.[93] It is not the anachronistic use of "energy" that misleads here, but, rather, the notion of potentiality, which goes against the grain of Spinoza's basic conviction that essence and power are identical, hence, that there is no power which is not actualized.[94]

6. The force of rest is, fundamentally, the force of resistance actually exercised by a body against the impingements of other bodies, whether or not the latter belong to the same complex individual to which the first belongs. This is Spinoza's express thesis in *PP* (*PP* II, P22, N; Land, 166; Hayes, 80) and presupposed throughout the "Physical Digression." One must keep in mind, however, that this resistance is not the sign of a body's inertness or passivity, but is an activity, an expression of the body's *conatus*. This interpretation fits in well with the general picture of the physical world Spinoza's positions imply, a world in which each individual is continually pressed from all sides by other bodies and must therefore secure its own persistence by overcoming the challenges posed by these others. Following a hint by Matheron, we might say that this world is that of Hobbes's *bellum omnium contra omnes* translated into the language of physics.[95] Consequently, the force of a body's resistance is at the same time the force needed to maintain itself in its antecedent state of rest, one way it has of thwarting external threats to its perseverance.

7. All of the preceding remarks serve to show that Spinoza's substitution of the ratio of motion and rest for Descartes' quantities of motion and rest is not thoughtless or arbitrary. Gueroult has proved that the two functions are not mathematically equivalent and that Spinoza's function is satisfied only under very restricted conditions.[96] This is an awkward disadvantage from the viewpoint of physical science in the strict sense; nevertheless, we can see Spinoza here, as elsewhere, trying to unify what struck him as disparate and independent elements in Cartesian physics. A complex individual (of whatever level) displays both motion and rest, as do its component parts; its *conatus is* its effort not to yield to external bodies so many grades or degrees of its total quantity of rest or of motion that its corporeal equation and, thus, its essence, will be lost. (Of course, no degrees of motion or rest are lost absolutely; the *facies totius universi* varies in infinite ways without giving up its integrity.)

8. So far I have considered motion and rest in isolation from the nature of the attribute of extension. The relationship between these is one of the darker mysteries in Spinoza's thought, not only for the reader, but for Spinoza himself, as his last exchange of letters testifies. His correspondent, Tschirnhaus, had pressed the question "How can the existence of bodies having motions and figures be demonstrated *a priori*, since in extension considered absolutely, nothing of the sort is found?" (*Ep.* 80) Spinoza first replies (*Ep.* 81) that the existence of

moving bodies in fact cannot be demonstrated from extension *if* it is defined as a quiescent bulk (*moles*) as it was by Descartes. In his final letter (*Ep.* 83) he asserts that "matter has been badly (*male*) defined by Descartes by means of extension; it must necessarily be defined by means of an attribute which expresses an eternal and infinite essence." These passages have been pressed too hard, I think, by commentators who want to see Spinoza taking an entirely new turn and hinting at a third attribute in addition to *cogitatio* and *extensio*.[97] The operative phrase in the last passage cited is "badly defined"; that is, Descartes' error was not to construe matter as extension *simpliciter*, but as extension defined as a quiescent bulk to which motion is *eo ipso* alien. We have already learned from *KV* that both motion and rest are equally eternal and equally intrinsic to extension; moreover, Spinoza's account of attribute (*E* I, Df. 6) insists that an attribute express an eternal and infinite essence. Consequently, his valedictory comments simply epitomize his earlier criticisms of Descartes.

This does not mean that no question remains. How, in detail, are motion and rest to be derived from extension? Had he lived longer Spinoza would have addressed himself to this paramount question. As it stands, only the briefest hints can be culled from his *oeuvre*. I shall examine these by way of concluding this excursus.

Two criteria must be met if 'a' is to be derived from 'b': First, the conceptual relationship between 'a' and 'b' must match the ontological relation designed by the term "express" (*exprimere*), that is, the nature and existence of 'a' must express, make manifest or outward, what is already implicated in the nature of 'b'.[98] Second, the vehicle of the derivation must be a genetic definition stating the process through which the *definiendum* (here, 'a') is constructed or constituted from the *definiens* ('b'). (Cf. *TdIE*,Land, 28–31; Elwest II, 35–7)

Motion and rest satisfy the first criterion, for they are themselves forces and what they express is God's essence, an essence identical with God's power of acting or, synonymously, His force of existing. However, these modes express that essence mediately, that is, insofar as He is *res extensa*. (*E* II, Df. 1.) Are the modes ontologically consonant with the attribute extension? Spinoza at least twice points in this direction, in *PP* (*PP* II, Df. 1; Land, 143; Hayes, 53), where three-dimensional, geometrical extension is distinguished from an *actum extendendi*, and in *KV* (*KV* II, chap 19; Land, 72; Wolf(b), 120), where extension is referred to as a "force of effectuation or production" (*deze kragt van uytwerkinge*) whose principal effects are motion and rest. So extension, too, may be brought under the rubric of force or activity.[99]

The status of the second criterion is less certain. Spinoza mentions only the unsuccessful attempt to derive quantity from motion. (*TdIE*, Land, 33; Elwes II, 39–40) I must leave it an open question whether one could reverse and modify this abortive procedure so as to derive the "intimate essence and properties" of motion and rest from that peculiar quantity, the "act of extending."

9. One final perplexity. Tschirnhaus demanded a demonstration of the existence of *bodies*, while I have been discussing the derivation of motion and rest. As we have seen, Spinoza closes the gap between bodies and motion and rest in *KV*, perhaps less hesitantly than he does in the *Ethics*. However this issue is to be resolved, it would be a deliciously seductive anachronism to see Spinoza moving toward the notion of a field of force[100], or, more venturesomely, toward a geometro-dynamical theory in which material bodies (*Natura naturata*) are a dependent function of the geometry of space, while that geometry is, in turn, a function of the play of forces.

NOTES

1. I shall refer to the following translations: Elwes, Wolf(b), and Hayes (see *Key to References*). However, all other translations are mine.

2. Stuart Hampshire, *Spinoza* (Harmondsworth, Middlesex, 1951), p. 115. All students of Spinoza are pleasurably indebted to a notable tradition of commentary and analysis. My debts are heaviest to the following works, which I shall cite now for convenience of subsequent reference: H.H. Joachim, *A Study of the Ethics of Spinoza* (Oxford, 1901); Richard McKeon, *The Philosophy of Spinoza. The Unity of His Thought* (New York, 1928); Harry A. Wolfson, *The Philosophy of Spinoza*, I–II (Cambridge, Mass., 1934); Sylvain Zac, *L'Idée de la vie dans la philosophie de Spinoza* (Paris, 1963); Gilles Deleuze, *Spinoza et le problème de l'expression* (Paris, 1968); Alexandre Matheron, *Individu et communauté chez Spinoza* (Paris, 1969); Rainer Specht, *Innovation und Folgelast* (Stuttgart/Bad Canstatt, 1972). I must single out for very special mention the first two volumes of Martial Gueroult, *Spinoza* (Paris/Hildesheim, 1968, 1974). This is by far the most detailed and the most useful commentary on the *Ethics*. These works will be cited by the name of the author and page number.

3. For a different approach to this same question, *see* Wolfgang Bartuschat, "Metaphysik und Ethik. Zu einem Buchtitel Spinozas," *Zeitschrift für philosophische Forschung*, 28 (1974) pp. 132–45. Bartuschat calls attention to the important distinction Spinoza draws at the end of the Scholium to Prop. 36 in Book V. It should also be noted that Spinoza here treats a demonstration as an *affectus*.

4. I am deliberately omitting Plato. For a suggestive comparison, *see* Leon Brunschvicq, "Le Platonisme de Spinoza," *Chronicon Spinozianum*, 3 (1923) pp. 253–68.

5. Exploration of the whole question of the relationships among the *epistemai* would probably make these simple claims much more complicated. For example, to what division does Aristotle's exposition of *politike episteme* itself belong? There is a good discussion of this and related matters in Gunther Bien, *Die*

Grundlegung der politischen Philosophie bei Aristoteles (Freiburg, 1973) pp. 124–37. *Cf.* also, Margot Fleischer, *Hermeneutische Anthropologie (Platon. Aristoteles)* (Berlin, 1976), pp. 235–53.

6. Marx Wartofsky, "Action and Passion: Spinoza's Construction of a Scientific Psychology," in: Marjorie Grene, ed., *Spinoza. A Collection of Critical Essays* (Garden City, N.Y., 1973), pp. 329–53, at p. 332.

7. *Oeuvres de Descartes* (A.–T. IX), p. 14: The roots are metaphysics, the trunk, physics, and the three principle branches are medicine, mechanics, and morality, "le dernier degré de sagesse."

8. On the history of Hobbes's plans for this trilogy, *see* F.O. Wolf, *Die neue Wissenschaft des Thomas Hobbes* (Stuttgart, 1969), pp. 24–29. Note, too, that in the Prefatory Epistle to the separately published text of *De corpore* (*Opera Latina*, ed., Molesworth, Vol. II), Hobbes makes clear that *body* is the unifying theme of the *Elementa*; "since man is not only a natural body, but is also part of a citizenry, that is . . . , of a body politic."

9. *Discours de la méthode* (A.–T. VI), pp. 7–8.

10. *Cf.* Manfred Riedel, "Kausalität und Finalität in Hobbes's "Natur-philosophie," in M.R., *Metaphysik und Metapolitik* (Frankfurt a.M., 1975), pp. 192–217.

11. On the new "anthropology," Wilhelm Dilthey's study ("Die Funktion der Anthropologie in der Kultur des 16. u. 17. Jahrhunderts," in *W.D.*, *Weltan-schauung und Analyse des Menschen seit Renaissance u. Reformation*, G.W., Bd. 2 (Göttingen, 1968, pp. 416–92)) still remains fundamental, despite his enthusi-asm for the role of Renaissance Neo-stoics in the formation of early seventeenth century thought. Some important differences are brought out in Hans Blumenberg, *Selbsterhaltung und Beharrung. Zur Konstitution der neuzeitlichen Rationalität*, Abhandlungen der Gestes-u. Sozialwiss. Kl. Akademie der Wiss. u. der Literatur, Mainz, Jg., 1969, #11 (1971). (This work is also valuable for the understanding of Spinoza's concept of *conservatio sui*.)

12. Consequently, the collateral campaign I am sketching may have the status of an "ideal-type." Descartes clearly begins with physics and mathematics; Hobbes, with Thucydides and Aristotle's *Rhetoric*. This difference is, to my mind, less im-portant than the fact that both brought the two disciplines into conjunction. A good account of some primary aspects of the campaign is in Amos Funkenstein, "Natural Science and Social Theory: Hobbes, Spinoza and Vico," in G. Taglia-cozzo, and D.P. Verene, eds., *Giambattista Vico's Science of Humanity* (Baltimore, 1976), pp. 187–212.

13. Descartes wraps the mysteries of his ethics in the enigmas of his psycho-physiology. *Cf.* Alexandre Matheron, "Psychologie et politique: Descartes, la noblesse du chatouillement," Dialectiques No. 6 (1974), pp. 79–98, for an illumi-nating study of these matters.

14. Published in Breslau, 1785. On the revival of Spinozism and the so-called "Atheismusstreit," *see* L. Bäck, *Spinozas Erste Einwirkungen auf Deutschland* (Berlin, 1895).

15. *Fragmente* #1770 in *Werke*, I, ed., E. Wasmuth (Heidelberg, 1957), p. 476.

16. *Gesammelte Werke* (ed. Glockner), Vol. XIX, p. 376.

17. *Ibid.*, p. 375. Hegel also discusses Spinoza at length in *Glauben und Wissen*, G.W., I, pp. 336–46 and in the *Wissenschaft der Logik*, II (ed., Lasson), pp. 164–69.

18. On the many further aspects of Hegel's "reading" of Spinoza, cf. Efraim Schmueli, "Hegel's Interpretation of Spinoza's Concept of Substance," International Journal for the Philosophy of Religion, 1 (1970), pp. 176–91; Stanley Rosen, "Hegel, Descartes and Spinoza," in James B. Wilbur, ed., Spinoza's Metaphysics. Essays in Critical Appreciation (Assen, 1976), pp. 115–32; Gueroult, op. cit., I, pp. 462–68; Zac, op. cit., pp. 248–51.

19. The literature devoted directly to Spinoza's physical principles is, unsurprisingly, meager compared to the literature dealing with his metaphysics and theology ,etc. However, there are a number of studies of considerable importance of which I have made use in trying to understand this topic. S. von Dunin Borkowski, "Die Physik Spinozas," in Septimana Spinozana (The Hague, 1933), pp. 85–101; L. Brunschvicq, "Physique et metaphysique," ibid., pp. 43–54; idem, Spinoza et ses contemporains (Paris, 1923), Ch. IX; Francois Duchesneau, "Du modèle cartésien au modèle spinoziste de l'être vivant," Canadian Journal of Philosophy, 3 (1974), pp. 539–62; William J. Edgar, "Continuity and the Individuation of Modes in Spinoza's Physics," in J.B. Wilbur, ed., Spinoza's Metaphysics. Essays in Critical Appreciation (Assen, 1976), pp. 85–105: Michele Giorgiantonio, "Intorno ad un tentativo di ricostruzione della meccancia e della fisica di Spinoza," Sophia, 22 (1954), pp. 326–30; A.R. Hall and M.B. Hall, "Philosophy and Natural Philosophy: Boyle and Spinoza," in Mélanges Alexandre Koyré. L'Aventure de l'esprit, II (Paris, 1964), pp. 241–56; Pierre Jacob, "La politique avec la physique à l'âge classique. Principe d'inertie et conatus: Descartes, Hobbes et Spinoza," Dialectiques, n.6 (1974), pp. 99–121; Richard McKeon, "Spinoza on the Rainbow and on Probability," in Harry A. Wolfson Jubilee Volume (Jerusalem, 1965), pp. 533–59; Albert Rivaud, "La physique de Spinoza," Chronicon Spinozianum 4 (1924/26), pp. 24–57; P. von der Hoeven, "Over Spinoza's Interpretatie van de Cartesiaanse Fysicaen Betekenis daarvaan voor het Systeem der Ethica," Tijdschrift voor Filosofie, 35 (1973), pp. 27–86; idem, "The Significance of Cartesian Physics for Spinoza's Theory of Knowledge," in Spinoza on Knowing, Being and Freedom, ed., J.G. van der Bend (Assen, 1974), pp. 114–25. Of these I have learned most from the papers by von Dunin Borkowski, Jacob, and Rivaud; van der Hoeven's long paper is detailed and provocative.

20. Gueroult writes that for Spinoza "physics was only an accessory preoccupation," op. cit., II, p. 568.

21. For useful criticisms of some of these alleged affinities, see S. Zac, op. cit., pp. 78–80 and H. Blumenberg, op. cit.

22. The first quite likely refers to TdIE. See H.H. Joachim, Spinoza's Tractatus de Intellectus Emendatione (Oxford, 1940), pp. 11–12.

23. C. Sigwart, cited by Joachim, ibid., p. 12, n. 1, seems to have missed the sense of "nondum ordine conscripta sunt." This does not mean that he had not written anything.

24. I shall keep the term "affections" (for affectiones) throughout, so that its close link with affectus will be apparent. Elwes' choices, "modifications" and "emotions," obscure the semantic kinship.

25. Op. cit., p. 85.

26. Cf. Leon Brunschvicq, Spinoza et ses contemporains, op cit., pp. 243, 266.

27. Descartes à Mersenne, 27 July 1638 (A.–T. II 268). But cf. the distinction drawn in the Entretiens avec Burman (A.–T. V, 160) between physics and mathematics.

28. On Descartes' battle against the Aristotelian theory of science, cf. Jean-Luc Marion, L'ontologie grise de Descartes (Paris, 1976).

29. Alexandre Koyré, *Études Galiléennes* (Paris, 1966), p. 319. On the *Regulae* and the scheme of a *mathesis universalis* see, above all, Jacob Klein, *Greek Mathematical Thought and the Origins of Algebra* (Cambridge, Mass., 1968), and Lüder Gäbe, "Einleitung," *Rene Descartes, Regulae ad directionem ingenii*, ed. H. Springmeyer, *et al.* (Hamburg, 1973), pp. xxi–xlix.

30. *Cf. Prin. Phil.*, II, 23.

31. *Cf. Prin. Phil.*, II, 10–15.

32. *Cf. Le Monde* (A.–T. XI), p. 33.

33. *Ibid.*, p. 37.

34. *Ibid.*, p. 39–40. *See* John Wild, "The Cartesian Deformation of the Structure of Change and its Influence on Modern Thought," *Philosophical Review*, 50 (1941), pp. 36–59.

35. *See* A. Koyré, *op. cit.*

36. From II, 4 to II 35, he discusses the *nature* of motion (in the plenum); from II, 36 to II 64, he discusses the *causes of motion* (in a void or vacuum). On this whole problem, *see* Martial Gueroult, "Metaphysique et physique de la Force chez Descartes et Malebranche," in M.G., *Études sur Descartes, Spinoza, Malebranche et Leibniz*, (Hildesheim, 1970), pp. 85–121; Henri Carteron, "L'idée de la force mécanique dans la système de Descartes," *Révue Philosophique*, 94, (1922) pp. 243–77; 483–511.

37. *See* R. Catesby Taliaferro, *The Concept of Matter in Descartes and Leibniz* (Notre Dame, Ind., 1964), pp. 19–21.

38. *Cf. Prin. Phil.* II, 39, with *ibid.*, III, 56. *See* Thomas A. Prendergast, "Descartes and the Relativity of Motion," *Modern Schoolman* 50 (1972) pp. 64–72. The best work on the entire subject, to my knowledge, is Alan Gabbey, "Force and Inertia in Seventeenth-Century Dynamics," *Studies in the History and Philosophy of Science*, 2 (1971), pp. 1–67.

39. On the reality of rest and its conservation in the universe as a whole, *see* Gueroult, *Etudes . . .* , *op. cit.* pp. 92–94.

40. Note that Descartes has obviously seen problems arising since composing the unpublished *Le Monde*. There God endows matter with rectilinear motion only (A.–T. XI, p. 46); now, in *Prin. Phil.* II, 36, God is said to "move the parts of matter in diverse ways (*diversimode*)."

41. This is why Koyré (*op. cit.*, p. 129) thinks the relativistic thesis is a sham, designed to camouflage Descartes' Copernicanism.

42. *Prin. Phil.* II, 25.

43. This line of interpretation gains in plausibility if one considers the strikingly similar *Fragestellung* motivating Leibniz's dynamics and metaphysics. His monads are a response to the twin demands of individuation and intrinsic causal explanation of movement and change. *See, e.g., De ipsa natura* (*Philosophische Schriften*, ed. Gebhardt, IV, 504–16. A very good recent account of these issues is by J.E. McGuire, " 'Labyrinthus Continui': Leibniz on Substance, Activity and Matter," in R. Turnbull and P. Machamer, eds., *Motion and Time, Space and Matter* (Columbus, Ohio, 1976), pp. 290–326.

Leibniz was, to be sure, as critical of Spinoza as he was of almost all his contemporaries and proximate predecessors. I cannot enter here into any further questions of their philosophical relationship. *Cf.* L.A. Foucher de Careil, *Leibniz, Descartes et Spinoza* (Paris, 1862); Ludwig Stein, *Leibniz und Spinoza* (Berlin, 1890); G. Dawes Hicks, "The 'Modes' of Spinoza and the 'Monads' of Leibniz," *Proc. Arist. Society* 18, (1918), pp. 329–62; Georges Friedmann, *Leibniz et*

Spinoza, edit., révue et augmentée, (Paris, 1962); and Martha Kneale, "Leibniz and Spinoza on Activity," in H.G. Frankfort, ed., *Leibniz. A Collection of Critical Essays* (New York, 1972), pp. 215–37.

44. See Meyer's Preface to *PP*, Land, 108; Hayes, 9.

45. The *Korte Verhandeling* seems to me to be in agreement with the *Ethics* in all that concerns the body considered for itself. *PP* is a more difficult text in this regard, since Spinoza explicitly withholds his endorsement of all the demonstrations. (*PP*, Land, 108; Hayes, 9) *Cf.*, however, Matheron, *op. cit.*, p. 27, n.12.

46. This disagreement is at the heart of his debate with Boyle. *Cf.* A.R. Hall and M.B. Hall, *op. cit.*, and R. McKeon, *lib. cit.*, pp. 130–57.

47. I shall adopt the convention of using an asterisk after the numeral to distinguish the second set of axioms from the first.

48. M. Gueroult, *lib. cit.*, II, p. 156. Later, Spinoza refers to (simple) bodies differing in "magnitudo." This raises the question whether there is a material or quantitative substratum of the *corpora simplicissima*. See also H.H. Joachim, *A Study of the Ethics of Spinoza* (Oxford, 1901), p. 83, n.1.

49. *Cf.* the theses of Deleuze, *op. cit.*, pp. 181–88 (infinitely small extensive parts), von Dunin Borkowski, *op. cit.*, pp. 90–93 (corpuscles of aetherial fluid), and Gueroult, *op. cit.* II, pp. 158–64 (modeled on Huyghen's theory of simple pendula).

50. *See* Pierre Jacob, *op. cit.*, p. 116.

51. Deleuze, *op. cit.*, p. 183–88, reads this as signifying that every individual body incorporates an infinite number of *corpora simplicissima*. This makes sense given the infinite *modal* divisibility of Substance under the Attribute of Extension. *Cf.* also *Ep.* 12 to Meyer on maximum and minimum (Elwes II, 317–323).

52. These correspondences suggest that *natura* in Lemma 4 should also be interpreted as *ratio* and not as volume, as Gueroult claims.

53. If there had been any doubt before, the Dutch usage settles the question that what Spinoza means in these passages of the *Ethics* by *ratio* is something more precise than Elwes' "relation" lets the reader see. Note, too, that *certa ratio* is stronger than *quaedam ratio* would have been. Its sense is possibly given in Spinoza's frequent use later on of the phrase *certa ac determinata*. In the same passage of KV, Spinoza's translator uses "wezentlijke proportie," probably to render *ratio essentialis*.

54. I add the parenthesis because of Spinoza's critique of numbers and of arithmetic generally, especially in *Ep.* 12 to Louis Meyer (see Gueroult, *op. cit.* I, pp. 413–26, on *entia rationis*, and *ibid.*, pp. 500–28, on the letter to Meyer). However, the elements in the ratio need not themselves *be* numbers; they can be any comparable magnitudes, for instance, lines or any other geometrical figure. This is, of course, the lesson of Descartes' *Regulae* and would have appealed to Spinoza, the great enthusiast of geometry. In any case, it is enough to establish that the ration *is* intended to be mathematically precise (*certa*) to see the error in van der Hoeven's claim that Spinoza drops the mathematics when he takes over Descartes' physics. *Cf.* van der Hoeven, "Over Spinoza's Interpretie . . ." *op. cit.*, p. 84; I also have difficulty understanding why van der Hoeven says, *ibid.*, that Spinoza eliminates Descartes' conservation principle.

55. Thus, in Lemmata 4–7, the *ratio* remains the same.

56. Matheron, *Individu et communauté chez Spinoza, op. cit.*, p. 48.

57. *Cf. Ep.* 32; Land 121; Elwes II, 291, where *communicare* and *transferre* are used interchangeably.

58. *Cf.* Rivaud, *op. cit.*, pp. 30–31, for a conjecture on Spinoza's reason for

rejecting only the sixth of Descartes' seven laws of impact. (*Ep.* 32, Land, 122; Elwes II, 293)

59. In particular, metabolism (E II, Post. 4) and brain activity (E II, Post. 5).

60. *Cf.* Jacob, *op. cit.*, pp. 115–18.

61. *Cf.* Gueroult, *op. cit.*, II, p. 166 sq.

62. *Cf. ibid.*

63. *Codex* here is a double pun; it denotes not a *code* in the cryptographic sense, but, rather, a volume (such as Galileo's "libro della Natura"), and, at the same time, a code of laws, as in the *Codex Justinianus.*

64. The phrase is a difficult one to interpret. It is used by Suarez, *Disputationes Metaphysicae*, Disp. 31, sect. 3 (*esse essentiae actualis*) in contradistinction from *essentia potentialis.* Spinoza may have wanted to stress that no essence is potential. Equally, he may have been hinting at a connection with God as *essentia actuosa.* (E II, P3, S)

65. This does not conflict with E II, P37, since each essence is constituted by its own unique *conatus*, but all essences have (or, are) a conatus.

66. Another synonym for "good" that could have added to the sequence is *laetitia*, or joyful pleasure, (E IV, App., Chap. 30), for this ties in with the affect of *acquiescientia*, and, later, with knowledge of the third kind.

67. *Cf.* Joachim, *A Study . . . , op. cit.*, p. 140.

68. Descartes, *Resp. ad IV Obj.* (A.–T. VI), p. 232; *Resp. ad III, Obj. ibid.*, p. 188.

69. Gueroult, *op. cit.*, II, p. 245.

70. This is the most marked difference between *Ethics* and the *Short Treatise*, for in the latter (KV II, Chap. 19 and 20), Spinoza is still toying with the Cartesian notion that the mind cannot move the body or bring it to rest, but it can "determine" it, that is, change its direction, which is not a component of Descartes' scalar "quantity of motion." *Cf.* Leibniz, "Reply to the Objections of Boyle," *Philosophical Papers and Letters* (ed. Loemker), p. 577: "The Cartesians have had poor success . . . in trying to maintain that the soul cannot give motion to the body, but that it can nevertheless give it its direction."

71. *Cf.* E III, P2, S: "When the body is at rest in sleep, the mind at the same time remains torpid together with it, nor does it have the power of cogitating, as it does when the body is awake."

72. *Fabrica* here has at least a double meaning. It refers to an artisan's workshop, as well as to the products of his workshop. *Cf.* Matheron, *Individu . . . , op. cit.*, pp. 558–60.

73. It is worth remarking that Elwes' translation of *reflectantur* as "refracted" is quite inaccurate.

74. *Cf.* Zac, *op. cit.*, p. 110 sq., with reference to *TdIE*, Land, 10–11; Elwes II, 11.

75. *Cf.* Gueroult, *op. cit.*, II, pp. 467–87.

76. I have not done justice to the pivotal concept of *acquiescientia*; this is all the more unfortunate since Spinoza asserts that it is "in truth, the highest thing (*summum*) we can hope for (IV, Prop. 52, Schl.). Indeed, *acquiescientia* is something of an Ariadne's thread leading us through the labyrinth of *Ethics*, Parts Four and Five. (E III, P51, S; E III, P53 & C; E IV, P55, S; E III Df. Aff. 25–26; E IV, P52; E IV, App., Cap. 4 & 32; E V, P4, S; E V, P10, S; E V, P36, S; E V, P38, S; E V, P42, S (bis)). For further references *cf.* E. Giancotti-Boscherini, *Lexicon Spinozianum, I* (The Hague, 1970), s.v.).

Spinoza takes the term, if not the whole concept, from the anonymous Latin translation (Amsterdam, 1650) of Descartes' *Passions de l'âme*, Art. 190, where *acquiescientia in se ipso* is the rendition of Descartes' *la satisfaction de soi-même*. (*Générosité*, the key passion for Descartes, is demoted by Spinoza to a subsidiary position alongside *animositas*, the second species of *fortitudo*. (*E* III, P59, S) The essentially egoistic, not to say, narcissistic, character of Spinoza's *acquiescientia* allows us to detect how false a scent he left when he used *philautia* as a synonym (*E* III, P55, S). In Aristotle (*EN* IX, 8), love of self is intimately linked with friendship with others, while Spinozistic self-love is necessarily comparative and competitive, like glory in Hobbes. Friendship in Spinoza's theory would have to be classed as a species of "friendship for the sake of/on account of the useful" in Aristotle's three-fold scheme (*EN* VIII, 3, 1156a5-32), unless, of course, one accepts Spinoza's equation of virtue with power. (*Cf. E* IV, P35, C1; *E* IV, P37; *E* IV, P20, Dm.)

77. To cite a single, capital example: Quantity of motion in Descartes cannot be represented as 'mv', since Descartes has no concept of mass and treats velocity as a scalar, rather than vectorial, quantity. Gueroult, *Etudes* . . . , *op. cit.*, p. 114, n. 4, among others, is guilty of imprudence on this score.

78. *Cf.* Sir Frederick Pollock, *Spinoza. His Life and Philosophy* (London, 1899), p. 103. Pollock's suggestion was endorsed by Joachim, *A Study* . . . *op. cit.*, p. 83, n. i.

79. *Cf.* Descartes, *Prin. Phil.* II, 36 and *Le Monde* (A.-T. XI), p. 40; also, *Prin. Phil.* II, 26 & II, 44. On occasion, Descartes drops "rest" from his formulations, *cf. ibid.*, II, 42; but these omissions cannot override the argument from basic principles. For Aristotle's position, cf. *Physics* V 6, 229b23-230a18.

80. *Prin. Phil.* II, 43. This passage has been construed in the most various ways; especially difficult is the construction *tum . . . tum* in the last line. For discussions of the quantity of motion, *cf.* Gabbey, *op. cit.*, p. 22; Patrick Suppes, "Descartes and the Problem of Action at a Distance," *Journal of the History of Ideas* 15 (1954), pp. 146–52; Pierre Costabel, "Essai critique sur quelques concepts de la mécanique cartésienne," *Archives internationales d'histoire des sciences* 20 (1967), pp. 235–52; Desmond M. Clarke, "The Impact Rules of Descartes' Physics," *Isis* 68 (1977), pp. 55–66. (Motion in the sense of local displacement is, of course, measured simply by the distance traversed, since Descartes eliminates the time-variable.) For the quantity of rest, *cf.* note 83, *infra*.

81. *Prin. Phil.* II, 29. Note that this statement of relativity occurs *after* the distinction between the vulgar and the strict definitions of motion in II, 24 & 25.

82. *Cf.* Gueroult, *Etudes* . . . *op. cit.*, esp. pp. 85-92. The extreme consequences of this view that causes and forces are extrinsic to the bodies on which they act were drawn by the Occasionalists. *Cf.* T.M. Lennon "Occasionalism and the Cartesian Metaphysic of Motion," *Canadian Journal of Philosophy*, Supplementary Volume I, Part I (1974), pp. 29–40.

83. For (i) & (ii), *cf. Prin. Phil.* II, 43; for (iii), *cf. ibid.*, II, 55. To the best of my knowledge, Descartes never discusses the common ground of these three functions. On the variable measure of the quantity of rest, *cf.* Koyré, *op. cit.*, p. 331.

84. *Cf. KV* I, chap. 2, Land, 12n., Wolf(b), 28n.; *KV* II, Praefatio, Land, 36-7, Wolf(b), 63-5, notes 7-15; *KV* II, chap. 19, Land, 72-3, Wolf(b), 120-1; *KV* II, App. 2, Land, 98-99, Wolf(b) 161-62; *PP* II, P11 S; *PP* II, P13. Only in *KV* I, chap. 9, Land, 37, Wolf(b), 57 does Spinoza mention motion without adding "rest."

85. Spinoza alludes to this argument again in *KV*, App. II; Land, 98–99; Wolf(b), 161. On the passage cited, *cf.* Gueroult, *Spinoza II, op. cit.*, p. 180. The text reads like a gloss on Descartes, *Prin. Phil.* II, 34 and thus has to do with the problem of the real indivisibility of infinite extension versus its modal divisibility *ad infinitum*. On the analoguous argument in *E* I, P15, S, *cf.* Gueroult, *ibid.* I, pp. 529–56; Douglas Lewis, "Spinoza on Extension," *Midwest Studies in Philosophy* 1 (1976), pp. 26–31 & Alan Donagan, "Spinoza and Descartes on Extension: A Comment," *ibid.*, pp. 31–33.

86. Other such instances would be his statement of a principle of simplicity or minimality used in the derivation of the rules of impact (*E* II, P23), his demonstration of the difference between force of motion and force of determination (*E* II, P27, S) and, finally, what seems to be the germ of a vectorial concept of velocity (*E* II, P36).

87. The parallel series would hold for rest as well. *Cf. Ep.* VI, 20: *motus, quies et eorum leges.*

88. This raises the sensitive problem of the compatibility between the thesis that causality is intrinsic because it rests on an infinite sequence of finite modes of the same attribute and the claim made here that the forces of motion and rest are intrinsic to each individual exhibiting one or the other or both. Spinoza's concept of essence and its identification with *conatus* (Ethics IV, Prop. 7) would have to provide the solution to this problem. On the general question of causality in Spinoza, *cf.* James G. Lennox, "The Causality of Finite Modes in Spinoza's *Ethics*," *Canadian Journal of Philosophy* 6 (1976), pp. 479–500.

89. *Cf.* Rivaud, *op. cit.*, p. 26 & 53, and E.F. Hallett, *Aeternitas, A Spinozistic Study* (Oxford, 1930), pp. 137–41.

90. For Descartes, *cf. Prin. Phil.* II, 44; for Spinoza, PP II, P22, C3.

91. Descartes, *ibid.*; Spinoza, *ibid.*, II, Prop. 22, Cor. 1 and II, Prop. 27.

92. Cohesion: von Dunin Borkowski, *op. cit.*, pp. 94–99; Equilibrium: Jacob, *op. cit.*, pp. 115–18. Gueroult, *Etudes . . . op. cit.*, pp. 118–19 brings out the weaknesses in the equilibrium-thesis. It should also be noted that Spinoza gives a somewhat different account of cohesion (*cohaerentia*) in *Ep.* XXXII to Oldenbourg, discussed above, pp. 90–91.

93. *Cf.* Pollock, *op. cit.*, pp. 106–107; A. Wolf, "Spinoza's Conception of the Attributes of Substance," *Proc. Arist. Society*, N.S. 27 (1927), pp. 177–92 & Leon Roth, *Spinoza* (London, 1929), pp. 83–84.

94. On the identification of *potentia* with *potestas* and the reduction of potentiality to actuality, *cf.* Gueroult, *Spinoza I, op. cit.*, pp. 387–89; Jacob, *op. cit.*, pp. 118–20; Deleuze, *op. cit.*, pp. 82–84 & Leo Strauss, *Natural Right and History* (Chicago, 1953), pp. 194–96. The key texts in this regard are *E* I, P34 & 35.

95. *Cf.* Matheron, *op. cit.*, p. 28. Matheron restricts this trope to the *corpora simplicissima*. On the other hand, it should be noted that Spinoza drops from the final statements of his political theory the Hobbesian notion of contract; that is, the state of nature and the civil state are no longer radically distinguishable. (*Cf. Ep.* 50, Land, 172, Wolf(b), 369 and *TP* II, 12).

96. *Cf.* Gueroult, *Spinoza II, op. cit.*, p. 563–69.

97. *Cf.* Jacob, *op. cit.*, p. 107.

98. The best account of the sense and roles of "expression" is in Deleuze, *op. cit.*, *passim.*

99. *Cf.* Zac, *op. cit.*, ch. 3. This observation does not settle the question of the character of extension in *natura naturata*, or, in other words, the vexing problem

of the material substrate or bearer of the relevant ratios of motion and rest. The expression *eiusdem aut diversae magnitudinis* in the Phyical Digression, is one crux among many. *Cf.* von Dunin Borkowski, *op. cit.*, p. 98–99, Joachim, *A Study . . . op. cit.*, p. 83, n.1, and Gueroult, *Spinoza II, op. cit.*, pp. 161–64.

100. *Cf.* von Dunin Borkowski, *op. cit.*, pp. 98–101 and Mendel Sachs, "Maimonides, Spinoza and the Field Concept in Physics," *Journal of the History of Ideas* 37 (1976), pp. 125–31.

Malebranche's Refutation of Spinoza

DAISIE RADNER
State University of New York at Buffalo

One of the major disagreements between Spinoza and his Cartesian contemporaries had to do with whether extension is an attribute of God or infinite substance. Spinoza had to make his God extended in order to preserve God's absolute infinity and special status as the sole substance. The Cartesians denied extension to God because they believed that extendedness implies divisibility and that divisibility is incompatible with the divine nature. Spinoza rejected the supposition that infinite extension is divisible. Malebranche objected that Spinoza's "atheistic" system rests upon a confusion between extension and the idea of extension. It is the idea of extension which is infinite, eternal, and indivisible; extension itself is none of these.

Is Malebranche right? Is Spinoza guilty of the confusion that Malebranche attributes to him? One has to see what is meant by the criticism and on what basis it is made before one can assess its worth. My procedure here is as follows. First, I outline the steps which led Spinoza to the conclusion that extension is infinite, eternal, and indivisible. Second, I give Malebranche's criticism, reconstructing it in terms of what he holds in common with Spinoza and what he rejects. Third, I consider what there is in Spinoza that serves as a reply to Malebranche. Finally, I evaluate Malebranche as a critic of Spinoza. My thesis is that Spinoza's unique conception of the substance-mode relation enables him to escape the criticism.

I.

Spinoza's extension is infinite, indivisible, and eternal because it is an attribute of infinite, indivisible, and eternal substance. The argument is clearly laid out in the *Ethics*.[1] (1) There cannot be two substances with the same nature or attribute. If there were two substances, they would be distinguishable either with respect to their attributes or with respect to their modes. If they are distinguished in terms of their attributes then they must have different attributes and consequently different natures. If they are distinguished in terms of their modes, the modes may be disregarded because they are only conceived through substance, but then the two substances are not distinguished at all. (E I, P5, Dm.) (2) One substance cannot be produced by another substance. For like can only be produced by like and, by (1), there is no other substance like it. (E I, P6, Dm.) (3) Every substance is cause of itself, i.e., it pertains to its nature to exist. (E I, P7) This follows from (2) and the definition of "cause of itself." (4) Every substance is infinite. If it were finite it would be limited by another of the same nature, for that is what it means to be finite. But, by (1), there is no other substance of the same nature. Thus there is nothing to limit it. Consequently it is infinite. (E I, P8, Dm.) (5) Every substance is eternal. This follows from (3) and the definition of eternity. (E I, P19, Dm.) (6) Every substance is indivisible. If it were divided, its parts would either be substances themselves or not. If they are substances, then each part will be infinite, by (4), and there will be a number of substances produced from one substance, which contradicts (2). If they are not substances, then the substances in being divided into parts will cease to be, which contradicts (3). (E I, P12, Dm.) (7) There are not two substances with different natures or attributes, but only one substance to which all attributes belong. The more reality a thing has, the more attributes it possesses. God or substance absolutely infinite is substance having an infinite number of attributes, each expressing its nature or essence. (E I, P10, S) Spinoza gives several proofs of the existence of such a being. (E I, P11, Dm. and S) (8) Extension is an attribute of God or of substance absolutely infinite. Individual bodies are modes which express the nature of God in a certain and determinate manner. Thus God possesses an attribute the conception of which is involved in all individual bodies and through which they are conceived. (E II, P2, Dm.)

Those who deny that extension is an attribute of God would have extended substance created by God, but this is impossible in light of (2) as well as (7). Extended or corporeal substance is not a substance in addition to God; it is God himself. Philosophers suppose that extension cannot be an attribute of God because they think of it as being composed of parts, thus not infinite, thus not an attribute of absolutely infinite substance. Spinoza cites three arguments designed to show that extension is not infinite. (E I, P15, S)[2] The first is that if infinite extended substance is divided into two parts, the parts are either finite or infinite. If they are finite then there is an infinite composed of finite parts, which is absurd. If they are infinite then there is one infinite twice as great as another, which is also absurd. The second argument is also based on the principle that one infinite quantity cannot be greater than another. Suppose that infinite extension is measured by units of one foot. There would be an infinite number of such parts. But each one-foot part can be divided into twelve one-inch parts. The number of one-inch parts would be an infinite number twelve times the infinite number of one-foot parts, which is absurd. The third argument is that if one supposes two finite lines AB and AC drawn at an angle from a single point A, points B and C will be at a determinate distance from one another, but as the lines are extended to infinity the distance between B and C becomes indeterminable. All these arguments purport to show that the supposition that extension is infinite leads to absurdities and thus must be rejected as false.

Spinoza's reply to these arguments is that the absurdities follow not "from the supposition that quantity is infinite, but from the supposition that infinite quantity is measurable, and that it is made up of finite parts." (E I, P15, S) Given that absurdities really do follow from the assumption that infinite extension is divisible (Spinoza has no quarrel with his opponents on this score), then there are two ways of getting around them. One is to deny that extension is infinite. The other is to affirm that extension is infinite, but to deny that it is divisible into parts. The others take the first way out. Spinoza chooses the second. The absurdities have to do with the nature of the parts into which infinite extension is supposedly divided, not with the infinity of extension as such. All the arguments show is that if extended substance is infinite then it is not divisible. Whether extended substance is infinite has to be decided on other grounds. Spinoza believes that there are other grounds; they have already been given, and what they establish is that extended substance is infinite.

Bodies are not parts of extended or corporeal substance, but modes of it. In the course of his polemic against those who deny infinity to extension, Spinoza writes: ". . . it is not less absurd to suppose that corporeal substance is composed of bodies or parts than to suppose that a body is composed of surfaces, surfaces of lines, and that lines, finally, are composed of points." (E I, P15, S) He is not merely giving examples of other equally absurd (but unrelated) claims. He is giving examples of the same kind of mistake. The point-line, line-surface, surface-solid relation is meant to serve as an analogy, to show how modes of substance differ from parts. Just as a line is not an aggregate of points, a plane not an aggregate of lines nor a solid of planes, so extended substance is not an aggregate of bodies. Just as a line is not divisible into points (but only into lines), a plane is not divisible into lines (but only into planes), nor a solid into planes (but only into solids), so extended substance is not divisible into bodies (albeit not into substances either).

It may be argued that a line is nevertheless conceived through a point, a plane through a line, and a solid through a plane, because a line is generated by a moving point, a plane by a moving line, and a solid by a moving plane. But to speak of moving a point, a line, or a plane is to presuppose a space through which it is moved. The generation of a solid by the motion of a plane presupposes three dimensions, the generation of a plane by the motion of a line presupposes (at least) two, and the generation of a line by the motion of a point (at least) one. One does not start with a point and work up, one starts with three-dimensional space and works down. It is more properly the point which is conceived through the line, the line through the plane, and the plane through the solid. For given any solid, one can always limit it at a plane; thus a plane may be defined as the limit of a solid. Given a plane one can limit it at a line, and given a line one can limit it at a point; thus a line is the limit of a plane and a point of a line. Similarly, bodies are conceived through extension in the sense that they are limits of it. The only way to get multiplicity out of the unity which is infinite extended substance is by limiting it, or rather by considering it as limited. This is what Spinoza means when he says that individual bodies or finite modes express God's nature or essence in a certain and determinate manner. (*E* I, P25, C; *E* II, Df. 1)

II.

Malebranche was asked by Dortous de Mairan to point out the paralogisms or mistakes in Spinoza's *Ethics*.[3] He answered that the main cause of Spinoza's errors is that he takes the ideas of things for the things themselves. What is apprehended as eternal, necessary, infinite, and indivisible is "intelligible extension" or the idea of extension, not created extension, which is the object represented by the idea. Spinoza, having convinced himself that creation is impossible, makes the ideal world into the material world and assigns to corporeal substance features which rightfully appertain only to the idea of it.[4]

Mairan is not satisfied. Surely no one is more careful than Spinoza to distinguish between ideas and their objects.[5] His theory of extension holds good within the context of that distinction. The idea of extension represents extension to us as infinite, eternal, etc. For what else does it mean to say that the idea is infinite but that it offers the mind an infinite representation? The so-called created world, the world of bodies, the world that is finite, temporal, and divisible, is not the object of the idea of extended substance but a mode of that object.[6] In the final analysis, Spinoza's view is not very different from Malebranche's own. Spinoza's extended substance, like Malebranche's intelligible extension, is infinite, eternal, and divine, and Spinoza's bodies relate to his extended substance as Malebranche's relate to his intelligible extension, not as parts but as modes.[7] Whether Mairan is right about Malebranche's theory is not at issue here. The question that concerns us is whether Malebranche is right about Spinoza, and Mairan insists that he is not.

Incensed by the accusation of Spinozism, Malebranche elaborates upon his initial criticism. Spinoza confuses ideas and their objects not in that he fails to acknowledge an idea-object distinction but rather in that he thinks that the object is infinite, eternal, etc., because the idea of it is. This error is the result of a misapplication of the Cartesian principle that one can affirm of a thing whatever one clearly conceives to be contained in the idea of it. This principle holds only with regard to the essence and properties of the thing and not with regard to the circumstances of its existence. I can infer that matter is divisible and movable because the idea I have of it represents it to me as such, but I cannot infer that it exists because the idea exists nor that it is infinite and eternal because the idea is.[8] The point Malebranche is making may be formulated in terms of Descartes' distinction between the formal reality and the objective reality of the idea. One can conclude nothing about the object of the idea from the formal properties of the idea; whatever is concluded about the object must be in the idea objectively or by representation. The idea of extension is formally an infinite idea, but it is not infinite in its objective realty, that is to say, it does not represent extension as infinite. The idea is eternal, but it does not represent extension as eternal. It is indivisible, but it does not represent extension as indivisible. It is necessary, but it does not represent extension as necessary.

As for Spinoza's claim that bodies are not parts of extension but modes of it, it is true that bodies cannot be conceived without extension, but it by no means follows that they are modes of extension. A body cannot be conceived without extension only because no substance can be conceived without its essence.[9] By Spinoza's own definition bodies are substances. For all that can be conceived alone is a substance, and a single cubic foot of extension can be conceived alone. Thus this cubic foot of extension is a substance, and its cubic figure is a modification of it.[10] At this point Mairan protests that it makes no sense to speak of a single cubic foot of extension existing all alone. If an extended thing is limited then there must be another extended thing which limits it. It cannot be said that it is limited by a possible extended thing, for that would be to suppose that there is a space around it which could be filled but is not, which in Cartesian terms is plainly absurd.[11] Malebranche replies that a portion of extension can be conceived to exist by itself without conceiving of anything beyond its surface serving to draw its boundaries; for the figure a body has is defined not in terms of its relation to other bodies surrounding it, but in terms of the relation its own parts bear to one anoher. A sphere, for example, is a three-dimensional figure all of whose surface points are equidistant from its center. That there is such a figure does not presuppose that there is anything else beyond it.[12]

When Malebranche says that one cannot infer that material substance is infinite because the idea of it is and that a single cubic foot of extension can exist all alone, he does not mean to imply that material substance is necessarily finite in extent or in dimensions. The idea of extension represents extension as capable of either finite or infinite extent. The material world may consist of a single cubic foot of extension all alone, or it may be completely unbounded, with parts beyond every part, or it may be of any magnitude in between. One cannot determine its extent simply by consulting the idea of extension. Its extent is determined by God's will, not by its own nature.[13]

There is a sense in which the material world *cannot* be infinite. Malebranche explains this sense of 'infinite' in the *Éclaircissements*:

> It is a characteristic of the infinite to be at the same time one and all things, composed, so to speak, of an infinity of perfections and so simple that each perfection it possesses includes all the others without any real distinction. . . .[14]

What Malebranche means here by 'infinite' is similar to what Spinoza means by 'absolutely infinite'. (See *E* I, Df. 6, Expl.) It is infinity or unlimitedness in the sense of absence of negation. It is having a feature without thereby being precluded from having any other positive feature. In the passage just quoted, Malebranche is referring to God, but it is clear from his other writings that he considers anything that is general to be infinite or unlimited in this sense. A circle in general, for example, is at the same time one and all circles, and it is an infinite, even though it is not *the* infinite which is one and all things.[15] Extension in general is not all things (for example, it is not thought), yet it is unlimited in a way in which no created extension, however vast, can be. A material object, in being circular, is thereby precluded from being square, but matter in general has each figure in it in such a way that it is not precluded from having any other in it. There is no such thing in creation as a material object in general. There are only particular bodies with particular figures. Figure in general and extension in general are only

118

ideas.[16] Even if the actual corporeal world is infinite in extent, it is still a particular world and hence not infinite in the sense of involving no negation.

An infinite substance cannot be limited or affected by modes, for a substance that is limited is a substance that is finite.[17] Spinoza himself prefers to speak of infinite substance as being "considered as affected" by finite modes. (E I, P28, Dm.; E II, P9, Dm.) The phrase seems to signal the confusion of which Malebranche accuses him. One forms the idea of a certain figure by conceiving of extension as limited in a certain way. One does not impose any limitation on extension in general by considering it as limited. The idea of extension continues to represent extension as capable of an infinite number of figures, even when one considers extension as bounded by a closed curve all points of which are equidistant from the center. On the other hand, to construct an actual figure is to impose a limitation on matter itself. The idea of extension in representing one figure is no less capable of representing all figures, but extension itself, given one figure, is thereby precluded from having others. Furthermore, the matter that is modified by figure is not *all* matter (supposing that matter is unlimited in extent) but only a portion of matter, and that portion is a substance just as the whole is.

If Malebranche is right then Spinoza must be wrong in his initial demonstration of the infinity, eternity, and indivisibility of extended substance. Virtually every step in that demonstration reveals some point of disagreement with Malebranchian doctrine. According to Malebranche, (1) there can be two substances with the same nature. The two are distinguishable in terms of their modifications. It is true that modes are conceived through substance, but it does not follow that they can be put aside or disregarded in this context. Modes follow from the nature of a substance in the sense that given the nature one can deduce all the modes of which the substance is capable. But one cannot deduce which modes it actually has. Two substances with the same nature would be capable of the same modifications, but they need not actually have the same modifications.[18] (2) One substance can be produced by another substance. Any substance produced by another is created by it from nothing, but in accordance with an idea or archetype. Only God is capable of an act of creation. (3) Created substance is not the cause of itself. To subsist by itself or to be conceived by itself does not imply being cause of itself. (4) Every created substance is finite or limited in that its having certain modifications (e.g., its being round) precludes it from having others (e.g., its being square). In addition, every created substance (with the possible exception of the extended world as a whole) is finite in extent, i.e., it has its properties (e.g., magnitude) to a limited degree. That a substance is finite in either sense does not presuppose that there actually are other substances of the same nature but only that such substances are possible. Other figures and greater magnitudes need not actually exist in order for a single cubic-foot block of extension to be considered finite; it is enough that they are possible. (5) Created substances are not eternal. How long they persist depends upon how long their creator keeps them in existence, and that is determined by his will, not by their nature. (6) Not every substance is indivisible. Extended substance, in particular, is not. Parts of extended substance are themselves substances with the same nature as the whole. (7) There are two substances with different natures, namely mind and matter. It cannot be said that the more reality a thing has the more attributes it possesses if the attributes are mutually exclusive, as thought and extension are. (8) Extension is not an attribute of substance absolutely infinite. Whatever is extended is capable of figure, magnitude, and motion, all of which limit the substance to which they belong. Even a formless mass of matter with a part beyond every part is limited in that there are modifications it is capable of having but does not have. Thus, in Spinoza's terms, it is not absolutely infinite.

III.

Is there anything in Spinoza that serves as a reply to Malebranche? It would be surprising if there were not, for Malebranche is operating within the Cartesian framework and Spinoza had that framework in mind when he composed his *Ethics*. Spinoza does not, of course, explicitly address the charge of confusing ideas and things because it was never put to him, but he does have some things to say about the tenets by which Malebranche supports that charge.

Malebranche claims that the statement that bodies cannot be conceived without extension does not imply that bodies are modes of extension, and that a body cannot be conceived without extension only because no substance can be conceived without its essence. Spinoza's retort is to be found in Part II of the *Ethics* in the Scholium to the Corollary to Proposition 10.

> ... I did not say that that pertains to the essence of a thing without which the thing can neither be nor can be conceived; and my reason is, that individual things cannot be nor be conceived without God, and yet God does not pertain to their essence. I have rather, therefore, said that the essence of a thing is necessarily that which being given, the thing is posited, and being taken away, the thing is taken away, or

that without which the thing can neither be nor be conceived, and which in its turn cannot be nor be conceived without the thing.

An individual body cannot be nor be conceived without extension, but that does not make extension its essence; for extension can be and be conceived without that individual body. When the "can neither be nor be conceived" relation holds only one way, between X and Y, and not the other, between Y and X, then Y is not the essence of X but rather X is a mode of Y.

Malebranche claims that by Spinoza's own definition bodies are substances, for what can be conceived alone is a substance and one can conceive a single cubic foot of extension all alone, without thinking of any other thing. But Spinoza's definition of substance is "that which is in itself and is conceived through itself; in other words, that, the conception of which does not need the conception of another thing from which it must be formed." (E I, Df. 3) It is not enough for a thing to exist by itself; it must contain in itself the reason for its existence. Anything that is caused by another thing is conceived through that other thing. (E I, A4) A thing is conceived through itself only if it is cause of itself, and it is cause of itself only if its existence follows from its own nature or essence. (E I, Df. 1) A single cubic foot of extension is not conceived through itself because it is not cause of itself. It cannot really be thought as existing all alone, for there must also be something which has caused it.

Malebranche would agree that a body must be caused by another thing, but not that its nature or essence is defined by reference to its cause. An effect cannot exist without its cause, but one does not discover what the cause is by examining the idea of the effect. All that we learn by examining the idea of a body is that a body has neither the power to create a body nor the force to move one, whether itself or another. What is the cause of bodies and their motions? To discover that, one must look to the idea of God or of infinitely perfect being. One sees that God is the sole being with the power to create. One does not see *what* He creates by consulting the idea of Him, but only (a) that He can create whatever He wills and (b) that whatever actually exists was created by Him.

Much of Malebranche's opposition to the argument by which Spinoza establishes the infinity, eternity, and indivisibility of extended substance stems from his notion of creation. According to Malebranche, not all that is possible is actual. What is actual is only what God chooses to bring into existence. The effects God produces follow not from His nature but from His volitions, and His volitions are free, that is, they could have been otherwise. This concept of divine creation Spinoza categorically rejects. "Things could have been produced by God in no other manner and in no other order than that in which they have been produced." (E I, P33) God is not free in the sense of being able to omit to do what He does. Things follow from God's nature "in the same way as it follows from the nature of a triangle, from eternity and to eternity, that its three angles are equal to two right angles." (E I, P17, C2, S) Those who would have God create material substance out of nothing by an act of will are ignorant of the power by which this is supposedly accomplished, "so that it is clear that they do not understand what they themselves say." (E I, P15, S) Does not Malebranche himself admit that he cannot explain how God's will gives rise to its effects and that he does not know in what the efficacy of the divine volitions consists?[19]

Malebranche claims that Spinoza ascribes to extended substance a kind of infinity that really pertains only to the idea of it. What kind of infinity pertains to the idea but not to extension itself? According to Malebranche, the idea of extension represents extension as capable of either finite or infinite extent. The material world may have very narrow limits or it may be boundless, with parts beyond every part. Is Spinoza's extended substance infinite in the sense of lacking boundary or terminus? The philosophers' three arguments against the infinity of extension are all arguments against extension infinite in extent. Does Spinoza, in rejecting them, opt for extended substance that is infinite in extent? That is, is the extension which he claims to be indivisible also infinite in the sense of having no boundary or terminus? It would seem not, for an extension without terminus is an extension with parts beyond every part, but to say that beyond every part there are further parts is to suppose that extension is divisible. Malebranche takes Spinoza to task for arguing that extension is necessarily infinite in extent because the idea of extension represents it as capable of being so. But is it Spinoza's extended *substance* that is infinite in extent or is it extension considered as a *mode*? In light of the letter to Meyer on the infinite (*Ep.* 12; Wolf(a), 115–122), in which Spinoza distinguishes between that which is infinite by virtue of its own nature and that which is infinite in virtue of its cause, and says of the latter that when it is considered abstractly, it "can be divided into parts and viewed as finite," it is evident that when one speaks of extension as infinite or unlimited in extent, one is considering extension as a mode and not as a substance.

The attribute of extension is immeasurable (E I, P15, S), not in the sense that one never comes to an end in measuring it, but in the sense that measurement does not apply to it. The question of how far or how large does not arise in respect to extension *per se* but only in respect to its modes. A body or finite mode of extension is limited by another thing of the same nature "because we can always conceive another which is greater." (*E* I, Df. 2) Extended substance is not limited by another thing of the same nature, not simply because there can be no extended thing greater than it, but because there cannot *be* another thing of the same nature. Extension as an attribute or expression of the essence of substance expresses that essence as definitive of a single thing.

If the infinity that pertains to the attribute of extension is of a kind that does not admit of division into parts, then is Spinoza's extension what Malebranche calls 'general'? Spinoza would have his extended substance affected or modified with all sorts of figures at once, but not with different figures in different portions of it because it is indivisible. Thus, Malebranche argues, his extension is really extension in general or the idea of extension. Spinoza might reply that extension *per se* is indivisible, but extension as figured is divisible, that is to say, it is a mode and not an attribute of substance. Is extended substance itself not really figured but only *considered* as figured? Then it is an idea, and what Spinoza calls the mode is the object of the idea. Spinoza's answer seems to be: To say that extension is not really figured but only considered as figured does not imply that in speaking of extension as figured one is merely saying of the idea of extension that it represents extension as capable of taking on all sorts of figures. It is not Spinoza's view that extended substance has all figures in itself; his view is rather that in itself it has none. Extension is not really limited by figure, in that it is not extended substance as such which takes on figure. It is only considered as figured, in that a figure is defined as a limitation of extension. When Spinoza says that finite modes are in infinite and indivisible substance, he does not mean that substance includes all finite modes in a unity, but rather that finite modes can be defined as limitations of substance.

My statement that modes are definable as limitations of substance seems at first glance to suggest a genus-species model of the substance-mode relation. H. A. Wolfson interprets Spinoza's doctrine on this model. He maintains that substance for Spinoza is the *summum genus*, or the genus that is not itself a species of another genus.[20] The model is inappropriate. Whatever Spinoza means by his claim that bodies are modes of extension, it is clear that he does not mean that they are species of extension. Limitation is not to be understood as differentiation. In the *Improvement of the Understanding*, Spinoza tells us what form our definitions ought to take, and that form is not one of genus and difference. A definition, he says, "must explain the inmost essence of a thing." He rejects the definition of a circle as "a figure, such that all straight lines drawn from the center to the circumference are equal" because it "does not . . . explain the essence of a circle, but solely one of its properties." To explain the essence of a circle is to explain how circularity is generated. Thus a circle is properly defined as "the figure described by any line whereof one end is fixed and the other free." (*TdIE*, Wild, 37–38) This definition explains how a line must be drawn in order to limit extension in the form of a circle.

Spinoza's attribute of extension is an amorphous, tridimensional structure. It is infinite in the sense of being indeterminate, unqualified, and undifferentiated. It would be incorrect to call it homogeneous, insofar as homogeneity connotes the having of parts. Parts are not distinguished in it, not because they are all alike, but because the very having of parts would render it determined. One cannot determine amorphous extension; one can only make determinations in it. To make determinations in substance is to work out the sequence of objects and events that its nature makes possible. Malebranche objects that an infinite substance cannot have finite modes because finite modes would limit it and hence render it finite. His objection misses the mark, for Spinoza's modes do not *modify* his substance. Modes are in substance and are conceived through substance, not in the sense that they are properties of substance, but in the sense that they are defined as limitations of substance. To define X as a limitation of Y is not to impose a limitation upon Y itself. Malebranche would make his own infinite substance finite if he gave it finite modes because for him modes are properties, and to have a finite property is to be finite. Spinoza, however, can grant his infinite substance finite modes since all he means by calling them 'modes' of it is that one explains their nature in terms of it.

IV.

Has Malebranche refuted Spinoza? Certainly not on Spinoza's own terms. His attack is launched from outside Spinoza's system, from premises that Spinoza would not accept. If 'infinite' meant 'general', then Spinoza would be guilty of confusing extension with the idea of extension when he asserts that the former is infinite. If "to be in itself and to be conceived through itself" meant merely "to be capable of existing by itself" and did not mean "to be cause of itself," then a body could be classified as a substance and extended substance would be divisible. But by 'infinite' Spinoza does not mean 'general' and by "to be in itself and to be conceived through itself" he does mean "to be cause of itself." Malebranche has refuted him only by misunderstanding him.

Malebranche's discussion is nevertheless of value, for it reveals something important about Spinoza. It is often said that Spinoza pushes the Cartesian ontology to its logical conclusion. For example, he takes Descartes' definition of 'substance' in the *Principles* as "a thing which so exists that it needs no other thing in order to exist," a definition which Descartes admits applies only to God, and concludes that God is the only substance and that everything else is a mode of Him. Malebranche show us that a strictly Cartesian interpretation of Spinoza's doctrine of substance and mode is unworkable. So long as one insists upon treating substance as a thing with properties and modes as the properties it has, it remains incomprehensible how an infinite substance can have finite modes. The only way a thing could have finite properties without being limited by them would be to contain them objectively or by representation. If Spinoza's modes were properties, his extension would have to include them objectively, but then, as Malebranche observes, it would be an idea. It is because modes are limitations or determinations of substance that Spinoza has room for finite modes in his ontology. Substance for him is not a thing with properties but an amorphous structure. Finite modes are not properties but are themselves things having properties. They are in substance neither formally nor objectively, and they are conceived through substance as that which is explained is conceived through that which explains it.

Spinoza is often accused of depriving bodies of reality and of turning them into "illusions."[21] How, it is wondered, can finite modes ever arise out of infinite substance? Spinoza's answer that substance is cause of finite modes only insofar as it is affected by other finite modes (*E* I, P28, Dm.) is dismissed as unsatisfactory. The question is not how this or that particular mode gets into the system, but how there can be any finite modes in it at all. The dissatisfaction comes from thinking of substance as a Cartesian agent, which produces modifications by acting upon the substance to which they belong (in this case itself). Spinoza's substance is cause of modes, not in the sense of being their author, but in the sense of being their ground or justification. Substance, for him, is that to which any adequate account of individual things must ultimately refer. Determination presupposes something indeterminate. Division presupposes something indivisible. The differentiation of extension into individual bodies cannot be accomplished by separation but only by limitation; but, for there to be limitation there must be something extended which is in itself unlimited and undifferentiated. Extended substance does not give rise to finite modes. One finite mode gives rise to another, limitations being produced by other limitations, but all are grounded in substance as limitations of it. If substance itself can be said to give rise to anything, it is only to the infinite modes, which are the general laws for limiting extension.[22]

The relation between the attribute of extension and finite modes of extension parallels that in Malebranche's system between intelligible extension and particular sensible ideas,[23] yet Spinoza manages to escape certain difficulties which plague Malebranche's account. Malebranche holds a representative theory of perception, in which material objects are not perceived directly but only through the mediation of ideas. What we see when we look out on a meadow are not trees and flowers themselves but ideas of trees and flowers. The space in which we see them is not actual or material space but the ideal or intelligible space which is the object of study of geometry. When we close our eyes and think of extension by an act of conception, intelligible extension is presented to us as it really is, infinite and indivisible. When we open our eyes in the middle of a field, this same intelligible extension is presented to us but now it is "rendered particular" by having sensations of color "attached" to it. The variety of colors serves to single out different portions of intelligible extension and to set them off from one another, so that we see a variety of sensible objects positioned in intelligible extension. The colors and other sensible qualities that render particular the general idea of extension are not themselves part of the realm of ideas or (direct) objects of the mind's acts of perceiving but species of those acts and thus modifications of the mind. That intelligible extension is rendered particular by sensible qualities therefore does not imply that any change has been made to it.[24]

The trouble with Malebranche's account is that intelligible extension, in being rendered particular, is also rendered divisible. The portions of intelligible extension that are singled out by color are not intelligible portions or ideas of portions, as Malebranche would have it, but real portions with real distances between them. When different colors are "attached" to different portions of intelligible extension, we see different parts, not merely different representations of parts, and we see a distance between those parts, not merely a representation of a distance between parts. The problem arises because Malebranche tries to identify intelligible extension, or the idea of extension in general, with the very extension we see and feel. The only way he can do this is to make intelligible extension somehow contain all sensible objects in a unity so that it can reveal each of them in turn. Spinoza gets around the problem because his amorphous and undifferentiated extension is not identified with the world of bodies. One can understand finite modes in terms of the attribute of extension without having to fish them out of it. Malebranche gets particular sensible ideas out of intelligible extension only by rendering intelligible extension actually particular, whereas for Spinoza the limitations of substance do not render substance actually limited.

NOTES

1. Quotations are from the translation in Wild.
2. Whose arguments are these? Certainly not Descartes' nor any Cartesian's. H.A. Wolfson considers the question of sources in *The Philosophy of Spinoza* (Cambridge, Mass.: Harvard University Press, 1934; New York, Schocken Books, 1969), I, Ch. VIII.
3. D. de Mairan to Malebranche (September 17, 1713), *Oeuvres complètes de Méditations chrétiennes et métaphysiques*, IX, 12, OC X, p. 100; *Entretien d'un* be cited as *OC*.
4. Malebranche to D. de Mairan (September 29, 1713), OC XIX, p. 855.
5. D. de Mairan to Malebranche (November 9, 1713), OC XIX, p. 860.
6. D. de Mairan to Malebranche (August 26, 1714), OC XIX, pp. 894–96.
7. D. de Mairan to Malebranche (November 9, 1713), OC XIX, pp. 861–62.
8. Malebranche to D. de Mairan (June 12, 1714), OC XIX, p. 883. See also *Méditations chrétiennes et métaphysiques*, IX, 12, OC X, p. 100; *Entretien d'un philosophe chrétien et d'un philosophe chinois*, OC XV, pp. 33–34.
9. Malebranche to D. de Mairan (September 6, 1714), OC XIX, p. 909.
10. Malebranche to D. de Mairan (December 5, 1713), OC XIX, p. 865.
11. D. de Mairan to Malebranche (August 26, 1714), OC XIX, pp. 897–98. *Cf.* Descartes to Chanut (June 6, 1647), *Oeuvres de Descartes*, eds. C. Adam and P. Tannery (Paris: Léopold Cerf, 1897–1912), V, p. 52; *Descartes: Philosophical Letters*, trans. and ed. A. Kenny (Oxford: Clarendon Press, 1970), p. 221.
12. Malebranche to D. de Mairan (September 6, 1714), OC XIX, pp. 909–10.
13. *Cf. Réponse à Régis*, II, 11, OC XVII-1, pp. 286–87.
14. *Éclaircissements*, X, OC III, p. 148. See also OC VI, pp. 52, 250; OC IX, p. 955; OC XII, p. 185.
15. *Entretiens sur la métaphysique et sur la religion*, II, 3–4, OC XII, *pp.* 52–53; *Dialogues on Metaphysics and on Religion*, trans. M. Ginsberg (London: George Allen & Unwin, 1923), pp. 89–90.
16. *Cf.* Malebranche to Arnauld (March 19, 1699), OC IX, p. 970.
17. Malebranche to D. de Mairan (June 12, 1714), OC XIX, p. 883.
18. There can be two substances with all actual modifications in common. Strictly speaking, however, the two substances would not share numerically the same modification, for a modification is defined as "the substance itself in this or that manner" and thus cannot be conceived except through the very substance to which it belongs.
19. See, for example, *Méditations chrétiennes et métaphysiques*, IX, 2, OC X, p. 96; *Entretien d'un philosophe chrétien et d'un philosophe chinois*, OC XV, p. 33.
20. Wolfson, *op. cit.*, I, pp. 75–76.
21. See, for example, A.E. Taylor, "Some Incoherencies in Spinozism," *Mind* XLVI (1937), pp. 147–48; in *Studies in Spinoza: Critical and Interpretive Essays*, ed. S. Paul Kashap (Berkeley: University of California Press, 1972), p. 200.
22. *Cf. On the Improvement of the Understanding*, in *Spinoza Selections*, p.

40. The causal power of substance (E I, 34–36) is explicated in terms of substance's necessary connection with its effects, not the other way around. Failure to recognize this fact has led some interpreters to view Spinoza's substance as a seat of activity or energy. See, for example, A. Wolf, "Spinoza's Conception of the Attributes of Substance," in *Studies in Spinoza*, pp. 16–27.

23. Mairan's understanding of the similarity between Malebranche and Spinoza is wrong on two counts: first, the relation in Malebranche which parallels the attribute-finite mode relation is that between intelligible extension and the ideas of bodies (not the bodies themselves); and second, this latter relation is not a substance-mode relation as Malebranche understands those terms.

24. This account of Malebranche's theory of perception is gleaned from a number of his writings, including *Éclaircissements*, X, OC III, pp. 127–61; *Conversations chrétiennes*, III, OC IV, pp. 58–85; Letter to Arnauld (March 19, 1699), OC IX, pp. 901–75; *Entretiens sur la métaphysique et sur la religion*, Préface, Entretien I, OC XII, pp. 7–48; *Entretiens sur la mort*, II, OC XIII, pp. 385–415; *Réponse à Régis*, II, 1–5, OC XVII–1, pp. 281–83.

Spinoza on Immortality and Time

C. L. HARDIN
Syracuse University

I.

H. A. Wolfson[1] differentiates two senses of "eternity" as it occurs in the history of philosophy. The first, the "Platonic" sense, excludes time, while the second, the "Aristotelian" sense, simply means endless time ("sempiternity"). The traditional reading of Spinoza has been along "Platonic" lines, and seems to be supported by numerous passages, chief among them E I, A8:

> By eternity, I understand existence itself, so far as it is conceived necessarily to follow from the definition alone of the eternal thing.
>
> Explanation.—For such existence, like the essence of the thing, is conceived as an eternal truth. It cannot therefore be explained by duration or time, even if the duration be conceived without beginning or end.

This interpretation has recently been challenged by Martha Kneale[2] and Alan Donagan.[3] Kneale concedes that Spinoza intended the Platonic sense early in his work on the *Ethics*, but she maintains he changed his mind as he worked on Part V. Donagan holds that Spinoza should be read throughout as intending by "eternity," "sempiternity." Both Kneale and Donagan agree that the chief function of the sharp distinction between eternity and duration is to mark the difference between that which is logically necessary and that which is not.

Why do Donagan and Kneale suppose this new interpretation of Spinoza to be required? There seem to be three reasons. First, Spinoza on occasion says of substance or the infinite modes that they always (*semper*) exist. Second, the immediate infinite mode of extension is motion and rest, and this clearly presupposes temporality. Third, only by understanding "eternity" in this way can we make sense of several propositions of Part V of the *Ethics*, notably Proposition 23: "The human mind cannot be absolutely destroyed with the body, but something of it remains which is eternal."

I have nothing useful to say on the first point, except that it cannot by itself be decisive. The second point I take to be the crucial one, even though Kneale does not mention it and Donagan, although stating it forcibly, does not dwell upon it. I shall be concerned to defend, as against Donagan, a position resembling that of H. F. Hallett.[4] The third point is the one to which both authors devote their chief attention. I shall focus upon what Donagan has to say because I believe that his account is more carefully thought out than Kneale's. His argument turns upon an interpretation of E II, P8, which I wish to reject. I shall take the failure of Donagan's argument to count against his reading of "eternity" and shall suggest that this reading compounds the problems of understanding E V, P22.

II.

It was J. M. E. McTaggart[5] who distinguished two senses of temporal order: past, present, and future (the "A-series"), and earlier and later (the "B-series"). McTaggart took the A-series to be the more fundamental of the two, and Donagan agrees, conceding, however, that Spinoza "had no term for 'time' in what I take to be its ordinary sense: namely that in which it stands for the passage of the future into the present, and of the present into the past. . . . I shall refer to time, in this sense, as temporal passage."[6]

Is it incumbent upon Spinoza to give an account of temporal passage as well as of temporal order? Only, I would suggest, if he regards temporal passage to be an objective feature of the world rather than just an appearance.[7] The fact that his use of "time" in the *Ethics* does not involve this notion would suggest that he did not regard it as fundamental. Furthermore, no proposition in the *Ethics* requires the notion of temporal becoming. Spinoza neither presents us with a theory of temporal order, nor does he attempt to acount explicitly for the "awareness of passage" which Kneale and Donagan find so central. Any attempt, therefore, to give a Spinozistic account of these matters is necessarily speculative. On the other hand, the materials for such an account seem ready to hand.

I would propose to ascribe to Spinoza a causal theory of time, in which temporal order is to be regarded as an appearance founded upon causal order,[8] with temporal passage as the sensory (and hence confused) representation of that order. To see how this works, let us for the moment abstractly represent the "face of the whole universe" under the attribute of extension by means of a space-time diagram with three spatial axes and one directed "temporal" axis.[9] Any two finite modal states *A* and *B* may be ordered with respect to one another according as *A* is a remote or proximate cause of *B*, *B* is a remote or proximate cause of *A*, or *A* and *B* either cause one another or have no causal relationship to one another. In the first case, we shall call *A* "earlier than"*B*, in the second we shall call *A* "later than" *B*, and in the third instance, we shall say that *A* is "simultaneous with" *B*. Our diagram will exhaustively represent all of the kinematic relationships among the modes, which is to say that it will depict motion and rest insofar as they may be regarded as *extrinsic* denominations of bodies. We should notice two additional features of this representation. First, there is nothing in the diagram which is to be interpreted as temporal becoming. Second, although sets of points within the continuum may be described as having temporal relations to one another, it would be downright misleading to describe the continuum itself as "existing in time" or as "existing at all times."

Spinoza would reject our Minkowski-type diagram as an accurate representation of *natura naturata*, but for reasons which do not, I believe, undercut our argument. First, he would see the diagram as artificial because it adopts metaphysically disparate sets of axes—an ordering of extension in the one case and causes in the other. This is a perfectly reasonable opinion to have adopted before 1900.[10] Second, and for our purposes more important, he would have seen it as distortingly abstract and external because motion and rest are, in his view, not simply extrinsic denominations of bodies, but rather comprise the very essences of individual physical things.[11] As such, they are the force by which the thing continues in existence and is causally efficacious. (*E* III, P7; *E* I, P36) The parallel between Spinoza's *conatus* and Leibniz' *appetitio* is instructive here. *Appetitio* is the metaphysical basis of succession, which is intra-monadic time, while a fixed proportion of motion and rest is the foundation of duration, or temporality in the individual considered as existing in abstraction from the order of nature. (*E* II, P45, S; *E* III, P8) In the Leibnizian case, the intrinsic force of the monad has an external aspect, *vis viva*. For Spinoza, the essence of a mode is extrinsically exhibited as relative change of position. In both instances, the extrinsic, public appearance is well-founded, but an appearance nonetheless.

The *conatus* of an individual expresses, in a fixed and determinate way, the power of God. (*E* III, P6) It is this power, viewed as a *whole* under the attribute of extension, which is the *immediate* infinite mode, motion and rest, whereby substance, in itself infinite and indeterminate, exhaustively differentiates itself in infinitely many ways.[12] God, thus differentiated, exhibiting all possible combinations of motion and rest, is the *mediate* infinite mode, the face of the whole universe. (*Ep.* 64) Duration and time make their appearance only at this point (*E* I, P21), duration insofar as finite individuals may be abstractly considered apart from one other, time insofar as they may be compared with one another.(Ep. 12)[13] Thus considered, there is no logical place for applying either the concept of duration or of time to the entire system. Our original representation of the mediate infinite mode as space-time was thus metaphysically superficial, but the conclusions we drew for motion and rest as physical concepts were not thereby erroneous.

In this way we may dispose of Donagan's remark that,

> Only by resorting to such speculative interpretations as Hallett's of motion and rest as not spatio-temporal . . . can we resist the conclusion that, since Spinoza held the immediate infinite and eternal mode of extension to be motion and rest, he must have conceived at least one eternal mode as being in time. The concept of timeless existence may be intelligible; that of timeless motion is not.[14]

But what has become of temporal becoming? It suffers, I suggest, the same fate as colors and smells: it is a confused idea of causal relationships in the physical world. Its adequate counterparts under the attribute of thought are relationships of logical entailment. No wonder Hume looked for causality in experience and found only temporal succession and perishing existence![15]

III.

Donagan's analysis of Spinoza's treatment of individual immortality in Part V of the *Ethics* is ingenious, simple, and seductive. It is also the only way that I can see in which Spinoza's pronouncements on the subject may be reconciled with the claim that God is sempiternal. I shall sketch the essential parts of Donagan's argument, suggest that crucial portions of it are incompatible with a plausible interpretation of a number of passages from the *Ethics* and from *On Improvement of the Understanding,* and thus infer that Spinoza's God is not sempiternal.

According to Donagan:

> Spinoza had laid it down that, if an essence were such that its existence would not in itself involve a contradiction, then what would call for explanation would be not so much its existence (if it existed), as its nonexistence (if it did not). Let us call such essences 'intrinsically possible.' His idea evidently was that an infinite substance

would bring about the existence, as a finite mode, of every intrinsically possible finite essence, unless its other finite modes made it impossible to do so. Here Spinoza anticipated Leibniz: his infinite substance necessarily brings into existence the most perfect intrinsically possible system of modes (E., I, xxxiii S2). *Natura naturata* is therefore what Leibniz would have called the best of all possible worlds. And, although strictly speaking only the essences of modes in the most perfect possible modal system have power of existing, every intrinsically possible essence has it loosely speaking: that is, every intrinsically possible essence has conditional power of existing—it would exist if some finite existent did not prevent it. Essences possessed of power of existing only in this loose or conditional sense are not actual.

Since the very same essence (for example, that of Socrates' body) may be actual at one time (say, 424 B.C.) but not another (now), it is useful to have an epithet to indicate when an essence is being spoken of with no implication that it is actual. Spinoza used 'formalis' ('formal') for this purpose. Hence, in speaking of essences of individuals merely as they are contained in the divine attributes, without any implication as to whether the divine finite modes are or are not permitting them to be actual, he called them 'formal essences' ('essentiae formales') (E., II, viii). The idea of an actual essence is therefore composite, and may be analyzed into the idea of a formal essence, and the idea of other existents being such as not to prevent its existence. Spinoza presupposed an analysis of this kind when he declared that 'something of the human mind' is eternal, namely, the idea of the essence of the human body. . . . The answer to the question what Spinoza took the eternal part of a mind to be . . . is: the idea of the (formal) essence of its body.[16]

Like most attempts to explicate Spinoza's views on immortality, this one runs into difficulty with the famous and fundamental proposition of *E* II, P7: "The order and connection of ideas is the same as the order and connection of things." Does this not, Donagan asks, "rule out the possibility that an eternally existing idea of the essence of a body should correspond to a body which, having been destroyed, does not exist at all?"[17]

Donagan's ingenious reply to this objection rests upon his interpretation of the puzzling Proposition 8 of Part II, which he translates as: "Ideas of nonexistent individual things must be comprehended in the infinite idea of God, just as formal essences of individual things or modes are contained in the divine attributes."

Consider, he suggests, a nonexistent individual, say, Vesuvius erupting in 45 B.C.

It is true that, just as our counterpart Vesuvius is not among the finite modes of extension, so [its idea] is not among the finite modes of thought. However, it is no less true that just as any finite mode of extension excludes the existence of incompatible finite modes, so the idea of such a mode implies the idea of the nonexistence of modes incompatible with it. Hence the true idea of a Vesuvius quiescent in the circumstances of 45 B.C. implies the idea of the nonexistence of a Vesuvius erupting in these cirmstances. . . . Such actual ideas of the formal essences of nonexistent individuals, since they cannot be finite modes of thought, must form part of an infinite mode of it, a mode which Spinoza referred to as 'Dei infinita idea.' This infinite mode of thought must contain *inter alia*, an actual idea of the formal essence of every individual body, existent or nonexistent.[18]

He readily makes the application to Spinoza's proof of immortality:

When a living human body is destroyed, the corresponding mind, as nonderivative idea of that body actually existing, perishes with it; for they are the same finite mode in two distinct attributes. However, that mind, as actual essence, had as a part the idea of the formal essence of that body. And the idea of that formal essence belongs to God *sub specie aeternitatis*: it is part of the infinite idea of God, which is an eternal mode of God in the attribute of thought. Therefore the part of a man's mind which consists in the idea of the formal essence of his body must be eternal: it must have pre-existed his body, and cannot be destroyed with it. Q.E.D.[19]

Will *E* II, P8 bear the weight of Donagan's interpretation? It is interesting to look at one of the first applications of this proposition, which occurs in the proof of *E* II, P11: "Therefore an idea is the first thing which forms the Being of the human mind. But it is not the idea of a non-existent thing, for then the idea itself (Corol. prop. viii, pt. II) could not be said to exist."

This counts against Donagan, but it is not conclusive. Spinoza in fact uses two senses of "exists" or "is actual," and one of them also pertains to the question of what it means for an idea to express the essence of a body *sub specie aeternitatis*. We must look at *E* V, P39, S:

Things are conceived by us as actual in two ways; either in so far as we conceive them to exist with relation to a fixed time and place, or in so far as we conceive them to be contained in God, and to follow from the necessity of the divine nature. But those things which are conceived in this second way as true or real we conceive under the form of eternity, and their ideas involve the eternal and infinite essence of God, as we have shown in Prop. xiv., pt. 2, to the scholium of which the reader is referred.

The latter reads as follows:

By existence is to be understood here not duration, that is, existence considered in the abstract, as if it were a certain kind of quantity, but I speak of the nature itself of the existence which is assigned to individual things, because from the eternal necessity of the nature of God infinite numbers of things follow in infinite ways (prop. xvi, pt. I). I repeat, that I speak of the existence itself of individual things in so far as they are in God. For although each individual thing is determined by another individual thing to existence in a certain way, the force nevertheless by which each thing preserves in its existence follows from the eternal necessity of the nature of God (see Corol. prop. xxiv, pt. I).

If we are to follow Donagan, we must be prepared to say that the idea of the counterpart Vesuvius *also* expresses the essence of a body *sub specie aeternitatis*. Now Spinoza requires that to be eligible to express the essence of a body under the form of eternity, an idea must be the idea of an actual body (in at least the second sense of actual). But Donagan acknowledges that "essences possessed of power of existing this loose or conditional sense are not actual." Only durational or eternal things can be said to follow from the necessity of the divine nature, which can exfoliate in one and only one way. (E I, P33)

But is the counterpart Vesuvius not *comprehended in* the infinite idea of God? And doesn't this mean that it *follows from* the necessity of the divine nature in some sense? The following passage from the *TdIE* suggests, I believe, the way we are to understand what it is to be comprehended in the infinite idea of God:

For, if we suppose that the understanding has perceived some new entity which has never existed, as some conceive the understanding of God before he created things (a perception which certainly could not arise from any object), and has legitimately deduced other thoughts from the said perception, all such thoughts would be true, without being determined by any external object; they would depend solely on the power and nature of the understanding. . . . For instance, in order to form the conception of a sphere, I invent a cause at my pleasure—namely, a semicircle revolving round its centre, and thus producing a sphere. This is indisputably a true idea; and, although we know that no sphere in nature has ever actually been so formed, the perception remains true, and is the easiest way of conceiving a sphere. (*TdIE*, Gebhardt II, 59)

This suggests that the concept of a nonexistent thing is comprehended in the divine understanding only as linked to the idea of its (nonexisting) proximate cause. What *follows from* the divine understanding is not the idea of the counterpart Vesuvius *simpliciter*, but a (propositional) idea of the form, "If such-and-such conditions were fulfilled, Vesuvius would erupt in 45 B.C." What this asserts is really just an instance of a general relationship of natural necessity. To the extent that it is *about* the counterpart Vesuvius, it is also about a world-history that is, in God's understanding, impossible. To the extent that the concept of the counterpart Vesuvius is more than a set of conjoined law-like propositions, it is logically *incoherent*. "If there be a God or omniscient Being, such an one cannot frame fictitious hypotheses." (*TdIE*, Gebhardt II, 28)

I conclude that Donagan's "purely formal essence" does not give us the key to existence *sub specie aeternitatis*, for this must apply to *actual* essences. But Socrates, whose mind must endure in part if any mind does, is not actual now (1977) in Spinoza's first sense of 'actual'. How, consistently with E II, P7 can he be actual in the second sense?

This is, of course, a problem for anyone who holds, as Donagan and Kneale do, that whatever exists exists *now*, and thus maintains that nothing can be actual in the second sense unless it follows *now* from the essence of the divine nature. On the other hand, it poses no problem for one who is not wedded to the view that temporal becoming is metaphysically fundamental. Indeed, it gives a follower of Spinoza one more reason for not embracing that view and, along with it, the thesis that God's eternity is sempiternity.

There remain, of course, the problematic passages, such as: "The human mind cannot be absolutely destroyed with the body, but something *remains* which is eternal." But why not follow Harris[20] in construing "remains" in the sense of "is a remainder" in arithmetic or "is a residue" in chemistry?

The toughest passages for my reading are undoubtedly those from the last paragraph of E V, P20, S: "I have now concluded all that I had to say relating to this present life," and "It is time, therefore, that I should now pass to the consideration of those matters which appertain to the duration of the mind without relation to the body." The first of these is perhaps made clearer by the use of "present" in E V, P29:

"Everything which the mind understands under the form of eternity, it understands not because it conceives the present actual existence of the body, but because it conceives the essence of the body under the form of eternity." Here "present" is not opposed to, say, "future," but rather serves to distinguish the *first* sense of "actual" from the *second* sense, as the scholium to the same proposition expresses it: "Things are conceived by us as actual in two ways; either in so far as we conceive them to exist with relation to a fixed time and place, or as we conceive them to be contained in God, and to follow from the necessity of the divine nature."

I am less confident of the interpretation of "the duration of the mind without relation to the body." Taken by itself, this sentence is read more naturally in the Kneale-Donagan manner than in mine. However, subsequent passages abound with expressions like ". . . we cannot ascribe duration to the mind except while the body exists," and "only in so far, therefore, as it involves the actual existence of the body can the mind be said to possess duration," which make me suppose that the problem sentence should either be regarded as a slip, or given a slightly strained paraphrase. For the latter, I submit the following candidate: "It is time, therefore, that I should now pass to the consideration of whether the mind might be said to endure without relation to the body."

Finally, it seems to me that the discussion of the preexistence of the mind which occurs in the scholium of Proposition 23 is intended to *dismiss* the reading of "remain" as "endure without the body," as well as to account for our sense of eternity *without* being forced to claim that this sense has its origins in the recollection of a previous nonbodily existence, because the latter would be impossible. I simply cannot grasp Donagan's claim about this scholium that in it, "although Spinoza did not expressly avow such pre-existence he argued against prenatal reminiscence in a way that presupposed it."[21]

I thus follow Joachim[22] and Hallett[23] in the unremarkable conclusion that, at least when he discussed the relation between eternity and duration, Spinoza meant what he said.

NOTES

1. H.A. Wolfson, *The Philosophy of Spinoza* (Cambridge, Mass.: Harvard University Press, 1934), Vol. I, pp. 358–66.

2. Martha Kneale, "Eternity and Sempiternity," *Proceedings of the Aristotelian Society* 69 (1968–69), pp. 223–38. Reprinted in Marjorie Grene (ed.), *Spinoza: A Collection of Critical Essays* (Garden City, N.Y.: Doubleday, 1973), pp. 227–40.

3. Alan Donagan, "Spinoza's Proof of Immortality," in Grene, *op. cit.*, pp. 241–58.

4. H.F. Hallett, *Creation, Emanation and Salvation* (The Hague: Martinus Nijhoff, 1962). It seems to me that Hallett is at the same time the most profound and the most gratuitously obscure of all the Spinoza commentators.

5. J.M.E. McTaggart, *The Nature of Existence* (Cambridge: Cambridge University Press, 1927), Vol. II, Book V, Chapter 33, reprinted in R.M. Gale, *The Philosophy of Time* (London: Macmillan, 1968), pp. 86–97.

6. Donagan, *op. cit.*, p. 242.

7. That temporal becoming is not a fundamental feature of the world has been frequently and powerfully argued by several recent authors, e.g., Donald Williams (in Gale, *op. cit.*, pp. 98–116) and Adolf Grünbaum (*Philosophical Problems of Space and Time* (New York: Alfred A. Knopf, 1963), pp. 314–29. This view is thus at least defensible by contemporary standards, so to ascribe it to Spinoza is not automatically to render his account of temporality inadequate.

8. This position, too, has had an honorable philosophical history, of which Kant is, of course, a part, as well as such a contemporary philosopher as Hans Reichenbach. Cf. *The Direction of Time* (Berkeley: Univ. of California Press, 1956).

9. Or, in other words, a nonrelativistic Minkowski diagram.

10. The diagrammatic representation of disparate magnitudes goes back to Oresme in the late medieval period and was, of course, a widely accepted *practical* device in the seventeenth century. But it was only after Einstein that one would have seen such a diagram as expressing a *profound* connection.

11. Cf. the discussion of the nature of simple and compound bodies which follows E II, P12.

12. E I, P16. Spinoza's intellectual ancestor here is Anaximander. With Hallett, I see substance *simpliciter* as the *indefinite*, which is determined first by discrimination into attributes, then by self-differentiation into modes.

13. My last phrase is a gloss on Spinoza. One might measure duration arbitrarily, of course, and thus form the notion of time. I am instead referring to the division of duration by means of a standard clock, in which we compare one duration to another.

14. Donagan, *op. cit.*, p. 246.

15. Whether a more detailed account of the phenomenon of becoming can be given is a nice question. Its answer will depend partly upon whether an adequate phenomenology of becoming is possible. Once we had this, we might be able to describe the physical counterparts of the ideas. Of course, the best account of counterparts would, like an account of the counterparts of color experiences, leave out something which is phenomenologically both essential and ineffable. But what else could have been expected? Spinoza never claimed to be a reductionist.

16. Donagan, *op. cit.*, p. 249–51.

17. *Ibid.*, p. 253.

18. *Ibid.*, p. 255.

19. *Ibid.*

20. E.H. Harris, "Spinoza's Theory of Human Immortality," in Mandlebaum and Freeman (eds.), *Spinoza: Essays in Interpretation* (La Salle, Ill: Open Court, 1975) pp. 245–61. I subscribe to Harris' view that immortality involves a transcendence of the body by the mind, but not a *temporal* transcendence.

21. Donagan, *op. cit.*, p. 247.

22. H.H. Joachim, *A Study of the Ethics of Spinoza* (Oxford: The Clarendon Press, 1901).

23. Hallett, *op. cit.*

Spinoza on Part and Whole: The Worm's Eye View

WILLIAM SACKSTEDER
University of Colorado

I.

Any relatively complete philosophy is so fabricated that various pairs of terms exactly opposed to each other run through its entire tissue. Often these paired terms are formative of the contexture governing that scheme, so that our efforts to understand it require us to trace their threads and interweaving throughout that philosophy before we can grasp it according to its own ordering principles. *Part* and *whole* sometimes make up one such opposed pair. Others which are often important are *one/many, internal/external, like/unlike, self/other, same/different*. Occasionally, one such pair might seem to be the woof through which all other strands are shuttled and whose contexture holds the entire pattern together.

I wish in this paper to illustrate these generalities by tracing one major pair, *part* and *whole*, which seems to sustain the design in the philosophy of Spinoza. It might appear that *part/whole* forms the ultimately determinate pair for Spinoza. It seems to be all over the place in his philosophy. However, the logic of its use and its correlations with other pairs is more often than not inarticulate or taken for granted. One passage seems definitive for this pair, although in puzzling ways. This is to be found in Spinoza's correspondence with Oldenburg, Letter 32. I shall indulge in extensive quotation and detailed commentary on this explication in an effort to untangle some of its perplexities. To this, I shall append many but abbreviated citations of the role this pair performs in the philosophy. By such loose suggestions and invitations to recall, I hope to illuminate various figures in the larger tapestry. Yet, if we inspect the weave with something of a squint, we find many familiar or common usages to be inverted. The employment of this opposed pair, and its correlations with others, violate assorted traditions or technical proprieties. They seem to do so in ways requiring caution in surveying both the grand design and lesser figures.

Before I enter into details, I should like to point out that this opposed pair is as critical as it is ambivalent in Spinoza's philosophy. The pair, *part/whole,* is ubiquitous, but its function is problematic. There is an initial plausibility in treating God as a whole—as *the* whole—so that any other items are admitted into this universe as parts. Yet to qualify this plausibility, I note that one distinguished commentator asserts, "The notion, sometimes entertained, that Spinoza's substance is a *totum* of which its modes are the parts is too *jejune* to merit refutation."[1] But, to the contrary, Spinoza explicitly states that our highest good is knowledge of the union existing between the mind—as a part, it might seem—and the whole of nature. (*TdIE*, Gutmann, 6)

More local perplexities are consequent to this principal one. Oddities concerning *part/whole* may be found in the Lemmata concerning the body to be found following Part II, Proposition 13. These become especially strange if we speak also of the mind as whole or part and exploit the parallelism of Proposition 7. Likewise, some disposition of part and whole seems inextricably implicated in distinguishing adequate from inadequate ideas, true from false, liberty from bondage, and similar invidious separations. Presumably, to pursue added knowledge or practical guidance thence derived requires inverse processes this progression traverses connections toward or away from objects which may also be parts or wholes relative to each other. Thereby principles are correlated with our modes of thought and expression. Particularly in a demonstration *more geometrico,* it might be thought that such termini are parts and wholes roughly spatial in character. In addition, we—if not Spinoza—feel anxieties knotting these terms in speaking either of our cherished individualization and self-hood, or in citing the ties that bind us to others of our kind. Finally, even short of severe organicism or contractual ingenuity, discussing political associations seems to require some redisposition of erstwhile parts and wholes as they adjust their relations to each other.

However, these more ultimate questions are suggestions merely from my present less ambitious project, which might be described as investigating the "logic" of a critical and systematic use of paired and opposed terms. By this, I mean the requirements and facilitations which they exact from us in expressing, applying, or understanding an articulate philosophic scheme. The following are some of the logical puzzles suggested in scrutinizing the pair *part/whole* in Spinoza: (1) Is this pair primitive in the sense that it is not defined by some more ultimate pair, or is it implicated by another such distinction? (2) Are other pairs in the same sense derivative from it, or otherwise correlated? (3) Is a comparative scale implied by the two, perhaps delimited by them as opposite poles or implied by inverse directions from location at midpoints between them? (4) Does one or the other of these two designata assume a true or real priority over its counterpart? (5) May our advancement in the direction indicated by either of them be pursued in indefinite regression, or does it culminate in a completion which may be called "least part," or "most inclusive whole?" Presumably, the last query, if answered in one or othe other affirmative, would locate something which could be called a "principle" in the philosophy. We are directed to that question by taking seriously the logic of employing paired opposite terms.

For brevity's sake, my remarks will be sketchy and suggestive respecting the whole scheme of Spinoza's philosophy. Conversely, they may be overly diagrammatic regarding what I have called the "logic" of opposing paired terms. To attain balance, I shall attend closely but not exclusively to Letter 32 as principal text for my remarks, deploying a running commentary on its argument. In preparation, we should recall that any assertions in Spinoza's correspondence may fit oddly into the scheme of his philosophy. Sometimes his letters illuminate his extremely condensed expositions elsewhere. Yet his epistolary style is just as often equally compact. Further, at some points he clearly suits doctrines or vocabulary to his correspondent. It is also possible that any given remarks may be *obiter dicta*, preliminary versions, or trial balloons elsewhere deflated. However, for present purposes, I shall take the following extract to define *whole* and *part* for Spinoza's philosophy.

> With regard to whole and parts, I consider things as parts of some whole, in so far as their natures are mutually adapted so that they are in accord among themselves, as far as possible; but in so far as things differ among themselves, each produces an idea in our mind, which is distinct from the others, and is therefore considered to be a whole, not a part. (*Ep.* 32, Wolf(a), 209–14)

Part and *whole* are here being effectively defined, and that by reference to another pair of terms, *agreeing* and *differing*. Here, *part* is correlated with the characteristic of being mutually adapted to others of a like nature. Parts "accord among themselves." Things are parts to the extent that they accord or agree together—*convenire*. Spinoza uses a phrase which seems for him to be opposite to agreement in order to define *whole*: "differing among themselves" or being diverse—*discrepant*. The opposition he cites proximately to define part and whole is that between agreeing and diverging.

Before proceeding with the example which follows, I note that the terms *agree* and *differ* figure prominently in Spinoza's political writings. As here, they are there accompanied by overtones strongly suggesting association and conflict. But in discussing political matters, Spinoza offers in turn a peculiar distribution of wholistic and particularistic suggestions, namely one which corresponds to the present redisposition whereby opposed terms are defined. He shapes these pairs in oddly unfamiliar ways. Very roughly, Spinoza is a contract theorist. In consequence, coming to agreement, for which the same expressions are used, is immensely important in forming any associative unit. Citizens are parts of that unit so far as they have become "of one mind," as he says often, or they "agree in nature." Conversely, an association is a whole, not because it is constructed of them as parts, as in organic theories. It is a whole respecting other political units so far as it differs from them or is accepted as ruling. The analogue of what has been called the "state of nature" does not consist of parts rebounding according to merely natural laws. It is formed of whole units insistent on their singularity and incognizant of those agreements in nature or accordance with law whereby they may regard themselves as parts in some common order. They live, in Spinoza's phrase, "after their own laws." Hence, they are wholes. Conversely, a sound political order in attained only to the extent that citizens can and do agree in nature—which is to say that they conform to common laws. To that extent only, the political order is formed as a larger whole, so that its citizens may be regarded as parts.

II.

The oddity—or even perversity—of this definitive correlation between pairs is emphasized by the example which follows:

> For instance, since the motions of the particles of lymph, chyle, etc., are so mutually adapted in respect of magnitude and figure that they clearly agree among themselves, and all together constitute one fluid, to that extent only, chyle, lymph, etc., are considered to be parts of the blood: but in so far as we conceive the lymph particles as differing in respect of figure and motion from the particles of chyle, to that extent we consider them to be a whole, not a part. (*Ep*, 32, Wolf(a), 209–14)

He adds here that agreement consists in mutual adaptation "in respect of magnitude and figure"; and difference is "in respect to figure and motion." Here also, correlation with another opposed pair, *one/many*, is being suggested. But, presumably, this pair is derived from those cited thus far, for it is emerging with some hesitation. With respect to the parts, Spinoza prefers to use the plural "they." He speaks of "one part";

but he can do so only by identifying the sense in which it is like many others, being one-among-many. Conversely, the plural tends to drop out when he talks about the whole, although other wholes serve to distinguish it. Hence also, his rather ambivalent use of *particle*, sometimes in reference to many parts, but more often in reference to a curiously spurious unity.

The logic behind this slippage is not difficult to find. *Whole/part, one/many*, and the like seem to be distinctions on a sliding scale, we might say, so that what is "whole" respecting one viewpoint or location is "part" respecting another. For us, the terms *part* and *whole* are normally relative. A given item may be a whole relative to parts included and at the same time a part relative to a "larger" whole in which it is included.

In these definitions, Spinoza is not pointing to things which are wholes or parts simply. Rather, they are one or the other *in some respect*, according to the manner in which we take this or that object of reference. Hence, some form of the verb *to consider* recurs constantly and at important points. Something may be *considered*—or may consider itself, as we shall see—to be whole or part only by adopting this or that viewpoint. Either designation is appropriate or correct relative to that consideration only. From these ambivalences follow also the emphatic use of "to that extent only" and the necessary qualification, "in so far as" (*quatenus*), which occurs in each definition. This Latin word is found throughout Spinoza's philosophy. As a sort of qualification or limitation, it is often essential to his logic for making any significant statement whatsoever. We might say, citing the apparent logic of opposed pairs, that such bracketed designation and attribution is necessary *just because* we employ the terms with which we make reference in a scalar fashion. Assertions depend always on whether we observe an item from this direction or from that. It may be or may be conceived to be thus or so relative to one or another relationship, or so we might suppose, when regarding a scale. *One/many*, like *whole/part*, is a pair which is two-faced, we might say, whether among our linguistic devices, in our ways of conceiving various items, or in the ontological status we attribute to them.

This duplicity seems to infect Spinoza's disposition of questions— important to us, if not to him—concerning "individuation" or the nature of the "self." Under such headings, we seem to seek some preeminent item—both one and whole—which may stand opposed to many others and which may contain parts. We want a sort of rock-bottom particular entity. In place of this cherished ideal, I am interpolating the neutral word *item*—with a modicum of pretense to keeping questions open and vocabularly vacuous. It would seem that according to Spinoza's use of these pairs, as I have assigned them thus far, such solid entities evaporate among the interplay of "viewpoints." Or they are dislocated on a sliding scale which permits antithetical references and attributions. Let me anticipate another pair, *universal/particular*, in order to express these tensions as paradoxically as possible. We seem to want, for designation of ourselves, *particulars* defined as real *units* which may stand in fulsome *opposition* to each other—with *many others*, we might say, likewise distinct and agreeing in autonomy only. Conversely, we seem to want to dismiss universals—what is said "according to the *whole*," as our Greek tells us—as mere abstraction of *common* traits, thus formative of a solely intellectual unit indirectly from *many* real beings—a spurious *unity*, we might say, which omits the *discrepancies* whereby each of us is truly himself. It might seem that we want to have our cake and eat it, too.

These odd antitheses are apparent when we reconsider Spinoza's disposition of political ideals. In matters political, it is this switch in the unit of currency which permits Spinoza to emphasize agreement in such a way that democracy becomes the best form of government.[2] His preference for wholes justifies political power only insofar as the political unit is governed by common laws. But in this respect it is opposed only to other units. Its citizens are not "discrepant" with that whole; rather, they share in the patterns of accommodation whereby any parts agree with each other. Citizens are not ultimate or least units, potentially opposed to the state, as with more blatant contractualists. They are parts thereof only so far as their agreement in common nature and laws binds them to its rule. What we should call men's "particularities" make them oppose each other as warring wholes, whereas their union consists in conformity to their own nature and to common laws. That is, "agreeing" and "differing" control Spinoza's understanding of the ways men form associative units. Respecting its citizens, the political orders shares with them that rationality which is "equally in a part and in a whole."

This much seems clear. Both urgent questions and preferable answers require a terminology of opposition subject to dislocation and inversion suggesting degrees of sorts. In consequence, assertions are relativized to a "viewpoint" or to inverse polar directions. They may be ascribed only to "some extent." If they are corrigible, it is by altering correlations between pairs. But such correction depends on *who* is doing the considering, and from *what location* on any of several scales, and with what epistemological *faculties*. Which brings me to the worm.

III.

As if the definitions and first example citing blood were not puzzling enough, Spinoza is immediately stimulated (by his example, we might say) to complicate both with the much extended analogy introducing the worm.

> Let us now, if you please, imagine that a small worm lives in the blood, whose sight is keen enough to distinguish the particles of blood, lymph, etc., and his reason to observe how each part on collision with another either rebounds, or communicates a part of its own motion, etc. (*Ep.* 32, Wolf(a), 209–14)

It is this worm's reflections on part and whole which supply my subtitle for this paper. (We might find some such neologism as "microbe" less offensive in naming Spinoza's minute thinking thing. However, I shall identify him by employing Wolf's somewhat discomfiting Anglo-Saxon choice.) Notice that the worm is endowed with roughly humaniod faculties of sight and reason. Hence, wherever his suppositions and errors differ from our own it is rather because of his location respecting his world than because of his lesser powers. I use "view," or metaphors suggestive of differing "viewpoints," to signal that Spinoza's definitions of *part, whole* and attendant phrases are thereby made relative to the position of the knower, to the locus of the mind which surveys the world and its place in it. The worm has a certain location respecting the things in our world. His ways of considering and mentioning both "part" and "whole" are conditioned thereby. Any usage of vocabulary associated with *part* and *whole* is a function of what we, or the worm, or some other knower considers it to be. Hence, the prominent use of "consider" and "in so far as" mentioned above. In this case, the worm considers (at first) that all the particles, himself included, are wholes rather than parts. Thus the items *we* suppose we know to be parts, condescendingly calling them (with the worm himself) "particles" (*particulae*) in the blood, are mistaken by the worm. He finds himself different from them, and more or less in conflict. Thus in his ordinary language, he calls them and himself "wholes," and he pursues his opposition to them. It is because the worm is in battle-stance—collision and rebound—with other particle-sized objects that he sees himself as opposed and differing from them and according calls himself and them "wholes."

We reflect rather patronizingly that the worm is mistaken concerning himself. For he is "truly" a part, namely of ourselves or our blood, to both of which he is in some sense subject. Whatever he may suppose, he agrees in nature both with fellow particles and with the nature of the blood including all of them. But the point of Spinoza's fiction is that whole and part suggest ambivalent positions on a shifting scale. Despite our passing glimmer of superiority to the worm, we share one predicament in common with him. We, too, may consider ourselves to be one way or another both parts and wholes. We likewise occupy some intermediate point on one or several scales. We are tempted to look to our blood (and even to the worm) as included in ourselves, in some sense as parts. But in Spinoza's vocabulary, we are parts along with them so far as we share in common laws concerning figure, magnitude, and such. In this regard we are parts respecting other items in the universe which agree with us in nature, especially our fellows. However, we are wholes respecting whatever differs as some other opposed to us— which might include either obnoxious worms inside or enemy humans outside.

Not only do we share location somewhere mid-scale with the worm. The epistemic powers assigned to him are very like our own. The fiction Spinoza constructs requires that the worm should be able to see distinctions, and should have sufficient reason to observe. Presumably, what the worm has enough "reason to observe" is how parts collide, rebound, and communicate motions. Reason does not observe parts themselves, but rather the laws of adaptation whereby they accord. And conversely, his "sight is keen enough to distinguish" wholes. Although we wrench language somewhat to say it, the *wholes* perceived by the worm are such other particles as he can distinguish from himself by sight. Both of us *see* wholes, according to their differences; we *reason* about parts according to the laws interrelating them. Although it seems inverted, the worm's epistemological equipment is perfectly sound, if we understand that wholes appear to differ from each other, whereas parts agree according to laws. Parts and wholes are not isolated facts or items to which we apply or misapply empirical or rational techniques. Rather they are systematic functions respectively attending our rational cognition of laws and our discriminatory sensations. The worm designates parts and wholes alternatively, depending on where he is—or where he takes himself to be—with respect to either. He is inside or outside, so to speak. It is important to Spinoza's analogy that the worm "lives in the blood." It is consequent to this residence that he takes "each other particle"—the lymph, chyle, etc.—to be a whole, and not a part. Each is called "whole" inasmuch as he bumps up against them in ways he regards as random and discordant. He is taking himself as another whole among them, precisely to the extent that he remains ignorant of his agreement with others according to mutually adapted motions.

From our privileged position, we might be inclined to say that the blood is the "true whole." Relative to it, he and other particles are "in fact" parts accordant with each other by its laws. However, our privileged standpoint is not free from ambiguities. We, like the worm, regard ourselves as *one* whole. For some purposes we might take the blood to be a whole regulating lymph, chyle, and worm. However, we are even more inclined to take it as a part, namely of us. We might say that it accords in organic fashion with other parts more or less regulated by our bodily nature. In these opinions we are doubtless correct in some sense. One function of Spinoza's analogy is to boggle the worm's-eye view against our own, and to encourage a sort of double vision whereby things may be either wholes or parts according to the way in which they are considered.

The identity crisis of middle-sized beings like ourselves and the worm arises because each of us, in reflecting on himself, may consider himself to be either a whole or a part. That is, we may locate our "self-image," our "individuality," or whatever non-Spinozistic word we choose, either among our discrepancies or among our agreements. In the former case, taking ourselves to be wholes, we are in a more or less embattled stance respecting other middle-region beings from whom we see that we differ. These "others" may be inside us, as the worm is, or outside, like footstools we trip over, or persons we oppose or expect to be like to us in kind and kindness. Respecting persons, we may also take ourselves to be parts, citing some degree or concordance with fellows sharing a common nature in addition to middle-region status and interactions. For we observe by our reason that we agree in rebound, communication of motion, and the like. Both worm and footstool agree with us to this extent.

It is not our differences but the perplexities we share with the worm that Spinoza is calling to our attention: "That worm would live in this blood as we live in this part of the universe, and he would consider each particle of blood to be a whole, and not a part." (*Ep.* 32, Wolf(a), 209–14) As for him, our own dilemmas concerning our identity arise because we are mid-scale beings who boggle between alternate ways of considering ourselves. We take ourselves either to be wholes differing from other wholes more or less opposed in nature, or to be parts accommodated to them by our common nature. We are satisfied with our own identity just because we can protest that rational and discriminatory capacities have been conferred on the worm only by an honorary fiction.

We flatter ourselves that we are better than the worm only because we suppose that we know something he fails to know:

> And he could not know how all the parts are controlled by the universal nature of blood, and are forced, as the universal nature of blood demands, to adapt themselves to one another, so as to harmonize with one another in a certain way. (*Ep.* 32, Wolf(a), 209–14)

The worm lives in the blood as a part, although he neglects that fact, at least at first.[3] We correct his error by inverting for him his notions of self-identity. We insist on his status as a part that harmonizes with others and is controlled by a universal nature.

Our superiority to the worm lies in our capacity to correct our considerations respecting ourselves, our environment, and our fellows. We do so, however, by adjusting our disposition of parts and wholes and by assigning a certain priority to the latter respecting the former. Opposed pairs of terms tend to slip-slide, or to flip-flop on the scale implicated with them. Occasionally, we find it possible to avoid these perturbations by making one criterion to the other. Accordingly, any other matters determined by their logic are reoriented. In some systematic sense—which includes evaluation—we distinguish up from down by such a priority, so that the opposed pair is asymmetrical. One is subordinate or derivative from the other.

It is by reason, at least in the first instance, that we are able to reassort priorities among part and whole and to reconsider ourselves in a more enlightened manner. The Preface to Part IV of the *Ethics* admonished us to define Good and Evil according to a"model of human nature which we set before us." The origin of that model is not random experience, the imagination whereby we combine scattered (and opposed) private perceptions into a general but limited view. It is accomplished instead by *reason* which discovers that which is "equally in part and whole." All wholistic functions which the dictates of reason prefer to us are disclosed in that model of human nature wherein the parts agree with each other and with the whole. Only by reference to that whole do we agree as parts, whether with each other or with our common nature, or with our "true selves," we might say, invoking non-Spinozistic language. Otherwise, when we differ or stand in opposition to each other, we are wholes referent each to our private character, being neither accommodated to each other, nor to another whole in which we are parts and in whose laws we share. We thus violate the dictates which our own reason could observe, as they cite that which is equally in part and whole. We middle-region beings may view ourselves and companions alternatively either as part or as whole. Either perspective may be taken as rule and source of guidance. The fact is that we both differ and agree among ourselves. We may understand and we may seek guidance by either mode of consideration. It is to the extent that we consider and follow what is equally in the part and in the whole that we follow the dictates of reason.

This redisposition of our self-consideration—so that we refer ourselves as parts to a common whole—shapes the normative thrust in the final books of the *Ethics*. Accordingly, the criterion is a sort of preference for a whole of sorts over parts. Reason dictates recognition of that whole whereby many parts agree with themselves in a whole. Thus we correct the viewpoint previously adopted, after the style of the worm, whereby we are wholes discordant in nature and accommodated to no other whole of which we are aware. In this way, we recognize only other wholes related to ourselves roughly by enmity. Reflections thus limited are misleading, rather than false. The viewpoints they provide are counter-normative because they are irrational in the strict sense, being unable to locate that in which part and whole agree and are adapted to each other.

The function of a whole has been modified by an unexpected shift. It is the presumption of being self-contained which permits any of us or the worm to take himself as a whole differing from others. But no mid-region beings are completely self-contained, although they may so assert themselves. They are impinged on by others and impinged on them in turn, in which mutual stance both are subject to various governing laws. Indeed, such antagonists may be conceived, and may conceive themselves, through laws rather than through their differences. They exist as inclusions in the region characterized by those laws, in which sense they are parts. The self-contained whole to which they had previously attended is the whole they are not, as it turns out. It is replaced by a further whole, although this in turn may produce "an idea in the mind, which is distinct from the others."

This progression among ideas of ourselves is more subtle than replacing falsities by truths. Neither is our former idea an "appearance" and the enlarged one "reality," as some commentators would have it. Not even my talk implying degrees on a scale is appropriate. Rather, we make a discrete switch, attending now to a more adequate idea whereby we assess our identity. No doubt our idiosyncracies and our "rights to do our own thing" abscond when we resolve anxieties over identity in these ways. It is by mutual agreements that we so relocate our identity, whether by concordance with our common nature or by mutual consent to our union. Only regarding ourselves as parts so adapted do we realign our self-hood. Presumably we thus cite that human nature in which we all participate or by which we are ruled, willy-nilly. But such seeming submissions are extended by noting the specifically human partnerships in which we engage, such as love, political associations, or scientific pursuits. Thus we are truly humanoid and rational in our self-identification.

We might express our dilemmas concerning mid-region status by debating in which direction we ought to turn, whether toward "larger" wholes or toward more "minute" parts. However, this issue is decided by the corrected alignment of parts to wholes, and by the peculiar advantage of reason in disclosing ways in which they are conformed to each other according to the nature or laws of the whole. The dictates of reason result. The epistemic distinction between adequate and inadequate ideas seems also to depend on distinguishing the partial or imperfect character of the latter as distinct from their accommodations to the former as governing whole. *Adequate* means correspondent by equation, rather than merely sufficient, as the English word suggests. From this invidious separation develop others, those between *action/ passion, liberty/bondage* and *consent/tyranny*. It is the function of reason to invert these discriminations. It returns us to understanding and following laws of interconnection which are equally in part and whole. Such correction is among the powers of any middle-region being which possesses "reason to observe" collision, rebound, and communicated motion among parts. Which returns me to the worm, as he was imagined not inferior to us in capacity for this correction.

V.

The worm's error is a reflexive one. That is, he errs in considering himself and in assigning his own place in the scheme of things. Moreover, his error misjudges his respective characters as part and as whole. In this sense, he suffers a sort of identity crisis. For he overlooks the ways in which he is a part agreeing in nature with others and conforming to the more universal nature which is his environment. Instead, he seeks identity in his difference from others, namely in a deficient whole. That viewpoint is inadequate self-consideration, and it inverts the order of criteria. That which is equally in part and whole indicates a relatively more self-sufficient whole, namely the "universal nature of blood." Respecting that, the whole he had thought himself to be is an ephemeral and fictitious abstraction. It is a mistaken resolution of his identity crisis. But we, too, are liable to the same error. Indeed, we invoke it at a higher level when we imagine ourselves correcting the worm:

For if we imagine that there are no causes outside the blood to communicate new motions to the blood, and that outside the blood there is no space, and no other bodies, to which the particles of blood could transfer their motion, it is certain that the blood would remain always in its state, and its particles would suffer no changes other than those which can be conceived from the given relations of the motion of the blood to the lymph and chyle, etc., and so blood would have to be considered always to be a whole and not a part. (*Ep.* 32, Wolf(a), 209–14)

However, we have no cue to be smug about our lurking recall that to some extent we, too, control and harmonize the blood and the worm along with it. For in the fiction whereby we improve our reflections on the worm, we take the blood to be a whole in the same incomplete fashion. The worm's fallacy might be characterized as mistaking what is a part to a more enlightened view for that whole he supposes constitutes his identity. What he wants is to view himself as one, simple, integrated, and self-controlled. But he has mislocated these desiderata, supposing that they are found in a whole which is opposed to other wholes. We make the same error in attempting to correct the worm. For we cite the blood as if it were such a whole, holding in reserve our own superiority to blood and worm alike.

Various other opposed pairs of terms correlate with this corrective inversion, namely *one/many, simple/complex, constant/changing, autonomous/dependent,* and possibly *universal/particular.* We are inclined to regard each of these as defining its own scale, as does *part/whole.* Thus mid-range beings may be characterized relatively as being "greater" or "more" such and such respecting another. As the contrary-to-fact conditional respecting the blood indicates, the blood may be considered a larger whole, or even *the* whole—relative to the worm. So taken, it is also relatively unitary, simple, constant, autonomous, and universal. Indeed, we deflate the worm's identity by insisting that he is none of these. We say that he is more adequately characterized as an opposite to that whole—he is multiple, complex, etc. Correction by reason consists in realigning *whole* and *part* in proper correspondence to the others. We do this by citing the blood as a whole rather than a part. Accordingly it is a unit, simple, constant, autonomous, and universal.

One pair, *autonomous/dependent,* I shall reserve for later scrutiny along with *inside/outside,* whose mention I have omitted thus far. In the letter to Oldenburg, the others—saving *universal/particular,* which is trickier—can be clarified by unpacking the word "nature." In defining *parts* it was their *natures* which agreed or were mutually adapted. Thereby parts are referred to some whole other than themselves. In relation to it they are multiple, complex, and changeable. *That* identity constitutes at least a relative whole possessing unity, simplicity, and constancy such as the worm had claimed for himself in considering himself as if he were a whole. It is in accordance with this redisposition that we refer to the universal nature of blood. When we correct the worm, we suppose blood to be a larger whole containing and controlling parts by its "universal nature." Such nature as parts possess is found in *its* nature. Respecting it, they are multiple, having complexities in conjunction with others and reduced to simplicity only by laws of the blood. The worm mistakes when he finds his own unity, simplicity, and constancy in a distinctive nature wherein he differs from others or from the medium he occupies. We do likewise, when we locate our private nature in our discrepancies, overlooking our common agreements and the model of human nature we should set before us.

Spinoza's original explication of *part* and *whole* in Letter 32 was not as neutral in this regard as I have pretended. Rather, there is a curious asymmetry about it, and a certain evaluative ambivalence. In a way—which I shall exaggerate now, having hidden it thus far—*part* and *whole* are not merely correlatives. Rather the former is defined in terms of the latter. Wholes are not summations attained by adding parts, as we might be tempted to describe them in an alien vocabulary. Things are considered "parts of the same whole," according to their mutual adaptions. But this adaptation consists in agreement in their shared nature—including magnitude and figure—and in conformity to the laws to which all of them are subject. Strictly speaking, parts are defined by the kind of connections interrelating them. Only by an "idea in our mind" are they so distinct that they are "considered to be a whole not a part." I have withheld thus far the following preamble to the discussion of part and whole in Letter 32: "By connection of the parts, then, I mean nothing else than that the laws, or nature, of one part adapt themselves to the laws, or nature, of another part in such a way as to produce the least possible opposition." (*Ep.* 32, Wolf(a), 209–14) We should notice that the way which produces "the least possible opposition" requires that the including whole and its laws or nature is more simple than parts which are engaged in complicated interconnections. In this sense it is properly wholes which are simple and parts which are complex.

The metaphor of scale that I am explicating suggests a special inquiry which I shall mention only briefly, namely whether there is a terminus to the implied scale in either or both directions. Effectively, either such limit would determine the scale itself. The question of a "greatest whole" will occupy me later. However, while discussing *simple/complex*, I should like to question whether some minimal or perhaps "most simple" part is indicated by the present scheme. The answer must be negative in one sense. For it is wholes, not parts, which are simple. Parts lack a nature of their own. One is supposed for them only by a limited fiction. They are simple only to the extent that they may be substituted for each other in a common nature or in a constant pattern. We mistake Spinoza's scheme when we interpret *part/whole* terminology by imagining wholes attained by compounding or adding contained parts—spatially or organically, as we might say. Parts are complex by variable interfaces respecting others or by participation in a containing nature having multiple aspects. Their supposed simplicity among oppositions is deficient and corrigible.

Conversely, we might seek least parts by operations progressively subdividing a proper whole. However, we can never arrive at an ultimate part, whether complex or simple, by this move. For a new act of the mind is presupposed by each step. In both organic and geometrical terms, each successive operation would seem to require a principle of division or the idea of a shared nature. If the parts differ—say as kinds of triangle differ—both distinction and common ground refer to one nature. If they are homogenous—say as "most simple bodies" are alike— both interchangeability and isolation alike refer to one nature. Such simplicity as is presumed in locating whatever minimal parts is always a function of an idea constituting them.[4] Any part, however minimal, is conceived through a whole. We and the worm are both prone to consider our insides to be partitioned into separate parts. Probably we err by renewed mislocation of a whole when we pretend atomic stoppage to this series on behalf of any supposedly ultimate particle.

Western thought has been preoccupied with the pair, *universal/particular*. On the linguistic side, we suppose a special correlation with *whole/part* in deriving *particular* and in the wholistic suggestions in *Greek-to-Latin* translation of *universal*. Yet, like the worm, we ordinarily insist on identifying ourselves with something we call "the individual particular." This we take ourselves to be so far as we differ from others, imagining a whole compiled from what we call its "particularities"—that is, those idiosyncratic characters wherein it *differs* from others. Such individuality we think abrogated by conformity to surrounding natures or by interchangeability among characterless individuals. Its "particular" identity is lost therein. But Spinoza correlates *universal/particular* in a manner neither traditional nor ordinary. He prefers Latin cognates of *singular* and occasionally *individual*, using

153

particular much less than his translators do in English. The relocation respecting *part* and *whole* which we urge on the worm indicates the reasons. What we might call our "integrity" or "true wholeness" consists in adherence to a model of human nature or to a circumambient universal nature which controls and defines, as blood does for the worm. That model, we must recall, is not pieced together by compiling observed common traits, for thereby it would be both fictitious and abstractive. More universal natures, for Spinoza, cite causes not self-originated and laws defeating what we profess for our individualized nature. The more universal constitutes a whole by containing, controlling, and guiding. So we see it is the proper corrective for the spurious particularity whereby we urge our discrepancies and a fictitious independence.

This redisposition we recommend to the worm by calling his attention to the blood. But in doing so we insinuate a further fiction, for we take or mistake the blood as a sufficient whole. Likewise, we envisage ourselves as containing both it and worm. We repeat the worm's error at a level only one step higher, so to speak.

VI.

It is our psyche, not the worm's, which Spinoza wishes to amend in Letter 32. In consequence, he cunningly elevates his analogy to a new stage, subjecting us to the same inversion we urged on the worm. We have presumptuously cited the blood as that whole which is constant and caused or controlled by nothing outside. It shares its nature with no other which limits it. The blood is thus mistaken for God, which mistake the worm presumably shares even at the extreme of his conceptual powers. But we know better, just by recollecting our own preeminence in turn to our blood.

> But, since there are very many other causes which in a certain way control the laws of the nature of blood, and are in turn controlled by the blood, hence it comes about that other motions and other changes take place in the blood, which result not only from the mere relation of the motion of its parts to one another, but from the relation of the motion of the blood and also of the external causes to one another: in this way the blood has the character of a part and not of a whole. (*Ep.* 32, Wolf(a), 209–14)

Our error has been to treat the blood as subject to no outside causes, to no others respecting which it is opposed. We consider it to have only insides, so to speak, and, hence, to be self-caused as is God or nature.

154

Blood so understood seems to us a sort of whole at some level. For any other—like the worm—is *in* it and controlled according to its nature and laws. But we know that blood actually to be a part just because it accords under common laws with others outside itself. It is caused according to laws and natures respecting which it is partial. We recall that we are a next more inclusive whole. But we are carried by a sort of momentum of analogy to the further recognition that we in turn are not whole in that sense, but subject, as is the blood, to outside causes and to containment in a more universal nature. "We live in this part of the universe" as the worm lives in his, namely blood and us. That is the point of this entire exercise.

No one of us is the whole we each might profess. We are parts inhabiting a more whole region of the universe.[5] For the moment, we helpfully understand that region as a controlling whole, although it is also part in a further whole. We refer ourselves as parts to a next whole, presumably larger and more inclusive by our conformity to it. But neither comparative enters Spinoza's vocabulary here, although both are handy in discussing part and whole. Instead, whenever we invert our understanding, a new dependence is cited, and paired terms are correlated anew. Although each step suggests a comparative series, it is accomplished by asking the questions, which caused what? what is outside or inside? and—again—which nature universal, which partial? *Self* and *other* are also implicated, but they have been with us all the time in a sense vacillating according to our adjustment of *whole* and *part*.

Among these, I take the governing pair to be *autonomous/dependent*, as we move in serial order from worm to blood to ourselves to our region of the universe and on to whatever comes next. For I understand something to be "autonomous" to the extent that it is caused by itself; and to be "dependent" to the extent that it is caused by something other or by a nature shared with others which are like it. When we recognize that the blood is controlled by other causes which are outside, although it communicates with them by laws of motion common with them, we may say that it "has the character of a part, not a whole." Conversely, we considered it a whole when we neglected outside causes and motions transferred by some law governing it as well as others. That which is imagined to be autonomous is a whole, to that extent differing from various possible others. That supposition may be corrected by taking others into account, in which case a whole is cited that is "larger" or "contains" the implied series. The erstwhile whole is considered a part relative thereto. For it is dependent on others or on that nature which is equally in a part and in a whole, that is, on a common nature in which it shares. Thus *whole/part* may be correlated with *autonomous/dependent*, although with two qualifications invoked on behalf of the worm and other middle-region items. (1) By *sight* and other imaginings, we may *distinguish* wholes, taking them to be distinct and autonomous, although they are so only by a fiction or to a limited extent. (2) And by *reason* and other conceptualizations, we *observe* laws or natures governing the mutual adaptations of parts. These qualifications correct our initial considerations. Instead of taking parts to assert themselves as if autonomous wholes, we take them as if dependent on common or more adequate expression of the natures in which they share.

Causing/caused thus correlates with *automonomous/dependent*, and indirectly with *whole/part* as corrected. So also does *greater/lesser*, so far as we properly infer such comparatives. *Containing/contained* may also pass, if we recall that no spatial relation is intended. "Containment" is possessing a nature sufficient to account for contents or other consequents; "being contained" is inclusion in a common or more adequately conceived nature. *Inside/outside* requires the same omission of spatialized interpretations, with like reference to the nature or dependence in question. Strictly speaking, anything over which another has autonomy is "inside" it, being a factor accordant with its nature. It is therefore a part to that extent in some whole. With like precision, another on which anything is dependent is "outside" it, being an opposed or differing nature, and therefore another whole discordant with it. These statements apply to any mid-region beings. They may be illustrated with some contortion by respective descriptions of the worm among our viscera. The worm is "inside" us, as far as it confroms to our nature and to our gross movements. It shares in communication of motions according to laws we and it both participate in. On the other hand it is "outside," for example, to the extent that following its distinctive nature it instigates a viral infection which is in that respect discrepant with ours or an external cause limiting us. Being spatially "internal" is beside the point. Our agreement with mankind is within us, although our enemy virus is without. So understood, *inside/outside*, *larger/lesser*, *containing/contained*, *causing/caused* may all be assimilated to *autonomous/dependent*. That correspondence may guide middle-region being as they reflect on part and whole.

The step whereby we adjusted paired terms asymmetrically invariably suggests a comparative scale determined by one or another or both opposites. Hence, we are almost compelled by any of them to project in serial fashion, presumably seeking a true principle at its limit. In the section just preceding, I spoke briefly about the impossibility of pursuing successive steps to a possible ultimate or limit on a scale in the direction of lesser or included parts. It should be apparent that in moving in the reverse direction toward wholes successively more adequate, autonomous, or complete, we encounter such a limit, namely God. For present purposes, it is enough to note that God is self-caused or strictly autonomous. Any other being is controlled by beings outside itself. But everything else is inside God. There is no other, inside or out, from which God differs—no others to interfere with Him or otherwise to control Him.[6] His nature suffices to account for any other and it encompasses all "parts of the universe" to which other beings might refer, not to mention ourselves and worms. Accordingly, His nature is not altered, and it is one and simple. A whole is not greater by composition from distinctive parts, but by their conformity to its nature. Respecting any lesser mid-range beings, God might be considered to be ultimate whole or final region of the universe in a sense salutary if also *jejune*. Certainly. He is not part respecting some *other* whole. But strictly, according to the definitions of Letter 32, neither is God a whole at all. For something is a whole by differing from some other which is also taken to be a whole. A more cautious alternate expression is the following. God is principle, just because He is that being to which the paired terms—*part* and *whole*—cannot be applied.

Both apply, however, to all beings other than God, that is, to anything mid-region like the worm and ourselves. For any of them may be considered or may consider themselves to be either whole or part. Both reflections may be quite sound. It is a question about the unit of currency, so to speak, and about the domain in which either is aptly exchanged. Each thing this side of God is to some extent a viable and autonomous unit: that is, it is a whole. In such consideration, other and different things are ignored or distinguished, both doubtless with some limited success and truth. For each has some nature distinctive enough to be so taken or to be self-assertive. But such consideration fails to exhaust its nature. Hence, such consideration is corrected by reference to some whole respecting which it is a part. Each thing this side of God is thus also a limited and dependent multiplicity: that is, it is a part. Upon such reconsideration, other and accordant things are recognized or assimilated, both doubtless with improved success and truth. For in this enlarged sense of its nature, it exists in and is conceived through something else, through similar others, through added aspects of its own nature, and—finally—through God. Such a being presumably lacks capacity to exhaust its full nature, although its assertions and self-assertiveness are corrected and are adequate to the extent that it is able to advance in this direction. A perfect understanding considering itself as solely a part would exhaust such nature as is its own. For that would be what it is—and the way it is adequately conceived.

VII.

One last admonition for worm or ourselves, as you prefer. All mid-region beings suffer a certain anxiety about their self-identity. They are beset by others, and they puzzle over the pair, *self/other*. In numerous familiar cases, others are variously redistributed, whether as wholes or as parts. Willy-nilly, we take numerous others to be wholes differing from ourselves—like the footstool we stumble over or the little fish we eat; and we take numerous remaining others to be parts joined to ourselves by a common nature—like the gravity we adjust to or the friends we love. Reason dictates that at various points of rub we should join ourselves to the second group as much as possible, referring however tentatively to wholes more perfect than we are and to our respective selves as partial. Despite our finest endeavors, the self we cherish is not God. Nor is it any irreducible self to which no tensions between opposed considerations are applicable, which preeminence would also equate each such self to God.

However, cherishing that self for what it is and for the nature or Nature through which it is conceived might obviate the need to contemplate it or its fellows as either parts or wholes. For lacking such invidious comparison, we should not relate by concord or difference to any other, similar or alien. Hence, various irrelevant servitudes would disappear: rub at the interface, rational guidance and correction, wholes opposed or cited, and parts joined or explicated—from these all alike such a self would be free. Although I am not certain, I suspect that somewhere at the horizon of this extrapolation is where we or the worm might find such blessedness as our faculties permit.

NOTES

1. H.F. Hallett, *Benedict de Spinoza* (London: The Athlone Press, 1957), p. 13.

2. My paper, "Spinoza on Democracy," discusses this facet of his political philosophy. Included in M. Mandelbaum and E. Freeman, *Spinoza: Essays in Interpretation* (LaSalle, Illinois: Open Court, 1975).

3. There is a gap at this point in my argument, or possibly in Spinoza's. He says the worm "could not know"—*nec scire posset*. Yet the worm is endowed with reason, which supplies the correction indicated in the present section. The minimal cautious statement is that the worm does not know outside influences and universal laws inasmuch as he considers himself a whole opposed to the former and neglecting the latter.

4. The extremely condensed argument of these two paragraphs needs amplification, particularly by reference to the Lemmata following Proposition 13 of

Part II of the *Ethics*—the source of the quotes around "simple." I intend such extension of this and a parallel paragraph in the next section for another paper, also to be concerned with the perplexities we share with the worm.

5. Wolf is quite accurate in using *part* in the snippet just quoted, although I shall occasionally substitute *region* to avoid confusion. Like ourselves and worm, our "region" of the universe is also a mid-scale notion.

6. One important sense of *infinite* corresponds to this statement. But I omit complication with the implied pair, which doubtless correlates with *autonomous/ dependent*.

Spinoza and Recent Philosophy of Religion

E. M. CURLEY
Australian National University

I invite you to participate in a thought experiment with me. We are to imagine that Benedict de Spinoza, having died on the 21st of February 1677, descended into Hell—surely, in the eyes of many of his contemporaries, the appropriate place for the author of the *Tractatus Theologico-Politicus*; that he spent three centuries there, talking philosophy with other condemned spirits—Bayle, Voltaire, Hume, Bertrand Russell—thereby illustrating the correctness of Mark Twain's observation that one should prefer Heaven for climate, Hell for company; and that one fine spring day three hundred years later he rose again from the dead and ascended into Harvard, where he sits on the right hand of Quine, and whence he shall come again, very soon, to judge what is living and what is dead in the philosophy of this century.

He will, I think, be very much interested in the current state of the area we now call philosophy of religion and will feel that this has once again become an exciting area. The demise of logical positivism has meant that there has been not so much preoccupation with the meaningfulness of religious discourse. The work of philosophical logicians has made it possible once again to use modal language without blushing. (Perhaps we should imagine Spinoza sitting on the right hand, not of Quine, but of Kripke.) And there is once again, among the religious, a tolerably tough-minded disposition to offer rational arguments for religious beliefs. There is even a renewed interest in and sympathy for such extravagances of philosophical theology as the ontological argument.[1] These are all tendencies of which I think our resurrected Spinoza will heartily approve.

But while there is a good deal in recent philosophy of religion that Spinoza will find congenial, there is one particular recent work which I conjecture he will find especially intriguing, partly because this work has certain affinities with his own, because it argues in a similarly *a priori* way for God's existence, but more importantly because this work does not, as some recent works do, neglect those problems about God's nature which caused Spinoza to break from the mainstream of the Western theological tradition. It combines an interest in the analytic reconstruction of natural religion with a considerable awareness of how much must be done in order to prove the existence of a being recognizable as the God of the Judaeo-Christian tradition.

The philosopher of whose work I speak in these laudatory terms is James Ross, and the book I shall be looking at is his *Philosophical Theology*.[2] This is an exceedingly complex and difficult book, more complex and difficult, perhaps, than it need be. I suppose it is not necessary to apologize for the study of difficult books to an audience reading about Spinoza. But I shall have to simplify Ross's argument considerably in order to give an account at all of its main themes, and it is only fair to warn that in simplifying I may unintentionally be distorting.

Ross is concerned, among other things, to establish the existence of God by rational argument. Central to his strategy is a principle he calls the Principle of Explicability,[3] which says (roughly) that necessarily, for any consistent state of affairs, p, involving the existence or the non-existence of something, it is possible that there should have been an explanation of p's being the case. The explanation of p's being the case may be either p itself (if so, $-p$ must be inconsistent) or some other state of affairs q (in which case, q must entail the existence of something).

This principle is supposed, in conjunction with certain logical truths and an appropriate definition of God, to entail that God exists. God is defined here[4] as a self-explanatory, uncausable, unpreventable, omnipotent, eternal, benevolent, personal, and perfect being, who is the creator of the universe and the ground of the being of everything other than himself.

The argument runs (very roughly)[5] as follows: Suppose God does not exist; if he does not, it must be possible for there to be an explanation of this state of affairs; if the state of affairs were to explain itself, then it would have to be impossible for God to exist, but it is not; so that state of affairs (i.e., that God does not exist) would have to be explained by some state of affairs other than itself; but this could not be; for in defining God as unpreventable, we implied that nothing external to God could cause his non-existence; so if God did not exist, there could be no explanation of this state of affairs; but for any possible state of affairs it must be possible for there to be an explanation of it; so our original supposition—that God does not exist—is not only false but impossible.

This argument proceeds, then, from a definition of God and an *a priori* principle about the possibility of explanations. Ross claims that his principle vindicates Leibniz's contention that if God is possible, he exists.[6] So far, his reasoning is at least reminiscent of various modal versions of the ontological argument advocated recently by Hartshorne and Malcolm, and at one stage Ross refers to his argument as the Modal argument, although he is more concerned to emphasize its affinities with the thought of earlier thinkers such as Aquinas, Maimonides, Scotus, and Spinoza.

We might, I think, have some reason for preferring Hartshorne's modal argument to Ross's.[7] Hartshorne does not rely, as Ross does, on the notion of God as a being whose existence cannot be prevented. We might want more discussion of this somewhat unusual property than Ross gives it. We might believe, for example, that we understand well enough what is meant when some event (say, a revolution) is said to be unpreventable, *viz.*, that the tendencies and powers of things now existing are such that it must come to pass, but that this cannot be what is meant when God's existence is said to be unpreventable (because God is not supposed to be brought into existence by anything, or indeed, to come into existence at all).

On the other hand, Ross does not (as Hartshorne, in effect, does[8]) take it as a premise that if God's existence is possible, it is actual, and we might think that to allow such an assumption to pass without argument is to make things too easy for the natural theologian. Ross's Principle of Explicability is supposed to give us a reason for saying that God, if he is possible, must be actual. In this respect, we might think Ross's version of the modal argument preferable.

It is very important to Ross, however, to distinguish his Principle of Explicability from the traditional Principle of Sufficient Reason. The Principle of Explicability entails that every consistent state of affairs is such that it is *possible* for it to have an explanation; the Principle of Sufficient Reason maintains that every contingent state of affairs is such that it *actually* does have an explanation. Ross is committed to the Principle of Explicability, but disavows the Principle of Sufficient Reason.

There are a number of reasons for this. First, he is somewhat sympathetic to a Humean critique of the Principle of Sufficient Reason.[9] That principle must be either analytic or synthetic. If it is synthetic, then because it is a universal generalization, our acceptance of it, if rational, must be based on induction. But induction can never establish the absolute universality of an unrestricted generalization. If it is analytic, its denial should involve a contradiction. But no one has ever succeeded in showing in this way, the necessity of the Principle of Sufficient Reason, and there is little reason to expect success in the future.

Ross is not *entirely* sympathetic with this line of argument. For one thing, he is in the same position regarding the statement that "God exists" as Spinoza would be regarding the principle that every contingent state of affairs has an explanation. He does not think anyone has convincingly shown that its denial involves a contradiction. Moreover, he has apparently been convinced by the Cambridge nominalists (Quine, White, Goodman, and company) that notions like analyticity and self-contradiction are too confused at this stage in the history of philosophy for Hume's objection to be decisive.[10] He does think there is a strategic advantage in using the weaker Principle of Explicability, which claims only the logical possibility of an explanation, and is therefore much more likely to be true *a priori*. Indeed, he argues that the Principle of Explicability must be either true *a priori* or false *a priori* because it is an explicitly modal principle, and principles about what is possible or necessary are, if true, necessarily true.[11]

More importantly, though, Ross does not think the Principle of Sufficient Reason is merely ill-supported. He thinks it is false and must be held to be false by any orthodox Christian. The Christian doctrine of the Creation implies the existence of a "glaring counter-example to the claim that everything has an explanation."[12] The Christian wants to maintain that although the world, in some sense, has its explanation in the existence of a necessary being, God, the existence of this world is nevertheless contingent. So it cannot, for the Christian, be the case that God's existence is *by itself* a sufficient condition for the existence of the world. For God's existence is necessary, and what follows from the necessary is itself necessary. The existence of the world must, therefore, for the Christian, follow from God's choice, a choice which cannot in turn follow from anything which is necessary, like God's existence or nature. If there is any explanation of God's choice, it must lie in something which is itself contingent and open to an extrinsic explanation; but there must ultimately be some contingent state of affairs which is not in fact explained.

Ross, then, accepts Hume's contention that "the Christian has even less reason than anyone else for thinking the principle [of Sufficient Reason] necessarily true."[13] His rejection of the Principle of Sufficient Reason is not, in the pejorative sense of the term, merely dogmatic. He offers an *a priori* argument that the Principle of Sufficient Reason must be false.[14] Summarizing very roughly again, we can state the argument as follows: let W represent the conjunction of true contingent propositions and N represent the conjunction of all necessary propositions; N cannot explain W, otherwise W would be necessary rather than contingent; W cannot explain itself, for only the necessary is self-explanatory. So although there is no particular contingent truth which is intrinsically inexplicable, there is necessarily no explanation for the totality of contingent truths. That is one reason why it is important for Ross to be able to argue for the existence of God without assuming anything quite so strong as the Principle of Sufficient Reason, one reason why he prefers instead the weaker Principle of Explicability.

So far we have, I think, much that Spinoza would sympathize with. Whether there would also be much in this that Spinoza would take issue with is a difficult matter of interpretation, which I do not propose to go into here. Ross plainly takes Spinoza to be committed to the Principle of Sufficient Reason in a form that would be excluded by his *a priori* argument. If the interpretation of Spinoza that I have offered in *Spinoza's Metaphysics*[15] is correct, the difference between them may not be so great as Ross supposes, although I do think Spinoza is committed to the Principle of Sufficient Reason in *some* form. But then so, perhaps, is Ross, in spite of himself. More of that anon. In the meantime, what interests me, and what I conjecture would probably interest Spinoza most in Ross's work, is the way Ross goes on to deal with questions about the nature of the God whose existence he professes to have proven.

Ross considers the following objection[16] to his argument for God's existence. The definition of God he has used has proceeded by a fairly traditional enumeration of attributes: God is a being who is omnipotent, eternal, self-accounting, personal, benevolent, uncausable, unpreventable, etc. But the only attribute taken from that list which has actually been used in the proof is unpreventability. So unless there is some necessary connection between the various attributes, there is no reason to say that the argument has proved the existence of a being possessing the full set of attributes listed in the definition, i.e., no reason to say that it has proved the existence of *God* (as understood in the tradition). Ross allows that this objection is sound, and that the argument I have sketched does not, without further ado, prove God's existence. But he thinks the required necessary connections exist. This is how he understands the traditional doctrine of God's simplicity: although statements like "God is omnipotent" and "God is omniscient" are not synonymous, they are logically equivalent.[17] He also thinks that on an adequate analysis of the relevant attributes, the equivalences can be established. In a subsequent chapter he offers analyses of two rather critical attributes, which, he says, "suggest that this equivalence will be found to hold in all the necessary cases."[18]

The two attributes he analyzes are omnipotence and omniscience, and it is to these analyses that I now wish to turn. Ross considers and rejects a long series of definitions of omnipotence in terms of what God can do. His own (plausible) way of articulating the traditional theological notion of omnipotence uses the concept of will, or effective choice:[19]

$$\text{OP}s \longleftrightarrow (p) \left[(\Diamond p \,\&\, \Diamond \bar{p}) \to (p \longleftrightarrow s\text{W}p) \right]$$

This may be read: s is omnipotent if and only if, for any contingent proposition, p, p is true if and only if s wills that p. To this definition Ross adds two further principles, which may be regarded as axioms implicitly defining the notion of effective choice:

(i) $(p)\, (s\text{W}p \to \Diamond \overline{s\text{W}p})$

(ii) $(p)\, (\overline{s\text{W}p} \longleftrightarrow s\text{W}\bar{p})$

Ross says that (i) and (ii) are "parts of our concept of 'W' or 'chooses effectively that',"[20] and this seems to mean that he takes them to hold of any subject that can be said to choose, not only of an omnipotent one. (i) is intended to express the contingency Ross feels is essential to the notion of choice, and says that for any proposition, p, if s wills that p, then it is possible that s not will that p. (ii) says that for any proposition, p, s does not will that p if and only if s wills that not-p. The effect of this is to rule out the possibility of s willing neither p nor not-p. Whether or not that is satisfactory in general, it does seem plausible to say of an omnipotent being that it cannot abstain from choice.

The definition of omniscience is similar to that of omnipotence, although one obvious difference is that a condition analogous to (ii) is built into the definition:

$$\text{OS}s \longleftrightarrow (p) \left\{ \Diamond p \to \left[(p \longleftrightarrow s\text{K}p) \,\&\, (\overline{s\text{K}p} \longleftrightarrow s\text{K}\bar{p}) \right] \right\}$$

I.e., s is omniscient if and only if, for any logically possible proposition, p, p is true if and only if s knows that p and s does not know that p if and only if s knows that not-p. But the inclusion of

$$\overline{s\text{K}p} \longleftrightarrow s\text{K}\bar{p}$$

in the consequent of this definition is not so important as it might seem at first. I take it that this conjunct is redundant, following in fact from

$$p \longleftrightarrow s\text{K}p$$

So (ii) could have been added to the definition of omnipotence without increasing the informational content of that definition.

A more significant difference between the definitions is that omniscience entails knowledge not merely of all contingent propositions, but of all necessary ones as well. So Ross would not accept an analogue of (i) for the concept of knowledge, i.e.,

(i) $(p)\ (sKp \rightarrow \diamondsuit\ \overline{sKp})$

for all p, s knows that p entails that possibly s does not know p, will not generally be true. It will hold for contingent propositions, but not for necessary ones.

From what was said earlier, you might expect at this point to find some argument to the effect that

$(x)\ (OSx \longleftrightarrow OPx)$

i.e., a subject is omniscient if and only if it is omnipotent. But that expectation will be disappointed. Ross offers no such argument; he merely suggests that perhaps one may be found[21] without giving any hints about how to find it. Insofar as establishing such equivalences between the divine attributes is essential to the completion of his argument for God's existence, that argument (and the rational reconstruction of theology to which it is integral) is incomplete. And the other attributes are not analyzed, much less shown to be equivalent. So there is a highly programmatic character to Ross's work, and it leaves, as he acknowledges, many questions unanswered. Still, it is a beginning, the program is an important one, and the analyses offered do allow us to discuss, in a reasonably precise form, questions usually not even asked these days.

Does omnipotence entail omniscience, and conversely? Intuitively, the prospects of establishing such an equivalence do not seem good. How, for example, are we to get from the premise that contingent propositions are true if and only if God wills them to a conclusion which says, *inter alia*, that God knows all necessary truths? Perhaps deriving that conclusion is not impossible; such matters are best left to those more proficient in logic than I am. I would only suggest that the consequence is sufficiently nonobvious that we need to be shown. On the other hand, it does look as though it will be fairly easy to establish *some* interesting equivalences from these definitions. For example, that

$(p)\ [(\diamondsuit\ \overline{p}\ \&\ \diamondsuit\ p) \rightarrow (sKp \longleftrightarrow sWp)]$

i.e., if p is contingent, God knows p if and only if he wills p.

It should be emphasized, however, that Ross does not offer these

167

analyses solely for the purpose of setting up the establishment of logical equivalences between the divine attributes. That is a consummation devoutly to be wished, but he has other, more fundamental ends in view. His particular approach to the proof of God's existence requires him—like Hartshorne—to say, at some stage, that it is possible that God exists, i.e., that the proposition that God exists does not involve a contradiction. For if it did, the proposition that God does not exist would be self-explanatory. Insofar as the analyses of God's attributes show the logical possibility of something's having those attributes, they make a very important contribution to the argument for God's existence. Ross's analysis of God's omnipotence is designed to avoid various paradoxes of omnipotence, and he contends that it shows how something may be conceived without contradiction to be omnipotent. So far as I can see, he succeeds in this.

But Spinoza, I suppose, would want to urge that it is not enough to show that each of the divine attributes is separately capable of exemplification. That is a necessary, but not (so long as we use the term "God" according to Ross's definition) a sufficient condition of proving God's possibility. If the God of Ross's proof is to be shown to be possible, we must have some argument tending to show that it is logically possible for the traditional attributes to be combined in one being. This is a much more modest project than showing that they entail one another, but I think it can fairly be said that this is one other area in which Ross's program is incompletely carried out.

There are, as Spinoza would wish us to see, real problems here. For example, the traditional list of divine attributes numbers personality among them. Ross does not offer any analysis of personality and he might reasonably say that no one has a satisfactory analysis of personality. Certainly recent debates about the rights of persons to life, etc., show a depressing lack of consensus as to what a person is. But he may also feel that insofar as we ascribe knowledge and effective choice to God (as we do in ascribing omnipotence and omniscience to him), we ascribe all that is essential for personality.[22]

Would this be correct? Spinoza might counter that it would be a somewhat thin notion of personality that would take the possession of knowledge and effective choice to be sufficient for personality. Perhaps the capacity for feeling joy and sorrow and for having desires is also essential to being a person. If so, we would need some analysis of those notions, and some showing that the capacity for feeling joy or sorrow or having desires is compatible with such other divine attributes as perfection.[23]

But even without venturing into that thicket, we might wonder whether the knowledge and effective choice here ascribed to God are sufficiently like human knowledge and choice to make the ascription of personality to God reasonable, or whether they are so radically different as to make the ascription of personality to God quite unreasonable. Philosophers dealing with the notion of choice apropos of human beings have tended to relate that notion to deliberation, and to see knowledge as setting limits to the area within which deliberation and choice can operate.[24] I do not deliberate about, and cannot will to be the case, what I already know to be the case—say some general law of nature or some statement about a past event. This is not merely a contingent incapacity of mine, but a consequence of our concept of choice: necessarily, if I know that p, then I do not will that p, p is true independently of my will. But as we have seen above, Ross's definitions of omnipotence and omniscience have the consequence that, for any contingent proposition, p, "God knows that p" entails that "he does will that p."

So if Spinoza were to be miraculously returned to us today to participate in this discussion, I think he would feel justified in reaffirming what he wrote in the scholium to Proposition 17 of Part I of the *Ethics*:

> If intellect and will do pertain to God's eternal essence, we must understand by them something different from what men generally understand by these terms. For the intellect and will which would constitute God's essence would have to differ entirely from our intellect and will, and could have nothing in common with them except the name.

If man's intellect and will and God's are as radically different as I have been suggesting, this would undercut any attempt to ascribe personality to God on the strength of having ascribed intellect and will to him. The analysis of the way in which God has the properties of intellect and will, i.e., the analysis of his omnipotence and omniscience, is incompatible with the ascription of personality to him in any sense which would require having intellect and will as we do. An analysis of the sense of the term "personality" as it is used in the definition of God is very much to be desired.[25]

I might add that there seems to me to be some difficulty about the way in which Ross has expressed his requirement that an effective choice must be contingent, i.e., about axiom (i). Without questioning the contingency of God's actions at all, one might not wish to express it so broadly. Few Christians, I suppose, have emphasized the contingency of God's will more forcefully than Descartes. Still, he would have wanted to say that once God had made his choice, it was no longer possible for things to be otherwise, that the possibility of their having been otherwise obtained only up until the time of God's action. Once the choice is made, there is a certain finality about it which did not exist previously. You might then want to reformulate (i) so as to bring in these temporal notions. Perhaps

$$(p)(t) \left\{ sWpt \rightarrow [(t')((t' \lessgtr t) \rightarrow (\diamondsuit \overline{sWpt'})) \& (t'') \right.$$

$$\left. ((t'' > t) \rightarrow (\overline{\diamondsuit \overline{sWpt''}}))] \right\}$$

would do. This is meant to be read: For all p and for all t, if s wills p at t, then at any time up until t, it is possible that s not will p at that time, and at any time later than t, it is not possible that s not will p at that later time. It would be surprising if this turned out to be fully satisfactory, but there does seem to be an intuition here struggling to be expressed, and I leave it to those more competent than I to express it. But I should forestall one probable cause of difficulty. This formula is not to be so construed that one and the same proposition might be at one time possible and at another time impossible. The modal operators in the consequents govern different propositions.

Now a classically oriented theologian like Ross may well object to any attempt to introduce temporal operators in a way which would suggest that "s wills p at t" might have different truth values at different times (where "s" is understood as a singular term designating God). But if Ross did say that, it would raise further doubts about the propriety of ascribing personality to God; for it would be one more indication of a radical difference in meaning between properties ascribed to God and those ascribed to man. Certainly for personal subjects other than God, the sentence frame "s wills p at t" will be open to having different truth values for different values of t (s and p being held constant).[26]

A further problem about the consistency of the traditional list of God's attributes arises in connection with the doctrine of creation. As we have seen, on Ross's explanation of this doctrine, it entails the falsity of the Principle of Sufficient Reason. Not every contingent state of affairs in fact has an explanation. Specifically, some contingent proposition of the form "s wills p" (where "s" designates God) does not in fact have an explanation. The most that can be said is that no contingent state of affairs is intrinsically inexplicable.

The difficulty about this is that, as Ross has defined omnipotence, every contingent state of affairs *will* in fact have an explanation. For every contingent p, if p is true, then God wills that p. And God's willing that p is sufficient for p's being the case. So God's omnipotence implies the truth of the Principle of Sufficient Reason and that in turn (if Ross is right about the doctrine of the creation) implies the falsity of the doctrine of the creation. There would, then, be an incompatibility between God's omnipotence and his being the creator.

Indeed, I believe Ross is committed by his definition of omnipotence to a view sometimes ascribed to Leibniz, *viz.*, that each act of God's will gives rise to an infinite regress of explanatory acts of will.[27] Suppose it is contingent and true that there is light. Then by the definition of omnipotence, it is true that God wills that there be light. Ross insists that each act of God's will is contingent. So it is both contingent and true that God wills that there be light. So it will follow, again from the definition of omnipotence, that God wills that God wills that there be light. It is clear that the definition generates an infinite regress.

The moral I draw so far, then, is that when contemporary philosophers of religion put behind them the task of proving the existence of a self-explanatory being, and turn to the question of whether that being has the attributes traditional Christian theology ascribes to God, they may find it difficult to resist Spinozistic conclusions. The example of Ross suggests this: his analysis of omnipotence calls in question his account of creation and his analyses of both omnipotence and omniscience raise questions about the propriety of ascribing to God either knowledge or will in anything like their normal sense. So far it appears that God's omnipotence may be incompatible both with his being a creator and with his being personal. If this is correct, it would follow that the traditional list of attributes contains properties that are inconsistent with one another and that the God of Ross's definition is not a logically possible being.

This is a conclusion which we might reach by other routes. Ross, for example, includes eternity among God's attributes, and there are strong grounds for supposing that if eternity is identified with timelessness, it is incompatible both with God's omnipotence and his being personal. But perhaps this merely shows that theologians do best not to identify eternity with timelessness, that that identification represents an illicit incorporation of Platonic ideas into the Biblical tradition.[28]

More interesting—because not so easily dismissed—is the question of whether God's omnipotence is compatible with his acting purposively. These attributes are firmly rooted in the Biblical tradition.

Acting purposively, I suggest, involves an end desired, E, and an act, A (or a series of acts A, A', etc.) where doing A (A', etc.) is a cause of the coming about of E. For A to be a cause of E's coming about, its relation to E's occurrence must be logically contingent: by itself A must be neither a logically necessary nor a logically sufficient condition of E. Moreover, for A to be a cause of E's occurrence, A must be instrumental to the occurrence of E in the sense that it completes a complex set of conditions, which set, in conjunction with the laws of nature, is logically sufficient for E, but which would not be sufficient for E if either the laws of nature were different or some member of this set were missing.[29]

For example, suppose I want some boiling water for tea, I fill the kettle, place it on the stove, turn on the burner, and wait. The concurrent conditions and laws of nature being what they are—the electricity is turned on, electricity passing through a wire generates heat, etc.,—before too long I have my boiling water. Perhaps none of these actions or conditions is necessary without qualification. For example, suppose there had been a power failure, but some elaborate solar heating device was available. In those circumstances, putting the kettle on the stove, etc., would not complete a set of conditions sufficient for boiling the water, but running the water through the solar heating device would.

In this example, the actions we take involve bodily movements, and in thinking of human actions, we are apt to think of such cases. But this is not essential. For example, I may wish to know the answer to some question, say "How old is my father now?" To come to know this, I may think to myself, "Well, he was born in June 1905, and this is April 1977, so he will be 72 this June and is 71 now," nothing which is obviously a bodily movement here. What is essential is that although the answer to my question may follow from the truths of which I remind myself, still it is a contingent fact that I can bring myself to thinking of these things in this way. The laws of nature being what they are, and I being constituted as I am, I can only get the right answer to such questions by going through such mental calculations. Other people, of course, may have other recipes, and I might learn some other means of bringing about this end.

Now the problem is this: In these paradigms, my acting purposively seems to entail that I am not, in the sense in which Ross defines the term, an omnipotent being. In acting purposively, I do certain things as a means to an end which is both contingent in itself and contingent in relation to the means I employ. But it would make no sense to say that I do these things to achieve this end, if I were omnipotent. If I am omnipotent (as Ross defines the notion, at any rate) and I choose some contingent end (e.g., that this water should boil, that I should know the answer to some question), then my choosing that end is logically sufficient for its occurrence, and it is not necessary that any other condition be satisfied to achieve this result. And if that is the case, it cannot be said that my doing anything else is instrumental to achieving the result.

Now Ross does consider this problem, although not quite in the way in which I have presented it. He takes up the question of whether God can do immediately whatever he can do by secondary causality—a question which Occam had answered in the affirmative. Ross thinks the answer should be no. If we consider some particular event produced by a secondary cause, say, my writing this page, "it is absurd to say that God can produce numerically the same event . . . without the mediation of the secondary cause,"[30] for the numerical identity of the event logically involves the agent that produces it. So God can bring about that event only through my mediation.

Now surely this is right. Occam's principle must be false if "secondary causes" are logically necessary conditions of the events in question. On the other hand, if we think of secondary causes in the way reflection on purposive action suggests, as antecedent conditions contingently related to the event, then it seems that Occam's principle would be correct. Consider one of Spinoza's favorite examples of a miracle,[31] the crossing of the Red Sea by the Israelites in Exodus 14. God wished that the Israelites might cross the Red Sea on dry land. To that end he caused a strong east wind to blow all night and drive back the sea. Here God is pictured as causing one event in order to bring about another, where the first event is causally related to the other. But if God is omnipotent, he could have produced the second event immediately. Indeed, his willing that that event occur was logically sufficient for its occurrence. And the question is, "How can we understand the suggestion that the first event was instrumental to the second when it was neither logically nor causally necessary to the occurrence of the other?" A reconciliation of God's omnipotence with his acting purposively would be one of the things to be desired in an adequate analytic reconstruction of natural theology.

If we set aside literacy fictions about resurrected philosophers, what I have tried to do in this paper has been to look at recent work in the philosophy of religion from what I take to be a Spinozistic point of view. I have not been much concerned with questions of interpreting Spinoza. Presuming a certain interpretation, I have tried to put to that work the questions and objections I think Spinoza would have wished to put. This illustrates one way in which the study of philosophy's past can and should interact with the present practice of philosophy. The history of philosophy sets us problems which we neglect at our peril.

1. The best known example, perhaps, is Norman Malcolm's "Anselm's On-tological Arguments," *Philosophical Review*, 69 (1960), 41–62. Charles Harts-horne has argued independently along similar lines, see his *The Logic of Perfection*, (LaSalle, Illinois: Open Court), 1962. Alvin Plantinga's recent *The Nature of Necessity* (Oxford: Clarendon Press, 1974), is much more favorable to the argu-ment than his earlier *God and Other Minds* (Ithaca, N.Y.: Cornell University Press, 1967). In *Descartes Against the Skeptics* (Cambridge. Mass.: Harvard University Press, forthcoming in 1978), I argue that the Cartesian version of the argument is not open to the objections most often raised against it.

2. James F. Ross, *Philosophical Theology* (Indianapolis: Bobbs-Merrill, 1969).

3. *Ibid.*, p. 124.

4. *Ibid.*, p. 130.

5. *Ibid.*, pp. 131–32.

6. *Ibid.*, p. 88.

7. Hartshorne, *op. cit.*, p. 51.

8. The first step of his argument—If a perfect being exists, it exists necessarily—being equivalent to Leibniz's principle—If it is possible that God exists, then God exists.

9. Ross, *op. cit.*, pp. 96–97.

10. *Ibid.*, p. 122.

11. *Ibid.*, p. 128.

12. *Ibid.*, p. 99.

13. *Ibid.*, p. 97.

14. *Ibid.*, pp. 298–304.

15. The view taken in my *Spinoza's Metaphysics*, (Cambridge, Mass.: Harvard University Press, 1969, ch. III), is that Spinoza's commitment to the Principle of Sufficient Reason does not involve a commitment to the doctrine that the totality of singular facts has an explanation, but only to the doctrine that each singular fact has an explanation.

16. Ross, *op. cit.*, p. 132n.

17. *Ibid.*, p. 62.

18. *Ibid.*, p. 132n.

19. *Ibid.*, p. 211.

20. *Ibid.*

21. *Ibid.*, p. 214.

22. Cf. Nelson Pike, *God and Timelessness* (London: Routledge & Kegan Paul, 1970), pp. 123–24.

23. Cf. *Ethics*, Part I, Appendix.

24. Aristotle, for example: "Choice will be deliberate desire of things in our power. . . . Deliberation is concerned with things that happen in a certain way for the most part, but in which the event is obscure, and with things in which it is indeterminate." *Nicomachean Ethics* III, 3.

25. Cf. Spinoza, CM II, 8: "We are not ignorant of the term *personality*, which theologians commonly use to explain [how God's essence, intellect and will are to be distinguished]. But though we are familiar with the term, we do not know its signification, nor can we form any clear and distinct concept of it" (Gebhardt I, 264, my translation).

26. Pike (*God and Timelessness*, pp. 176–79) suggests an analysis of God's immutability according to which "God is immutable" does not entail "God can-

not change in any way whatsoever." On Pike's analysis, some of God's properties cannot change, while others can. For example, God is necessarily omniscient, but the specific content of his knowledge is subject to change as the objects of his knowledge change. Pike contends (rightly, I think) that this concept of immutability is closer to the Biblical tradition than the approach that would say that whatever is true of God must be true of him timelessly.

27. See, for example, my "The Root of Contingency," in H. Frankfurt (ed.) *Leibniz, a collection of critical essays* (Anchor, 1972), pp. 69–97.

28. This seems to be Pike's conclusion. *Cf. God and Timelessness*, pp. 189–90.

29. The account of causation assumed here is broadly Humean, of course, although I adopt certain refinements from modern writers, such as H.L.A. Hart and A.M. Honore, *Causation in the Law* (Oxford: Clarendon Press, 1959). Spinoza is sometimes held to have a very different concept of causation, but if the argument of *Spinoza's Metaphysics* is correct, that interpretation is mistaken.

30. Ross, *op. cit.*, p. 217.

31. The example is used in *KV* I, 3 (Gebhardt I, 36), in *CM* II, 8 (Gebhardt I, 265), and in *TTP* (Gebhardt III, 90).

Spinoza and La Peyrère*

RICHARD H. POPKIN
Washington University

From the earliest biographies of Spinoza to some of the popular literature about him today, he has been seen as a key figure in Western
thought, whose ideas developed after he was expelled from the Portuguese Synagogue of Amsterdam in 1656. According to this rendition,
it was only after Spinoza's excommunication from the Jewish community that he had the opportunity to learn Latin and to discover
modern philosophy, especially in terms of Descartes' expression of it.
Then, as the story goes, Spinoza, with the help of some of his new
friends in the left-wing Protestant movement of the Collegians, worked
out his analysis of Descartes' philosophy and pushed Cartesianism to its
logical conclusions, namely the pantheism of the *Ethics*.[1]

This version of the philosopher's journey, which I doubt very much,
has more than a tinge of antisemitism to it. Spinoza only became part
of Western thought *after* his excommunication. Before that he was
supposedly ensnared in the clutches of a rabidly intolerant Jewish community, which was unable and unwilling to consider any of the new
ideas being discussed in the non-Jewish world. This picture is reinforced
by the story of Uriel da Costa, as it appears in his autobiography (now
recognized by several scholars as a dubious source.)[2] The story in the
autobiography, which does not correspond to the facts in the case as
gleaned from the Inquisition records,[3] claims that Da Costa, a cleric
in Portugal of Jewish ancestry, became convinced of the truth of
Judaism through reading the Bible. He started practicing his Biblical
Judaism, and had to flee Portugal for Amsterdam to avoid being caught
by the Inquisition. When he arrived in Amsterdam around 1618, he
found the Jewish community carrying on practices which did not correspond to his Biblical Judaism. He wrote in opposition to various
Jewish leaders, and in 1623 wrote a work declaring the doctrine of the
mortality of the soul as the actual Jewish view. He was expelled from

*I should like to thank the National Endowment for the Humanities. Part of
the research for this paper was done under grant RO-22932-75-596. I should also
like to thank the Memorial Fund for Jewish Culture for its assistance.

the Amsterdam community for this. He wandered for several years in complete loneliness, and finally begged to be readmitted to the Amsterdam Synagogue. The story in the autobiography goes on to say that he was publicly scourged in the synagogue and all the members wailed over him. He was readmitted, but began his opposition anew. He was accused of urging two Iberians not to join the synagogue and was again expelled. Rhetorically in the autobiography, he declared that he did not want to be an "ape among apes." He did not want to be a Jew or a Christian, just a man. The autobiography espoused a kind of generalized Deism.[4] The Da Costa story, as it has come down to us, is that he committed suicide after his second excommunication, a victim of rabbinical intolerance.[5]

Da Costa's case has been taken as the prelude to Spinoza's.[6] Both are supposed to be examples of the closed and prejudiced minds of the rabbinical authorities, who were presumably living in a medieval ghetto and not the modern era. There is some hypocrisy in seeing only the intolerance of the Amsterdam Synagogue, while ignoring the much greater intolerances of the churches, Catholic and Protestant, of the time. For example, Galileo was condemned in this period. Nicholas Anthoine, a convert from Calvinism to Judaism was burned at the stake in Geneva in 1632.[7] Both the Spanish and Portuguese Inquisitions were having regular *auto-da-fés* all through this period.

To complete the legend of St. Spinoza, he was despised for his ideas but admired for his saintly character. In the French Enlightenment he became a hero for what Bayle said of him, that he was the first to have reduced atheism to a system. The German Enlightenment, and especially the Romantic metaphysicians after Kant saw him as the central modern figure before themselves.

I may have presented the common picture of Spinoza and his influences with a bit of bias. This is due to the fact that I think the hagiography of Spinoza is *prima facie* implausible, *and* also that we now have information which makes much more sense of Spinoza's development. First, I would like to deal with a few implausibilities, then with Spinoza's own contribution to a false or misleading picture, and finally with some new information, some gathered by myself and some of recent discovery by other scholars.

One feature of the Spinoza story that I think is not only implausible but downright false, is that he had to escape the clutches of the synagogue in order to learn Latin. Almost all of the leaders of the Amsterdam Jewish community had been raised as Catholics or Protestants in Spain, Portugal, Italy, France, Belgium, etc. Most were college graduates, having attended classes taught in Latin. Several of these leaders in Amsterdam edited or wrote Latin works (including Spinoza's teacher, Menasseh ben Israel). Hence, a knowledge of Latin was not rare in the Jewish community. Also, if one's native language is Portuguese, as Spinoza's was, it is not very hard to make out Latin.

Three vignettes of leaders of the Amsterdam community will show (a) that it was unusual for a Jewish community of the time, and (b) that it was amazingly cosmopolitan. I have shown elsewhere that the Portuguese and Spanish Jews who formed the Amsterdam community did not all arrive at once with a common background, but that they came over a period of thirty to forty years with different kinds of Christian backgrounds before they returned to Judaism in Amsterdam.[8] The chief rabbi who led the expulsion of Spinoza, Saul Levi Morteira, was a graduate of the University of Padua, and a student of the famous rabbi, Leon de Modena. Morteira became the court secretary of Queen Marie de Medici's doctor in Paris, and worked in the Louvre for six years with Dr. Elijah Montalto (who wrote Latin medical books that his secretary had to transcribe). Thus Morteira functioned in one of the leading palaces in Europe. When Montalto died, Morteira took the body for burial in Holland where there was a Jewish cemetery. Morteira stayed there and became the chief rabbi.

He was obviously quite cosmopolitan, with his background in Italy and France. An Inquisitional document found by the late I. S. Révah indicates a very tolerant side of Morteira. A non-Jewish Portuguese youth, aged 9, stowed away on a boat from Lisbon to Amsterdam. He lived there, without becoming Jewish, in the Jewish community, attending the Jewish schools. After about ten years, he got into Morteira's *Talmud* class and raised Christian objections to what he was being taught. Morteira, knowing the youth was not a Jew, let him stay on, and the youth finally decided to drop it all and go back to Lisbon.[9] This episode shows that Morteira could tolerate the most deviant views, namely Christian ones, being raised against him without going into a rage.

A second example of a cosmopolitan figure among Amsterdam Jews is Spinoza's teacher, Menasseh ben Israel. Menessah was born in Portugal and went to school in the French Protestant stronghold of La-Rochelle. At age eighteen he went to Amsterdam and became a printer and teacher (and a friend of Rembrandt van Rijn, who painted his portrait). Menasseh wrote in Latin, Spanish, Hebrew, and in one case, English. He printed books in a wide variety of languages. From his writings he became known as *the* Jewish philosopher of the time. He was consulted by learned men from all over Europe and traveled to Brussels to meet with Queen Christina of Sweden, and to London to meet with Oliver Cromwell. Menasseh was a Cabbalist and Messianist, and through him the Christian world learned of the latest developments in these Jewish theories. One can hardly categorize Menasseh as a bigoted, narrow-minded rabbi locked into the Middle Ages.[10]

A third example of an Amsterdam Jewish intellectual is Isaac Orobio de Castro. Spinoza had claimed that the whole Jewish community was up in arms about his views. Orobio de Castro is the only one we know of who wrote a reply, and he did that after Spinoza was dead. Orobio was raised and educated in Spain, studied medicine and metaphysics, and became a royal physician and medical professor. He wrote a work in Latin on fevers. The Inquisition arrested him for carrying on secret Jewish practices. When he was released, he escaped to Toulouse where he became a professor of medicine. From there he went to Amsterdam, where he joined the Jewish community and practiced medicine. Late in his life he became engaged in a disputation with Philip van Limborch over the truth of the Christian religion. John Locke was apparently present and wrote a long account of the affair.[11]

Orobio, who was probably the best philosopher among the Amsterdam Jews after Spinoza, also was not locked into a ghetto outlook, but used his knowledge of modern Spanish and other philosophies to fight against his several opponents.

If a quick look at some of the leading figures in the Amsterdam Jewish world of Spinoza's time suggests that Spinoza was not battling an entrenched, narrow-minded orthodoxy, then what was going on? Spinoza himself helped to provide ammunition for the traditional view. The two works of Spinoza published in his lifetime suggest that first, he had to work through Descartes to become Spinoza, and second, he had to reject totally the Jewish world. In 1666 Spinoza published *The Principles of Descartes's Philosophy*, which shows that when Cartesianism is made consistent it becomes Spinozism. Hence, it is easy to construct the view that Spinoza worked out his philosophy through studying Descartes. Spinoza's second and last publication during his lifetime, his *Tractatus-Theologico-Politicus* exhibits his total rejection of the Jewish world-view and his preference for the Gentile one—Old Testament prophets are rejected, Jewish ceremonies are now unnecessary, the religious data of Judaism is dubious. Only Jesus of the Biblical figures escapes as a teacher of a genuine Divine morality. Hence, Spinoza can be seen as rejecting everything Jewish in order to generate his rational ethical position.

In spite of how Spinoza's two publications may have aided his posthumous image, there have been serious attempts to reclaim Spinoza for the Jewish world and to claim that he is *the* major *Jewish* figure in modern thought. During the Romantic period, especially in Germany, for those liberal Jews who equated Judaism with a universalistic ethical view, Spinoza (and Uriel de Costa before him) became the founders or the sources of a modern Judaism, then emerging in the Reformed Jewish movement.

More recently, in fact quite recently, scholars like Harry Austryn Wolfson and Leon Roth[12] have sought to show Spinoza's relation to medieval Jewish thought. Wolfson, especially, in his magisterial two volumes on *The Philosophy of Spinoza*[13] has tried to show that the issues Spinoza was dealing with, especially in the propositions in the *Ethics*, the positions he was considering, and the stand he took, all made sense when considered in relation to the issues dealt with, and the solutions offered by, a wide range of medieval Jewish philosophers and theologians. (Spinoza certainly cited enough of these writers in the *TTP* to justify a claim that he had fully immersed himself in this material). In terms of connecting Spinoza with medieval Jewish thought, Wolfson portrayed him as the culmination of rationalistic tendencies that had been current three hundred years earlier.

Some of us have felt, Wolfson's work notwithstanding, that Spinoza's thought was probably related to more immediate issues in the Jewish world. No matter how loudly Spinoza screamed at Maimonides in the *TTP*, his immediate circumstances in the 1650's probably had more, or at least something, to do with the formation of his outlook and his position. Some have suggested that the Cabbalistic interest of some of the Jews in Amsterdam of the time may have affected him. This is still conjectural. A more direct influence has been found by the late I. S. Révah in his studies on Spinoza and Juan de Prado, and on the immediate circumstances of Spinoza's excommunication.[14] Révah found that Spinoza was expelled with two others, Prado and Daniel Ribera. Information exists about their expulsions but not Spinoza's. Prado, ten years older than Spinoza, was a Spaniard who had developed irreligious views in Spain. In Holland he had written a book on why the law of nature takes precedence over the law of Moses. This book has not been located, but two answers to it by Orobio de Castro exist, and from them one can get some idea of Prado's position.[15] Révah's data in his two studies show first of all that one can date Spinoza's change of opinion toward Judaism from the contribution records of the Amsterdam Synagogue. Spinoza, although a young man, gave really substantial donations. Suddenly, a few months before the excommunication, he dropped his giving to practically nothing.[16]

Second, from the charges and testimony against Prado and Ribera, one gathers that they were casting doubt on the Bible, both through points emerging from the embryonic Bible-criticism of the day, and through ridicule and satire.[17] Assuming, as seems reasonable, that Spinoza at the time held similar views to those of his fellow excommunicants, this would account for the charge in the *herem* (the excommunication decree) that he held atrocious views. Spinoza, Révah found, stayed in contact with Prado at least until 1658–59, and that the earliest knowledge of their fundamental views comes from that period. This will be discussed after considering what may be another major element in the development of Spinoza's view.

Spinoza, Prado, and Ribera were expelled in 1656. One year earlier, Isaac La Peyrère's bombshell, *Prae Adamitae*, was published in several editions in Holland and immediately became the most shocking event in the intellectual world. The author spent six months in Amsterdam while the book was being printed. And as a result of the book, plus some of his other writings, La Peyrère became the greatest heretic before Spinoza. I cannot prove that La Peyrère ever met Spinoza or talked with him, but there is ample evidence that La Peyrère greatly influenced Spinoza. Leo Strauss has suggested that La Peyrère was a major source of Spinoza's Bible-criticism.[18] I suggest that he was a major source of the development of Spinoza's religious skepticism and helped to force Spinoza to find a nontheological base for his theory of God.

Who was this mysterious Isaac La Peyrère? I have tried for over a decade to make him one of the central figures in modern thought, but have not yet succeeded in completely rescuing him from obscurity. La Peyrère, 1596?–1676, was born in Bordeaux and reared as a Calvinist.[19] A number of scholars think he must have been a Marrano, that is, a Jew forcibly converted to Christianity, and his views certainly indicate this.[20] He became a lawyer. In 1626 a Calvinist attempted to have him expelled for heresy.[21] (Nothing is known about the charges, but some of La Peyrère's statements would indicate that his pre-Adamite theory was involved). In 1640 La Peyrère became a secretary to the Prince of Condé and moved to Paris, where he became part of the *avant-garde* circle around Mersenne, Hobbes, Gassendi, Grotius, La Mothe Le Vayer, and others. In less than two years, La Peyrère completed his two most important books, *Prae-Adamitae* and *Du Rappel des Juifs*.[22] The second was printed in 1643, while the first was banned. La Peyrère's overall theory contains, among other heresies, the claims (1) that Moses was not the author of the Pentateuch; (2) that we do not now, in the seventeenth century, possess an accurate text of the Bible; (3) that there are many men (and women) born before Adam; (4) that the Bible is only the history of the Jews and not the history of all mankind; (5) that the Flood was merely a local event in Palestine and did not extend to the rest of the world; (6) that the world with people in it may have been going on for an infinite or indefinite period of time; (7) that the only human history that is important is that of the Jews; (8) that Jewish history began with Adam, and this history is divided into three major periods: the election of the Jews covering the epochs from Adam to Jesus, the rejection of the Jews, covering the period from Jesus to the middle of the seventeenth century, and last, the recall of the Jews which will occur very soon; (9) that the Messiah expected by the Jews is about to appear; and (10) that everyone will be saved, no matter what he believes or whether he or she is a pre-Adamite, an Adamite, or a post-Adamite.

The theory behind these claims is a mixture of a novel form of Bible criticism for its day, a hard-hitting evaluation of the Bible in terms of classical pagan histories and modern anthropology, as well as a bizarre form of French Messianism.

Scholars before La Peyrère had realized that there were conflicts within the Biblical texts and that the Scriptural accounts, such as the Creation story, were at loggerheads with ancient histories and new-found discoveries. They found ways of reconciling the passages and discounting the conflicts.[23] What La Peyrère claimed to be doing was taking the possibility of the existence of men before Adam seriously and erecting what he called "a theological system" on this supposition.[24] The central claim that leads to the others in his system is the separation of Jewish history from world history, with Jewish history being central to what has happened and what will be happening. In order to make the separation of Jewish history, La Peyère has to show that the Bible, in the form that we possess it, is inaccurate and cannot entirely be taken as Divine Revelation, *and* that the Bible does not encompass the early history of the non-Jews. The first point involves developing a criticism of the Biblical text. The second involves showing the plausibility of the evidence that there were people before Adam and that people exist now whose genealogical history is independent of Adam.

La Peyrère was the first to amass a sizable number of contradictions in the Biblical text *and* to advance serious reasons why there must have been several authors of the text. He showed that Moses could not have been the author of the passages in the Pentateuch about Moses' death and the events thereafter. He also showed that Moses, living so long after the events in *Genesis*, seems to have used antecedent sources. The result for La Peyrère is a truly revolutionary and skeptical view:

I need not trouble the Reader much further to prove a thing in it self sufficiently evident, that the first five books of the Bible were not written by *Moses* as is thought. Nor need any one wonder after this, when he reads many things confus'd and out of order, obscure, deficient, many things omitted and misplaced, when they shall consider with themselves that they are a heap of Copie confusedly taken.[25]

The evidence for the pre-Adamite theory starts from a text in St. Paul's *Romans*, where Paul spoke of sin beginning with Adam. La Peyrère pounced on this as indicating that there was a sinless world *before* Adam.[26] And La Peyrère, who knew neither Greek nor Hebrew, reconstructed the Pauline passage so that it definitely made his point. Then, turning to *Genesis*, La Peyrère tried to show that the text clearly showed that there was another source of people than Adam and Eve. For years he had been struck by the fact that after Cain killed Abel, and there were only three people on earth mentioned by the Bible—Adam, Eve and Cain—God put a mark on Cain's head so nobody would injure him for his crime. But why should God bother, if Adam and Eve knew what had happened, and they were the only other people around? Furthermore, Cain went off to a place of human habitation *and* he got married. To whom? La Peyrère insisted that Cain's having a wife proved that non-Adamic people existed according to the Biblical account.[27]

Next, switching to ancient history, La Peyrère argued that the Babylonian literature, especially its calendar (which he learned about from his friend, Claude Sarmaise), the Greek literature, and the Egyptian all showed that there were people living earlier and much earlier than 4004 B.C.,[28] Archbishop Ussher's date for the beginning of the world (about 5 per cent more time than the Hebrew calendar).

Lastly, on this subject, La Peyrère introduced the evidence that was to be most convincing to his contemporaries, that resulting from the voyages of Exploration. Could the Chinese, the Mexicans, the Peruvians, the Eskimos be accounted for in terms of the Adamic world? They all would have had to be descendants of the seven survivors of Noah's Flood, and then be descendants of people who managed to get from Mount Ararat to China, to the New World, to the far north, to the Pacific Isles. La Peyrère suggested that what is known of these civilizations, such as the great antiquity of the Chinese and the Mexicans, clearly indicates some kind of polygenetic development of mankind, rather than a monogenetic one.[29] La Peyrère wrote two books on the Eskimos, and was the leading European authority on them.[30] What he had learned about them definitely indicated a separate origin.

184

If there were diverse origins of people, as well as peoples like the Chinese, the Mexicans, the Babylonians, the Greeks, the Egyptians, whose history antedated Biblical history, then there must have been people before Adam—pre-Adamites. (La Peyrère's polygenetic theory, through no fault of his own, soon became the basis of a virulent theory of racism directed against the American Indian and the Negro slaves.)[31]

If the evidence supported the pre-Adamite hypothesis, then La Peyrère could advance his theory of Jewish history without having to integrate it with world history. Jewish history began with Adam. Before him there were lots of people living in a state of nature of the character that Hobbes was to describe, that is, living a life that was nasty, brutish, and short. Since the pre-Adamite world was getting nowhere, God decided to create Adam and begin Jewish history, a divine drama with a point.[32] Jewish history is *the* Messianic history, which other peoples participated in by "mystical imputation."[33] Its course has been the election of the Jews as the actors of Divine history (Adam to Jesus); the rejection of the Jews and the grafting of the Gentiles onto their stock as replacements in the Divine drama (Jesus to 1650?); and finally, the Recall of the Jews when they, as converts to Christianity, become the actors in the final drama when *their* Messiah arrives. The Jewish Messiah will, according to La Peyrère, rule the world with *"un roi universel,"* the King of France, and the Jewish Christians will be the central figures of the Messianic establishment, to be run from a rebuilt Jerusalem, and leading to everybody's salvation.

La Peyrère's Messianic views appear chiefly in his *Du Rappel des Juifs* (1643) and are summarized at the end of *Prae Adamitae*.[34] These did not seem to cause any scandal or concern. The Bible criticism and polygeneticism of *Prae-Adamitae* apparently made it impossible to publish it when written. La Peyrère showed the manuscript to many people. Hugo Grotius wrote a refutation in 1643, twelve years before the book was published. (Grotius claimed the American Indians were Norwegians descended from Lief Erikson's expedition and, hence, were part of the same Biblical world as the inhabitants of Norway.)[35] There is evidence the manuscript grew as La Peyrère consulted scholars in France, Holland, and Scandinavia.[36] What finally brought it to the light of day was La Peyrère's encounter with Queen Christina of Sweden after she had abdicated her throne. La Peyrère was living next door to her in Brussels in 1654–55. When he showed her his manuscript on the pre-Adamites, she urged him to go immediately to Holland to have it published. Some accounts say that she paid for its publication.[37] After the book appeared, the author gave a less plausible account of how it got printed. He said this happened through no fault of his own.

When he went to Amsterdam, he said, he had to carry his manuscript with him because he had no place to leave it. La Peyrère reports that when he got to Amsterdam "il tombay dans une foule d'Imprimeurs" who wanted to print his work. The manuscript was large, and he could not carry it everywhere. La Peyrère said he was afraid of losing it. So, as he says, "ie me voyais obligé par cette raison, à me servir de la commodité des Imprimeurs d'Amsterdam, & de la liberté que j'avois de publier mon livre."[38]

La Peyrère lived for several months in Amsterdam at this time. We do not know much about his life there, but he was in contact with some diplomats (probably as part of his service to the Prince of Condé), and may have been in contact with some of the local Messianists and Millenarians. Menasseh ben Israel favorably cites *Du Rappel des Juifs* in a work written in early 1655, as evidence that some learned men know the Messiah is coming.[39] Later in 1655, a millenarian friend of Menasseh's, Paul Felgenhauer, wanted Menasseh's help in arranging a debate with the author of *Prae-Adamitae*. They both had read the work before publication, and each prepared a refutation later on.[40]

In the second half of 1655, five printings of *Prae-Adamitae* were made, three by Elzivier, one in Basel, and one of as yet unknown origin. La Peyrère left Holland to attend to the Prince of Condé's business in Spain (where people thought "je fusse quelque animal fantastique" because of his Hugenot and pre-Adamite views),[41] and elsewhere. Somehow an English edition of his book was arranged and was published in 1656 with the title *Men before Adam*. La Peyrère returned to Belgium to meet a storm of refutations and accusations. His book was banned in Holland in November 1655.[42] Pastors and priests were grinding out answers. At Christmastime in 1655, the Bishop of Namur condemned *Prae-Adamitae* and had La Peyrère censured in all of the churches in his diocese "comme Calviniste & comme Juif."[43] And in February 1656, he was arrested by order of the Archbishop of Malines as *"unheritique detestable."*[44] Thus La Peyrère's book was a *cause célèbre* in the intellectual world of Holland and Belgium in 1655–56.

Before relating La Peyrère to the young Spinoza, I will briefly describe the rest of La Peyrère's career, starting with how he got out of jail. His employer, the Prince of Condé, was unable to have him released. It was suggested that if La Peyrère became a Catholic and personally apologized to the Pope, he would be released.[45] He agreed to this and went to Rome, where he was well received[46] and presented Pope Alexander VII with a most hypocritical apology. La Peyrère claimed that his theological errors were due to his Calvinist upbringing. As Calvinists accepted no authority save reason, inner spirit, or the reading of Scripture, La Peyrère asserted that he, as a Calvinist, had to accept the pre-Adamite theory because it accorded better than any other interpretation with right reason and the natural sense of Scripture. La Peyrère claimed that he was not trying to deny Scripture or the Christian faith. Instead he contended that the latter could be more solidly and firmly demonstrated by his hypothesis. In addition, the pre-Adamite hypothesis appeared to fit better with the histories of pagan nations, with the information about the newly discovered people, and with the theory that the world is eternal. La Peyrère said he had only put forth his theory tentatively as a hypothesis. He asked people to tell him if there was anything that was contrary to Scripture, or to any article of the Christian faith. La Peyrère said that when such a scandal broke out about his book, he looked around for somebody whose judgment he could trust to evaluate his work. The proper person was obviously the Pope. "Sa volonté sera ma raison & ma loy."[47] La Peyrère abjured the pre-Adamite theory, although he said that it was not contrary to reason or Scripture. What he now saw as the main problem with his theory was that it seemed to be contrary to the whole Christian and Jewish tradition. La Peyrère then went on in his apology to convince the Pope of his Messianic theory from *Du Rappel des Juifs*. He maintained that his main aim was to convert the Jews, and now that he knew that the Synagogue had rejected his pre-Adamite theory and his Biblical criticism, he felt he had to give them up. However, he intended to go with his Messianic activities. And to soften the Pope's heart, La Peyrère now announced that the Pope, not the King of France, would rule the world with the Messiah. Pope Alexander VII would accomplish what Alexander the Great had started.[48]

After La Peyrère submitted his abjuration, giving up most of his heresies, he was offered a benefice by the Pope.[49] He prudently declined the offer and returned to Paris to be the librarian for the Prince of Condé. He also became a lay member of the Oratorians and lived in their establishment near Paris the rest of his life. He spent a good deal of his time gathering further evidence for the pre-Adamite theory and in reworking *Du Rappel des Juifs*. La Peyrère discovered that it was reported that Adam died of gout and that gout is a hereditary disease. He found a mention in Jewish literature that Adam had a teacher. He tried to convince the great Bible-critic, Richard Simon, of these points, and Simon had to indicate to his senior Bible-critic that there was nothing to these claims. Simon said that all that Le Peyrère did in his religious retreat was to read the text of Scripture to fortify his views, especially concerning the coming of a new Messiah for the Jews.[50]

In the last years of his life, La Peyrère made two efforts to get his ideas published. One was in terms of the footnotes he was writing to Michel de Marolles' French translation of the Bible. Near the beginning of *Genesis*, La Peyrère placed notes indicating passages which seemed to imply that there were people before Adam. He contended that this view was not contrary to the Holy Scripture, but had been judged false by the Church, and one should submit to its decrees. This Bible-project was suppressed by the time it reached *Leviticus* 23:30.[51]

If La Peyrère could not express his ideas in carefully framed footnotes to the Bible, he would try another tack, one of redoing his book on *Du Rappel des Juifs*. He sent it to Richrd Simon in 1670.[52] Simon indicated that there would be difficulties in getting it published because of the two-Messiah theory, one for the Gentiles and one for the Jews. This theory, Simon declared, "vont à ruiner entierement la Religion Chretienne, laquelle est fondée sur la verité d'un seul Messie."[53] Simon was right in that the censor refused to approve it. A final version was written in 1673, and even though La Peyrère dropped his pre-Adamite theory in the hope of being able to publish his Messianic views, he apparently still could not get permission to publish. The manuscript at the Condé archives at Chantilly was his last attempt to get his message to the world.[54] He died in 1676. One of his friends told Pierre Bayle, "La Peirere étoit le meilleur homme du monde, le plus doux & qui tranquillement croyoit fort peu de chose."[55] Even on his deathbed he refused to retract his pre-Adamite and Messianic theories.[56] One of his friends wrote as La Peyrère's epitaph:

> Here lies La Peyrère, that good Israelite
> Hugenot, Catholic, finally Preadamite
> Four religions pleased him at the same time
> And his indifference was so uncommon
> That after eighty years when he had to make a choice
> The good man left and did not choose any one of them.[57]

If we now return to La Peyrère's climactic year 1655–56 played out in Holland and Belgium, La Peyrère and his heresies must have been known to a large number of people in the Lowlands. And, as his ideas became a shocking sensation and he became a martyr to his ideas (for a while), the intellectual community could not have avoided knowing about his case and what horrendous views he stood for. We know as pointed out earlier, that Spinoza's teacher, Menasseh ben Israel had a copy of La Peyrère's work before it was published and that he wrote a refutation by 1656.[58]

A bright young intellectual concerned with Biblical questions, Baruch de Spinoza must have heard of the sensational claims made by

La Peyrère. I wish I could prove that they met in 1655 and that this is when Spinoza's heterodoxy began. Unfortunately no document attesting to this has been found.

Two undatable items show that at some time Spinoza got some of his ideas from La Peyrère. The *Prae-Adamitae* was in Spinoza's library, but there is no way of finding out when he obtained the book.[59] Second, Spinoza used material from *Prae-Adamitae* in the *TTP*. The late Leo Strauss listed the borrowings, but there were actually even more items.[60] The *TTP* was published in 1670, but contains material written in 1656 to answer the rabbis who had excommunicated him, plus later items. The parts borrowed from La Peyrère seem logically to belong to the 1656 material, where Spinoza was using Jewish materials to answer the charges of Amsterdam Jewry. But one can only speculate about this because Spinoza's friends destroyed the *Urtractatus* when he died in 1677.[61]

What connects Spinoza more directly with La Peyrère in the crucial period when he became a heretic is the use of themes from La Peyrère by his fellow excommunicant, Juan de Prado. As Révah discovered, Prado was charged *at the same time* as Spinoza's excommunication with holding that the world was eternal and that human history is older than Jewish history. Prado's evidence for the latter claim was the same as La Peyrère's namely that Chinese history is 10,000 years old, a figure like that introduced into discussions about China by La Peyrère.[62] A little later, when Orobio de Castro answered Prado, he challenged the madness of those [Prado, etc.], who affirm that although it is true that God created the universe, this creation took place thousands and thousands of years ago, and not at the period that we believe on the basis of the Bible. This is certainly a La Peyrèrean thesis that is being attacked.[63]

Prado, the eldest of the three excommmunicants, seems to have been their leader in 1656. Introducing themes from La Peyrère, he stirred up some embryonic Bible-criticism. Spinoza was to go on to develop a full-fledged Bible-criticism based on a thorough analysis of the kinds of knowledge-claims made for the Bible and in the Bible. The impact of La Peyrère's attack on the Bible seems to have generated a small rebellion in the Synagogue. Prado and Ribeira were accused of Bible-criticism and of making fun of the Bible, and Spinoza (whose case we do not possess) of holding atrocious views and practices.[64]

The denial of the Mosaic authorship was certainly a key issue in developing a skepticism about revealed religion. At the end of the seventeenth century, the Catholic theologian Louis-Ellies du Pin, who composed encyclopedias about religions, declared that, "De tous les Paradoxes que l'on a avancez en nôtre siècle, il n'y en a point à mon avis de plus temeraire, ni de plus dangereux, que l'opinion de ceux, qui ont osé nier que Moise fût Auteur des Pentateuch."[65] Ellies Du Pin lists Hobbes, La Peyrère, Spinoza, and Richard Simon as holding this view.[66] As he makes clear, the whole relation of the supposedly revealed document, the Bible, to the truth becomes problematic, and one can doubt the veracity of all of Scripture. Moses provided the critical link of man to God, since supposedly God told him what is in the first five books. If the author or authors are not Moses, then the Bible becomes questionable.

The rabid Bible-critic, Tom Paine, said in the *Age of Reason* Part II, "Take away from Genesis the belief that Moses was the author, on which only the strange belief that it is the word of God has stood, and there remains nothing of Genesis but an anonymous book of stories, fables and traditionary or inverted absurdities or downright lies."[67]

If the question of the Mosaic authorship is so vital in developing a skepticism about revealed religion, it is worth noting that of modern authors, Hobbes is given the credit of first saying this in the *Leviathan* in 1651. Without diminishing Hobbes's importance, it should be pointed out (a) that La Peyrère's manuscript was finished in 1641, and Hobbes probably had access to it; and (b) that Hobbes holds a very weak form of the denial of the Mosaic authorship. "But, though Moses did not compile those books entirely, and in the form we have them; yet he wrote all that which he is there said to have written."[68] La Peyrère's stronger and wholesale denial of the Mosaic authorship was to flower in Spinoza's Bible-criticism and to become part of the basis for Spinoza's full-blown religious skepticism.

If La Peyrère helped trigger the Spinoza-Prado-Ribera situation, the three heretics only took materials from one side of La Peyrère's book, the negative and skeptical side of his Bible-criticism, and as far as we know, they ignored his Messianism. They may have mixed La Peyrère's criticial views with Uriel da Costa's deism, and developed a full-fledged naturalism about the Bible. The combination of La Peyrère's Biblical criticism and Spinoza's naturalistic metaphysics eliminated the supernatural dimension and transformed religious history into an effect of human fear and superstition.

La Peyrère had called what he was writing a "theological hypothesis," and he really seems to have believed it. We learn from a Spanish Inquisition report in 1658–59 that a spy, Fr. Tomas Solano y Robles, went to a theological discussion club in Amsterdam with people of many persuasions. Spinoza and Prado were there, and they held the view that God exists but only philosophically.[69] Spinoza's career was the working out of this claim, which left no room for supernatural religion, but was built on a critique of it. La Peyrère supplied some of the underpinning of Spinoza's position. However, his theology was totally rejected. La Peyrère's Messianic view led him to secularize all human history except Jewish history. Spinoza's philosophical God led him to secularize all human history, *especially* Jewish history. Spinoza provided a metaphysics for this new secular and natural world. "God exists, but only philosophically" became the theory that Spinoza unfolded in the *Ethics*.

If Spinoza ended up a partial disciple of La Peyrère, and much more of an original thinker, it is interesting to note that some of his contemporaries saw La Peyrère lurking in the background. Jacob Thomasius in 1670 said that Spinoza might have been influenced by La Peyrère.[70] Orobio de Castro, who wrote an answer to Spinoza, said in his disputation with Philip van Limborch that three kinds of enemies of the Bible are "Praeadamitae, Athei, Theologi politici."[71] The last is, of course, Spinoza, and the first, La Peyrère (and maybe Prado is the atheist).

To sum up, if Spinoza's excommunication was part of a small rebellion of Prado, Ribera, and Spinoza, I submit that part of what shaped their heretical views was the dramatic entry into the Amsterdam scene of La Peyrère and his heretical views. La Peyrère was offering a skepticism about the present Bible to buttress his Messianic theological hypotheses. The young rebels in the Synagogue just took over his critical and skeptical views and ignored his positive ones. The full rejection of La Peyrère's Messianism in the formula "God exists but only in philosophy," led Spinoza to develop the first full-fledged naturalistic metaphysics of modern times.

NOTES

1. This kind of story appears in, for instance, Frederick Copleston, A *History of Philosophy*, Vol. IV (London, 1960), "Descartes to Leibniz," p. 205; Johann Eduard Erdmann, *A History of Philosophy*, Vol. II, (London, 1892), p. 53 (he has Spinoza studying Latin and Descartes, and that leading to the excommunication); Bertrand Russell, *A History of Western Philosophy*, 2nd ed. (London, 1961), p. 552. Madeleine Francès did much to cast doubt on the usual account in her *Spinoza dans le pays néerlandais de la seconde mortié du XVIIᵉ siècle* (Paris 1937).

2. Mr. Joseph Kaplan of Jerusalem, Prof. H.P. Salomon of the State University of New York at Albany, and I have all voiced doubts, because (a) the manuscript of the biography is not in Da Costa's hand, (b) it skips large parts of his life, although the manuscript is continuous, and (c) it is at variance with facts Révah found about Da Costa's early life. See note 3.

3. I.S. Révah, "La Religion de Uriel da Costa," *Revue de'Histoire des religions*, Tome 161 (1962), pp. 45–76.

4. Uriel da Costa, "Exemplar Humanae Vitae," in Carl Gebhardt, *Die Scriften des Uriel da Costa* (Amsterdam, 1922), pp. 105–23.

5. Gebhardt, *op. cit.*, "Einleitung," pp. xxvii–xxxiii.

6. There is a nineteenth-century painting of the young Spinoza sitting on Da Costa's knee. This painting by S. Hirzberg and Romantic literature about Da Costa are described in B.B.'s appendix to my article, "Costa, Uriel da," in the *Encyclopedia Judaica*, Vol. V, p. 988.

7. See Elisabeth Labrousse, "Vie et Mort de Nicolas Antoine" *Études Théologiques et religiéuses*, Annéc 52 (1977), pp. 421–33.

8. R.H. Popkin, "The Historical Significance of Sephardic Judaism in 17th Century Amsterdam," *The American Sephardi*, Vol. V (1971), pp. 18–27.

9. I.S. Révah, *Spinoza and Juan de Prado* (Paris and The Hague, 1959), pp. 10–11.

10. See, for instance, Cecil Roth, *A Life of Menasseh ben Israel* (Philadelphia, 1945); and R.H. Popkin, "Christian Millenairianism and Jewish Messianism in the 17th Century," William Andrews Clark Library Series (forthcoming).

11. Joseph Kaplan of Jerusalem is completing a dissertation on Orobio with much new material. Locke's account of the affair is the review of Philip van Limbroch's *De Veritate Religious Christianae, amica collatio cum erudito Judaeo* (Gouda, 1687) in *Bibliothèque universelle et historique* for 1687.

12. Leon Roth, *Spinoza, Descartes and Maimonides* (Oxford, 1924).

13. Harry Austryn Wolfson, *The Philosophy of Spinoza: Unfolding the Latent Processes of His Reasoning* (Cambridge, Mass., 1934).

14. Révah, *Spinoza et Juan de Prado*, and "Aux Origines de la rupture spinozienne; Nouveaux documents sur l'incroyance dans la communauté Judeo-Portuguese d'Amsterdam à l'époque de l'excommunication de Spinoza," *Revue des Études juifs* Tome III (CXXIII) (1964), pp. 359–431.

15. Révah, *Spinoza et Juan de Prado*, pp. 84–153.

16. Révah, "Aux Origines de la rupture spinozienne", pp. 367–68, 385–87.

17. *Ibid.*, pp. 370–73, 391–408.

18. Leo Strauss, *Spinoza's Critique of the Bible* (New York, 1965), pp. 264, 327.

19. The most detailed picture of La Peyrère's life appears in Jean-Paul Oddos, *Recherches sur la vie et l'oeuvre d'Isaac La Peyrère* (1596?–1676), Thèse de 3eme Cycle, (Grenoble, 1974). For a shorter account, *see* R.H. Popkin, "The Marrano Theology of Isaac La Peyrère," *Studi Internazionale di Filosofia* V (1973), pp. 97–126. Oddos believes that La Peyrère was a true Calvinist, and that this led to his philosemitic ideas. I find this very doubtful.

20. See my "Marrano Theology of La Peyrère," plus Hans Joachim Schoeps, *Philosemitus in Barok* (Tübingen, 1952), pp. 14–18, and *Barocke Juden Christen* (Bern and Munich, 1965), p. 24; Leo Strauss, *op. cit.*, chap. 1; Léon Poliakov, *Le Mythe aryen* (Paris, 1971), pp. 127–29; and Miriam Yardeni, "La Religion de La Peyrère et 'Le Rappel des Juifs'," *Revue d'Histoire et de la Philosophie religieuse* LI (1971), pp. 245–59. For other interpretations considering La Peyrère as a *libertin* and a desist, see note 7 of my "Marrano Theology."

21. He was charged with atheism and impiety. No further details appear in the documents. Sixty pastors supported La Peyrère and the charges were dropped. *Cf.* Popkin, "Marrano Theology," note 8.

22. A letter of Gabriel Naudé to Cardinal Barberini in 1641 indicated that *Prae-Adamitae* had already been completed, and because Cardinal Richelieu had

banned it, people were trying to obtain copies of the manuscript. Bibl. Vat. Barberini, Lat 6471, fol. 22v.

23. See, for instance, Menasseh ben Israel's *Conciliador*, 4 parts, ([Frankfurt] Amsterdam, 1632–51).

24. In my paper, "The Preadamite Theory in The Renaissance," in E.P. Mahoney, ed., *Philosophy and Humanism, Renaissance Eeesays in Honor of Paul Oskar Kristeller*, pp. 50–69, I have discussed views antecedent to La Peyrère suggesting there were people before Adam. See also my paper, "The Development of Religious Scepticism and the Influence of Isaac La Peyrère's Pre-Adamism and Bible Criticism", in R.R. Bolgar, ed., *Classical Influences on European Culture*, A.D. 1500–1700, (Cambridge, England, 1976), pp. 271–80.

25. Isaac La Peyrère, *Men before Adam* (London 1656), p. 208; Lib. 4, cap. 1, in *Praeadamitae*, ([Amsterdam], 1655), p. 189.

26. La Peyrère, *Men before Adam* and *Praeadamitae*, Lib. 1, cap. i-ii.

27. La Peyrère, *Men before Adam* and *Praeadamitae*, Lib. III, cap. IV.

28. La Peyrère, *Men before Adam*, and *Praeadamitae*, Book III, caps. 6–11; and Popkin, "The Development of Religion Scepticism," pp. 276–80.

29. La Peyrère, *Men before Adam*, "Discourse," p. 22, and *Praeadamitae*, "Exercitatio," p. 29.

30. La Peyrère, *Relation du Groenland* (Paris, 1647), and *Relation d'Islands*, (Paris, 1633).

31. *Cf.* R.H. Popkin, "The Philosophical Basis for Modern Racism," in Craig Walton and John P. Anton, *Philosophy and Civilizing Arts, Essays Presented to Herbert W. Schneider on his 80th Birthday* (Athens, Ohio, 1974), pp. 126–64, and "Pre-Adamism in 19th Century American Thought: 'Speculative Biology and Racism'," *Philosophia* (forthcoming). From the late seventeenth century onward, supporters of racism and slavery claimed Africans and American Indians were pre-Adamites, and were inferior to the Adamites (Caucasians). La Peyrère himself was not a racist. He stated that the Jews "were made up of the same flesh and blood as Gentiles, and were temper'd with the same clay of which other men fram'd." *Men before Adam*, p. 59.

32. La Peyrère, *Men before Adam* and *Praeadamitae*, Lib. III, cap. i–iii.

33. La Peyrère, *Men before Adam* and *Praeadamitae*, Lib. V, cap. ii–iii.

34. La Peyrère, *Du Rappel des Juifs* (Paris, 1643), and *Men before Adam* and *Praeadamitae*, Lib V, cap. ix.

35. Hugo Grotious, *Dissertatio altera de origine Gentium Americanarum adversus obstractatorem* (n.p. 1643).

36. *Cf.* Popkin, "Marrano Theology of La Peyrère," pp. 104–105 and notes 49–53.

37. *Ibid.*, p. 105. Sven Stolpe, *Christina of Sweden* (New York, 1966), p. 130; and Rene Pintard, *Le Libertinage érudit* (Paris, 1943), pp. 399, 420.

38. La Peyrère, *Lettre de la Pèyrere à Philotime* (Paris, 1658), p. 118.

39. Menasseh ben Israel's letter in Paul Felgenhauer's *Bonum Nunciam Israeli*, (Amsterdam, 1655), pp. 89–90.

40. *See* R. H. Popkin, "Menasseh ben Israel and Isaac La Peyrère," *Studia Rosenthaliana* Vol. VIII, p. 61. Felgenhauer's answer to La Peyrère was entitled *Anti-Prae-Adamita* (Amsterdam, 1659). Menasseh's was called *Refutatio Libri qui titulus Praeadamitae*, and was apparently never published.

41. La Peyrère's letter to the Prince of Condé, 8 Oct. 1655, *Condé Archives*, Chantilly, P, XV, fols. 347–48.

42. The President and the Council of Holland stated on Nov. 26, 1655, that the book was banned because "it was found to be scandalous, Godless and against the interests of the State." The British Library has a copy of this declaration.

43. La Peyrère, *Lettre à Philotime*, pp. 123–24.

44. Popkin, "Marrano Theology of La Peyrère," note 74, p. 122.

45. *Ibid.*, p. 107 and note 74, p. 122.

46. The Pope is supposed to have said, "Embrassons cet homme qui est avant Adam," cited in Richard Simon's letter to Z.S. on "Quelques particularitez touchant l'Auteur & l'Ouvrage des Preadamites," in *Lettres choisies*, Vol. II (Amsterdam, 1730), p. 27.

47. *Cf.* La Peyrère, *Lettre à Philotime*, and *Apologie de La Peyrère* (Paris, 1663). The quote is from the *Lettre*, p. 139.

48. La Peyrère, *Lettre à Philotime*, pp. 157–62.

49. Richard Simon, letter to M.Z.S., *Lettres Choisies*, Vol. II, pp. 24–25.

50. See Richard Simon's six letters to La Peyrère, 1670–71, in *Lettres choisies*, Vol. II, pp. 1–23, and Vol. IV, pp. 36–45.

51. La Peyrère said in one of his first footnotes, "Toutefois cette opinion [pre-Adamism] est rejettee, quoy que ceux qui la voulaient establir n'entreprenoient point de la faire contra l'authorité des Saintes Escritures, à laquelle ils rendoient tout le respect qui luy est deub. Mais l'Eglise en ayant autrement jugée, on s'est soûmis à ses Decrets & aux sont de tous les Saints Peres." Michel de Marolles, *La Livre de Genese* (n.d. n.p.), p. 2. Both the Bibliothèque Nationale and the British Library have copies of this rare work.

52. According to Simon's letters, he received La Peyrère's manuscript between May 20, 1670, and May 27, 1670. *Cf.* Simon, *Lettres choisies*, Vol. II, p. 14.

53. *Ibid., loc. cit.*

54. The manuscript is at Chantilly, Ms. 191 (698).

55. Letter of Jean Francois Morin du Sandat Pierre Bayle, cited in Bayle's *Dictionnaire*, art. "Peyrere, Isaac La," Pemark G.

56. When pressed to retract on his deathbed, he said, quoting from the letter to St. Jude, "Hi quaecunque ignorant blasphement" (cited in Richard Simon's letter to Z.S., *Lettres choises*, Vol. II, p. 30).

57. Cited in Gilles Ménage, *Menagiana* (Paris and Amsterdam, 1715), Vol. III, p. 69.

58. *Cf.* Popkin, "Menessah ben Israel and La Peyrère."

59. Jacob Freudental, *Die Lebensgeschichte Spinoza's* (Leipzig, 1899). Item 54 is "Praeadamitae 1655."

60. Leo Strauss, *Spinoza's Critique of the Bible*, pp. 264, 327.

61. What I call the *Urtractatus* is the work listed in Lucas's life of Spinoza as "apologie de Benoît de Spinoza où il justifie sa sorte de la Synagogue." The work was in Spanish, but was never published. *Cf.* Freudenthal, *op. cit.*, p. 25.

62. Révah, "Aux Origines de la rupture spinozienne," pp. 378, 393.

63. Révah, *Spinoza et Juan de Prado*, p. 43.

64. Révah, "Aux Origines de la rupture spinozienne."

65. Louis Ellies du Pin, *Nouvelle Bibliotheque des Auteurs Ecclesiastiques*, Seconde Edition (Paris, 1690), Tome I, p. 4.

66. *Ibid.*, p. 30.

67. Thomas Paine, *The Age of Reason, Part the Second, being an Investigation of True and Fabulous Theology* (London, 1795), p. 14.

68. Thomas Hobbes, *Leviathan*, Part III, chap. xxxiii.

69. Cf. Révah, *Spinoza et Juan de Prado*, pp. 31–32, 64 (where the Spanish text is given.)

70. Jacob Thomasius, *Dissertationes LXIII Varii Argumenti* (Halle, 1693), p. 574. I should like to thank Professor Asa Kasher of Tel Aviv for bringing this reference to my attention.

71. Limborch, *De Veritate Religionis Christianae*, p. 148. I should like to thank Mr. Joseph Kaplan of Jerusalem for bringing this text to my attention. I should also like to thank him for the valuable discussions we have had on the subject of this paper and related topics.

The Geometrical Method, Personal Caution, and the Idea of Tolerance

EFRAIM SHMUELI
Cleveland State University

Although some recent schools of philosophy have used mathematical symbols and models, the method of geometery seems to the modern mind utterly unfitted for the presentation of philosophical theory. Many students of Spinoza's *Ethics* have complained about the discrepancy between the form of this volume, namely the network of axioms, definitions, propositions, corollaries, lemmas, and scholia, and its metaphysical content. The heavy mass of concepts and propositions, ordered and deduced mathematically, is considered by many not only an awkward but also an accidental instrument, a fad and a fashion of the seventeenth century which does not serve properly the real intent of Spinoza himself. H. Bergson described the geometrical method as "that complication of machinery, that power to crush which causes the beginner in the presence of the *Ethics* to be struck with admiration and terror as though he were before a battleship of the Dreadnaught class."[1]

The relation of Spinoza's method in the *Ethics* to its content constitutes one of those vexing problems to which the passing of years of scholarship seems to bring no satisfactory settlement. It is obvious to the reader that Spinoza laid great stress upon this method. It is announced on the title page of his book: *Ethica Ordine Geometrico Demonstrata*. Although Spinoza employed a variety of literary forms used traditionally in philosophical writings—the dialogue, the epigram, the autobiographical note, the epistle, the ordinary discourse, questions and answers—the main method with which he is identified by the reader and for which he was admired and blamed was certainly the geometrical method. It has been pointed out that Spinoza's experimenting with other literary forms had no bearing on his fundamental views. Thus, the question arises whether the geometrical method is only one of the literary forms employed or whether it is considered by him to be the most proper tool for the exploration of the universe conceived as a uniform whole governed by immutable laws.

If the geometrical method is merely a literary form without any apodeictic character, why did Spinoza prefer it to other forms? Does it perform additional roles and functions? On the other hand, if the geometrical method is a way to an indubitable body of truth, does it have also an ontological status, that is, are mathematical laws constructed by reason to order the universe, or are all physical phenomena essentially geometry incarnate? Finally, what is the role of the nongeometrical portions of the *Ethics*? It is my contention, indeed the main thesis of this paper, that those portions which I call "nongeometrical" bring into the clearest relief the limitations of the geometrical method when used in philosophy.

I.

In the vast literature on Spinoza's theory of cognition and the history of his conceptual framework, three main reasons have been given for his use of the geometrical method. It has been argued (1) that this method was merely a pedagogical device, (2) that Spinoza followed seventeenth-century scientists and philosophers, particularly Hobbes and Descartes, who, in search of a reliable method of investigation, came to believe that the mathematical model conveys the greatest certainty, and (3) that the geometrical method represents for Spinoza the coincidence between the act of cognition and the way reality is structured; it reflects truth and reality as they coincide in substance, as do the attributes of thought and extension.

In the following, I shall discuss the reasons given for Spinoza's employing the geometrical method in the order just mentioned, and I shall conclude with an account of the functions of the nongeometrical portions of the *Ethics*. But first, I think, it is worthwhile to consider briefly Euclid's *Elements* and the career of the geometrical method before Spinoza.

Euclid's book, *The Elements*, has played a decisive role in the thought of Western civilization. "Scarcely any other book, except the Bible, can have circulated the world over or been more edited and studied,"[2] writes Sir Thomas Heath, the latest translator of Euclid. For more than twenty centuries it has been used as an introduction to geometry, and only in the last hundred years has it begun to be supplemented by other textbooks. *The Elements* was without a rival in antiquity as well as in modern times and its fascination and efficiency were, indeed, remarkable.

The Renaissance scientists and philosophers, as long as they did not indulge in mystical contemplation, affirmed that the reality of nature consists of mathematical relations. This premise was widely accepted in the seventeenth century: mathematical principles are the characters in which God created nature, and the scientist has only to read this script rightly. Nature acts in accordance with the immutable laws established by the mathematical relationships as expressed in the rigorous order of Euclid's *Elements*. The scientists and philosophers, who dared to suggest ways of realizing the dream of man's conquest and mastery of the whole natural world, firmly believed in the possibility of developing and using the method which would lead to this conquest, would master and guarantee it.

Descartes proclaimed this belief in a famous passage which was highly praised by Marx and criticized by Heidegger:

> It is possible to attain knowledge which is very useful in life, and instead of that speculative philosophy which is taught in the Schools, we may find a practical philosophy by means of which, knowing the force and the action of fire, water, air, the stars, heavens and all other bodies that environ us, as distinctly as we know the different crafts of our artisans, we can in the same way employ them in all those uses to which they are adapted, and thus render ourselves the masters and possessers of nature.[3]

Seeking to establish a new world view on the basis of secure knowledge, many scientists and thinkers were attracted by the belief in the power of evidence of geometric demonstrations. The foundations of mathematics looked strong and solid, and the mathematically expressed properties of the physical world were considered really knowable.

One may suggest a further reason for the widespread belief in the power of Euclid's *Elements*. The essence of objects or matter was considered to be space, chunks of space solidified. Therefore, it was believed that objects could be mathematically described as geometry incarnate. In other words, extended objects, their shapes, motions and rest (or the "primary qualities," the source of all other physical properties), could be expressed through geometry and numbers. On the other hand, the "secondary qualities," like color or warmth, were thought not real, but rather a reaction of our mind to the fundamental realities of extension, shape, density, and motion. The real world, then, was the totality of mathematically expressible motions of objects in space and time, not an intangible labyrinth, but a great machine, all objects being space solidified.

I have omitted in this brief exposition the time element without which motion can hardly be understood. Euclidean geometry suggests that the notion of time could be eliminated in considering motion or any other relation between cause and effect. In this system of geometry, the properties of a circle, such as the length of the circumference and the properties of inscribed angles are all immediately determined as necessary logical consequences. Cause is nothing but reason, *causa cive ratio*. Only because of the limitations of our sense perception does the effect appear to follow the cause in time. Actually, only by sense perception do we apprehend events one by one and some as causes of others. But to the divine understanding, axioms and theorems are coexistent, and the temporal sequence illusory. To the divine understanding, the universe is comprehended immediately as one mathematical structure. It was believed that Euclidean geometry mirrors this understanding. No wonder that Spinoza was attracted by the geometrical method!

Coming back to the reasons given for Spinoza's use of this method, I shall state first the arguments of two exponents of the idea that Spinoza employed the geometrical method as a pedagogical device, rather than on philosophical grounds.

In the introduction to his translation to the *Principles of Descartes' Philosophy*, Halbert H. Britan states categorically that Spinoza "did not use the method because of the apodeictic character of its proof. This is conclusively shown by the fact that he used the method alike to present propositions in which he believed and those to which, as he said, he held the exactly opposite opinion."[4] The virtue of this manner was its unassailable cogency. The close form of propositions and demonstrations served not the purpose of establishing the truth of the conclusions but was intended for the pupil whom he was instructing. In short, Spinoza put Descartes' *Principles* in geometrical form because he believed that this was the form best adapted to educational requirements, the form in which the theory might most easily be learned and best understood. The method is simply a clear and forceful way to present ideas, strictly logical and thus pedagogically effective. In the *Ethics*, Britan maintains, the same method was employed for the same purpose. Because the warrant for truth for Spinoza was rational, not empirical, and the deductive method was the tenor of his age, it was only natural for him to employ "this dry stilted form" in which deductive logic reaches the height of consistency.[5] His purpose was to present first the theory of Descartes and then his own theory in a form adequate to the requirements of the mind of his pupils or readers.

According to Britan, there was no other justification for a new presentation of the truth which Descartes had taught than the forceful way provided by deductive geometry. On the other hand, Britan sensed some difficulties in this explanation of the use of the geometrical method in the *Ethics*. In this work, Spinoza expressed only what he firmly believed, and yet employed the geometrical method as the best form in which to express not mathematical but philosophical truth. Britan's answer is that Spinoza held that the old method of syllogistic deduction from premises previously and better known is not plausible enough as an organon of truth. It fails to take into account the impact of Descartes and the enthusiasm of the whole age for mathematical foundations.

Another exponent of the "pedagogical" explanation for the use of the geometrical method, Harry A. Wolfson, insists, against Britan, that Spinoza took the *Elements* of Euclid as a model for demonstration in philosophy in order to avoid the syllogistic proof identified with scholasticism. But Wolfson, too, emphasizes that the geometrical method was considered by Spinoza as a most convenient device of instruction because of the clearness and distinctness with which it was believed to delineate an argument; "It was used for the same reason that one uses outlines and diagrams."[6] Wolfson makes a distinction between the "geometrical" literary form and the mathematical way of looking at the universe. The former, he believes, is not a logical consequence of the latter. Spinoza had applied the geometrical method as a literary form to the philosophy of Descartes, whose method was analytic and not synthetic as Euclid's, and who did believe that the geometrical method "cannot so conveniently be applied to these metaphysical matters."[7] On the other hand, the *Short Treatise*, which is already based on the mathematical outlook, was written in the geometrical literary form. (The same could be said about Spinoza's two other Treatises). Therefore, concludes Wolfson, only pedagogical considerations moved Spinoza to employ the geometrical method. The clearness with which it enables the writer to state an argument was the decisive reason.

Wolfson adds a new and important consideration, namely, Spinoza's personal predicament as a teacher and author. Spinoza's philosophy was highly polemical and controversial. His axioms and propositions imply many denials and innovating views which were considered heresies. The *Ethics* was produced in a relatively cloistered atmosphere where little discussion was going on to challenge these explosive novelties. The *Ethics* is a peculiar piece of writing, because its arguments are not fully unfolded. In spite of its forceful method, the work has often been characterized as unclear and contradictory. Wolfson suggests that the geometrical method provided a tool of expression for a lonely thinker who had not had the benefits (and the distractions) of inquiring students and friends. Spinoza never revealed how he settled the problems which troubled him. His circle of educated merchants, students, and holders of public office could hardly serve as an effective sounding-board. Besides, he lived as a stranger among them, and although most of them were kind to him, he was cautious and not too communicative. But, as he did not wish to withhold from them his main ideas, he put his arguments in the geometrical form, which he thought would serve well for explaining them without dialogue or discussion. Besides, his students and friends were not sufficiently prepared for complicated inquiries, maintaining only a general interest in problems of theology and philosophy. This cautious and guarded attitude led to Spinoza's doctrine being put in the concentrated, impersonal form of Euclid's *Elements*. By this method he intended to avoid the need for arguing against opponents because the *Ethics* consists primarily of conclusions of an elaborate criticism of the traditional rabbinical and scholastic philosophies. Finally, Wolfson mentions Spinoza's desire to produce a work that would be different from all other philosophical books, even in its form. "He had something new to say, and he wished to say it in a new way."[8]

Both Britan and Wolfson rely upon the testimony of Ludwig Meyer's preface to the *Principles*. Indeed, this preface is most illuminating. It starts with the highest praise of the mathematical method: "The method by which conclusions are demonstrated from definitions, postulates and axioms is the best method of obtaining and imparting truth." However, Meyer goes on to explain that nobody can doubt the definitions, postulates, axioms of mathematics, "for definitions are but a very open explanation of the terms and names under which the subject is discussed, and the postulates and axioms of mathematics or the general ideas of the mind cannot be denied by anyone who understands the use of his vocabulary."[9] We shall return to this nominalistic qualification later. For those who regret the plight of philosophy, Meyer has a consolation. Descartes made it possible to establish many true propositions with mathematical certainty. However, he did not use the Euclidean form, the synthetic method, preferring analysis as the best way to discover truth, although both methods were recognized as kinds of apodeictic demonstration. Meyer describes those two kinds in the following manner:

> The one, Analysis, which Descartes showed to be the true method, by which truth is discovered methodically and as it were a priori;
> The other by Synthesis, the method by which a long series of definitions, in premises, and axioms and theorems, and problems is used so that if anything is denied in the conclusions, it is immediately

shown to be contained in the premises. By these means assent is extorted from the reader, however unwilling or unyielding he may be.[10]

The rivalry between the two kinds of demonstration seems to Meyer to be only an internal affair of the followers of Descartes, once the preference for the geometrical method in general was validly established by this thinker. While philosophy must follow mathematics in one or in both of the two kinds of demonstration, Meyer praises the synthetic Euclidean kind for its pedagogical efficiency. It can "extort assent even from the unwilling reader."

Britan, Wolfson, and many other scholars believed that Spinoza did not have any doubts as to the cogency of this form for the expression of philosophical ideas. They also stressed the fact that the use of geometrical method for philosophical subjects was not first suggested or invented by Spinoza. The influence of Descartes has already been mentioned. Thomas Hobbes had voiced the more radical call to treat ethics and politics in mathematical fashion in the preface to his *De Cive*, which we know Spinoza to have possessed.

II.

We can now summarize this line of "pedagogical" interpretation. The two scholars mentioned as representatives of this line maintain that the mathematical world-view made the old syllogistic device, transferred now into a geometrical method, a palatable instrument for expressing the ideas of the new age. However, Britan, Wolfson, and others believe that there is no logical connection between the substance of Spinoza's philosophy and the Euclidean form. "To the philosophers of the seventeenth century the blessed word 'mathematics' served as a veneer of respectability for the discredited syllogism."[11] The form provided mainly accuracy and precision. However, it seems to me, as already mentioned above, that the idea of the mathematization of philosophy was in the seventeenth century more than an external pedagogical or fashionable device or façade. Could it be that for Spinoza the geometrical form was first of all a sure way to cognitive certitude, and second, a reflection of the order of things themselves, rather than a mere form of instruction or a veneer of respectability?

The *Tractatus de Intellectus Emendatione* indicates clearly that Spinoza was in search of a method of knowledge that would direct his investigation according to fixed rules. The doctrine of mathematical evidence and the sure path of demonstration was first of all an attempt to escape doubt and ignorance. The validity of the geometrical manner

of Spinoza has been widely discussed. The assumptions and the inco-
herences have been pointed out by Joachim, Barker, Taylor, and Parkinson, to mention only a few of the most outstanding English scholars;[12]
there is no need here to travel the same ground. I would like, rather, to
indicate the function of this method as a weapon in fighting both
skepticism and dogmatism.

Spinoza rejects the Cartesian doubts about the validity of the geometrical method in metaphysics, namely Descartes' assumption that
even mathematical truths owe their certainty to the will of God. The
novelty of Spinoza's use of the geometrical method was to stretch the
mathematical doctrine from the rules of quantity and of logical necessity to the range of other categories, thus imposing demonstration of
eternal truth upon ways of arriving at a state of beatitude. The necessity
of things becomes identified with an absolute necessity in the divine
nature. The whole thrust of Spinoza's epistemological endeavors is to
show that the science of mathematics is able to arrive at a certitude in
all spheres of reality. The nature of the divine necessity removes doubt
and guarantees truth. This Spinoza learned from Descartes. However,
the aim of Spinoza's endeavors was different. Whereas Descartes'
purpose was, as suggested earlier, the reform of natural sciences in a way
which will allow man to become lord and master of the universe,
Spinoza's purpose was liberation from ignorance and doubt, the emen-
dation of the intellect in serving the free man to gain beatitude. The
nature of substance demands the identity of method in all sciences.
". . . It is evident that, in order to reproduce in every respect the faithful
image of nature, our mind must deduce all its ideas from the idea which
represents the origin and source of the whole of nature, so that it may
itself become the source of other ideas." (*TdIE*, Elwes II, 15–16)

Spinoza's explicit aim, then, was to reduce the universe to a unified
whole governed by unchangeable laws and thus overcome the dualisms
of God and material world, soul and body, thought and extension. This
unification eliminates the belief of design in nature, and also finds the
idea of free will inconsistent with the uniform universe. The geometrical method seemed to Spinoza to be the perfect instrument for such a
world view. It served as a demonstration of how the world was implicated in God and not created. The coextension of God and the world
leaves nothing which transcends the actual and turns all the actual into
the necessary, ruling out the other modal concepts of the contingent
and the possible as human illusions. Nothing can be, but what is.

Mathematical certitude was instrumental in emancipation from
authority. It replaces the evidence of Scripture. Most scientists who
sought to avoid conflict with the Church proclaimed, like Galileo, that

God discovers himself to us no less admirably in nature's action than in the sacred dictions of the Scriptures. Such scientists agreed that God designed the universe rationally, building on the foundations of mathematical relations, and that the discovery and explanation of the physical world is the revealing of God's grandeur and wisdom. But for Spinoza, the mathematical certitude yielded by the geometrical method presented a radical criticism of the main assumtion of the Bible. It questions the foundations. Spinoza believed that he who has gained mathematical certitude must be convinced of the inferiority of all other claims to knowledge, including the "wisdom" of the Bible and of ecclesiastical authorities.

The geometrical method, then, served Spinoza as a shelter against the "Pyrrhonic crisis" and as an indubitable way of seeking truth independent of any authority. In at least four famous passages, Spinoza triumphantly extols the idea that mathematical certitude is superior to any belief in authority, theological or otherwise. Three of these passages are directly pointed against Biblical authority. (1) Chapter 2 of the *Tractatus Theologico-Politicus* emphasizes that prophetic knowledge by revelation was not a mathematical but merely a moral certitude. (*TTP*, Elwes I, 28)[13] This thesis is elaborated in Chapter 15 of *TTP*, where Spinoza emphasizes that reason is the greatest of gifts and the mind "the true handwriting of God's word." (*TTP*, Elwes I, 192) In questioning the authority of prophetic revelation, he makes a clear distinction between the judgment of reason based on mathematical certitude and the moral conviction of prophecy which aims only to establish rules of right living. Whereas the Biblical conviction belongs to the sphere of "piety and obedience," the sphere of reason is "truth and wisdom." Because theologians cannot hope to attain greater certainty than the prophets, and the certainty of the latter was only moral and not theoretical (i.e., not mathematical), theological knowledge gained by the study of the Scriptures is inferior to scientific, philosophical certitude based on mathematics.

(2) In the same context, we have to understand Spinoza's response to Albert Burgh: "I do not presume that I have discovered the best philosophy but I understand the true one." (*Ep.* 76) The key concepts of metaphysical synthesis and their entailments lead to truthful propositions. The true philosophy relies upon the strictest methodological procedures founded on self-evident principles. It does not depend on subjective feelings, superstitions, and dogmatic assumptions reflected in judgments about the good or the best views. The criterion of the truth of an idea is its contents being clear and precise, a criterion independent of theological-political authority.

(3) The third passage is to be found in the Appendix to *Ethics,* Part I, where Spinoza argues that all "misconceptions" of religious beliefs in final causes stem from the neglect of mathematics. The theological axiom that God's judgments far transcend human understanding "might well have sufficed to conceal the truth from the human race for all eternity if mathematics had not furnished another standard of verity considering solely the essence and properties of figures without regard to their final causes." (*E* I, App.)

(4) Finally, in the *Tractatus Politicus,* Spinoza states his intention to consider social and political actions mathematically: "When I applied my mind to politics in order that I might inquire into the matters pertaining to it with the same freedom of mind with which we are wont to treat of a mathematical subject, I took care not to deride them, not to execrate them but to understand them." (*TP,* Chap. 1.4)

III.

So much for the geometrical method as a tool for liberating the mind from both skepticism and dogmatism. The ontological status of the method, that is, whether it is only a logical device of demonstration, i.e., a system of convincing truths and evidences construed by our minds, or whether it is based on the foundations of reality itself has been debated widely. The topic can only be mentioned here, even more briefly than in the previous section.

Spinoza's theory of parallelism, namely that given any adequate idea there is a mode of extension of which it is an adequate idea, and that, conversely, a corresponding idea must be found for any mode of extension, indicates the ontological status of mathematical truth. This parallelism or correspondence is a speculative *a priori* theory of a necessary connection between thoughts and objects. The mental-physical relationship for Spinoza is not a contingent nomological one; it is a representational relationship. In other words, given the system of infinitely many modes of extension, there is an adequate representation, i.e., knowledge, of this system and vice versa. "The order and connection of ideas is the same as the order and connection of things." (*E* II, P7) The correspondence of knowledge and its object is due to the fact that the all-embracing divine thought is nothing but the actualized connection of truth. Every thought is a part of the inner connection of the divine mind and corresponds point by point with the universal relation of material existence in space. The expression of the absolute universality of order, called substance, or God, is reflected in the geometrical method. The totality of conditions which are God's essence guarantees the reality of nature as constituting an unchanging objective order, and not a mere facticity of sense data. The general rules of method are thus converted into fundamental laws of things. The act of cognition and the structure of reality, or the operation by which God engenders both truth and reality, coincide. This coincidence between the act by which our mind knows truth and the structure of reality is central in Spinoza's system.

A comparison with Descartes' position may serve to clarify this point. Descartes' main reason for not employing the geometrical method in its literary form of Euclidean demonstration was probably that he did not conceive the universe as ruled totally by laws of necessity of a mathematical character. His world was still a world of final causes, divine intervention and providence, and free will. The mathematical method served his theories only as demonstrations for analogies.

We recall Meyer's statement about the validity of mathematical postulates and axioms that "cannot be denied by anyone who understands the use of his vocabulary," a statement which echoes Descartes' position. For Spinoza, however, the mathematical method seems to serve as a proof for the tight set of laws of necessity in the whole of nature: "I shall consider human actions and desires in exactly the same manner, as though I were concerned with lines, planes, and solids." (E III, pref.) It is obvious that Spinoza rejects the Cartesian assumption that even mathematical truths owe their certainty to the will of God. For Spinoza, the divine nature has no choices. It acts because it exists and as it exists. It cannot act differently or be anything different. It knows no antitheses of true and false, or right and wrong, but subsists exclusively in the affirmation of itself which the geometrical theory, axiomatized and deductive, reflects. The geometrical order, then, seems to be more than a form of instruction or a method of cognition; it has an objective ground in the order of things themselves. Full treatment of this complex issue, however, is beyond the scope of this paper. It has been discussed in connection with Spinoza's theory of attributes and with his attitude towards universals.[14]

Spinoza's concept of adequate, clear, distinct, and self-evident ideas suggests what is normally called "realism." His concept of substance, the origin of all modal things, of the attributes and of the common properties of the modes have the character of logical universalism. The nominalistic trend in Spinoza's doctrines cannot, however, be disregarded. He designates the concept of man as an example of an abstraction or *ens rationis* derived from the fortuitous impressions of this or that person. Even stronger is the explanation in the *Cogitata Metaphysica* of the notions of order and connection as modes of cognition "by which we can more easily retain objects in memory and image them." (*CM* I, chap. 5) They should not be conceived "as something in the essence of things." This clash between realistic and nominalistic tendencies makes it hard to understand how the geometrical method based on modes of thinking becomes a tool for knowing absolute reality. The premises of the system presuppose the common ground of thought and existence in a universal intelligibility. But the critical, nominalistic tendency suggests that the mathematical procedure was meant by Spinoza as an analogy rather than as an operation.

At present we must rest content, without further elaboration, by stressing this incompatibility. The reasons for employing the geometrical method discussed so far were probably not mutually exclusive in the mind of Spinoza. I shall turn now to the fourth reason which, as I have indicated, seems to me to have been most significant, if not decisive.

IV.

The geometrical method, I believe, provided for Spinoza a helm and a compass by which he thought he could steer safely between the Scylla of his own intellectual doubt and emotional agitation and the Charybdis of the dogmatic impositions of his unfriendly environment. *Caute* was inscribed on Spinoza's ring. It meant both a warning against political enemies and fanatics of all sorts, and a metaphysical caution that man is a frail being essentially threatened from within and without. Because the external dangers, he knew, were many and multi-faceted, Spinoza taught that "the virtue of a free man is seen to be as great when it declines dangers as when it overcomes them" (*E* IV, P69), and that "the free man is a man of courage in timely retreat from fighting as in actual combat." (*E* IV, P69, C) The reason why Spinoza adopted the geometrical form, I believe, was his wish to avoid, as a matter of caution, the personal touches which ordinary composition brings clearly into the light. This wish was supported by the traditionally philosophical conviction that truth is universal and impersonal, reflecting the objective order of the universe, and by the new view that the ideal way of stating it is the mathematical manner. The philosopher's task is to bring into the open the self-articulation of the universe according to the essence of things, man's emotions included. Philosophers should, therefore, consider human actions and desires in the same spirit as one would "lines, planes and solids." (*E* III, pref.)

My contention that the geometrical method was employed as a form of caution, and indeed, as a pedagogical device of self-restraint, will be supported in the following by the examination of the nongeometrical portions of the *Ethics*. By "nongeometrical portions," I mean the passages which are more or less unconstrained by the mathematical form. I refer to the prefaces, appendices, extended notes, and corollaries which belong only in a loose way to the geometrical skeleton of the work.

I consider as eminently nongeometric the appendix on design, final causes, and free will in Part I; in Part II, the short preface and the extensive last note on understanding, falsehood, and error; in Part III, the preface; in Part IV, the preface on perfection and imperfection, good and evil, and the appendix on emotions, as well as the notes to Proposition 25 and 36; and in Part V, the preface on freedom, and the extended notes to Propositions 10, 20, and 41.

What strikes me most, whenever I go carefully through the *Ethics*, is the difference between the restrained and detached, although controversial assertions dressed in the geometrical form, and the nongeometrical assertions loaded with harsh rebukes, refutations, ridicule, and scorn. Spinoza's interpreters still debate the question of whether the premises stated as axioms, definitions, and postulates are to be construed as descriptive elucidations of self-evident principles and of what can be deduced from them, or disguised normative positions, "persuasive definitions" (C. L. Stevenson's term) expressing commitments and exhortations and essentially arbitrary instructions. It is my contention that it is the nongeometrical portions that manifest some of the latter characteristics. This is the reason for William K. Frankena's distinction between Spinoza's metaphysics, epistemology, and psychology (referred to by him as *MEP*) as laid down in the form of a Euclidean system in Parts I–III of the *Ethics*, and the rest of the book, in which Spinoza supposedly deduces his "new morality."[15] Frankena maintains that Spinoza's ethical teachings do not follow deductively from his *MEP*. Although my concern in this paper is more restricted, I do believe that Frankena's observation supports my claim that the nongeometrical passages have a distinctive character. They seem to be often highly antagonistic, and whereas the geometrical form has cautiously disciplined the argumentation, the nongeometrical discourse gives vent to the aggressive impulses of the author. This leads me to the suggestion that the portions which I term "nongeometrical" are agitated by deep apprehensions and intellectual doubt, and thus indicate that the geometrical form served for Spinoza, consciously or semiconsciously, as a device for restraining his strong temper when dealing with views whose treatment by him might have annoyed the public. Such discussions indeed called for increased caution and for self-conquest.

Spinoza was living under theological ostracism not only from Jews.

With all his great patience and willingness to forego much for the quieting of angry adversaries, he was courageous in speaking out, sensitive to injustice, and annoyed at pretentious stupidity. Of course, in trying to communicate his ideas, he was careful not to flaunt his "heresies" in the face of others.

Leo Strauss has pointed out,[16] correctly in my view, that Spinoza used certain literary devices in order to conceal his seriously held views not only from the Calvinist theologians and the orthodox, but also from believers in general. As a matter of fact, he was extraordinarily bold in his whole enterprise of attacking orthodox Biblical theology. In this attack he could count, to a certain extent, on the sympathy of liberal believers, or, more precisely, on the sympathy of those who regarded moral teaching, as distinguished from dogma and ritual, as the chief purpose of Biblical revelation. The *TTP* expresses an extreme version of this liberal view. But Spinoza had to appease his liberal friends who remained Christian believers of various shades. Therefore, he concealed his partial but decisively important disagreement with these Christian liberals.

For this I shall give two examples, very different in kind. (1) There is a strong reason to interpret Spinoza's concept of God as the totality of being which does not think, as it does not laugh or desire. And yet, Spinoza used the religious language of a "loving God" with all the personal reverence and confidence which the phrase normally suggests. True, this phrase, "The love of God," with all its emotional power, could express Spinoza's feeling of awe for man's purest action, namely the triumph of reason in supporting an attitude by which man can view the whole universe in its necessary order and connections, as an object of awe and reverence. Such language, although strictly self-contradictory, was a suitably loose metaphor for his readers.

(2) In a letter to Oostens (*Ep.* 43), one of Spinoza's followers among the liberal Christians, Spinoza uses strong words against Lambert van Velthuysen, another liberal who sharply criticized the *TTP*. In the original of this letter, the most contemptuous expressions are struck out and replaced by milder terms. Of course, one has to take into account that rugged language was widely used in those days. Yet, it is odd to find words of such scornful anger in Spinoza's writings. However, after a while Spinoza asked Velthuysen to allow him to insert his critique and Spinoza's answer divested of all its harsh expressions ("you should be given full power to modify or expunge them") into a planned new edition of the *TTP*. He praises Velthuysen for his rare candor of mind and a single eye to truth.

Still, someone might object that Spinoza was well known for his affability and sweetness of temper, as described vividly by his biographers. Colerus, for instance, recounts that "his conversation was also very sweet and easy. He knew admirably well how to be master of his passions; he was never seen very melancholic nor very merry, he was besides very courteous and obliging."[17] Yet Spinoza's equanimity was obviously not gained without rigid self-conquest. The few vehement outbursts described by his biographers testify to his temper. His mind must have been troubled when not brought under the control of the *ordo geometricus* by which he found intellectual aquiescience in necessity. The nongeometrical passages in the *Ethics* in fact have a twofold character. They consist of mystical, or should we say anagogic ("for the eternal glory"), illuminations which transcend the naturalistic concept of self-preservation as self-perfection, and of vehement exhortations and scornful, grotesque descriptions and ironic arguments, contradicting the image of a composed lover of necessity.

What I have argued so far can be supported by an examination of a few of these nongeometrical passages in the *Ethics*. Such an examination will, at the least, provide a new clue to a proper understanding of one of the most important functions of the geometrical method in Spinoza's system. (1) How striking is the difference between the calmness of the definitions, axioms, and propositions in Part I, although their actual affirmations imply a serious denial of the concepts of design and final causes in religion and the invective against these same concepts at the end of this part! The nongeometrical appendix testifies to the purpose of the method. Mathematics, Spinoza argues, saves us from teleological "prejudice." The attempt to show that nature does nothing that is not profitable to man shows really that nature, the gods, and man are alike "mad" and the theologians "insane"—theology laid down as an axiom that God's judgment far transcends human understanding. Such a doctrine amounted to "concealing the truth from the human race" until mathematics furnished another standard of verity in considering solely the essence and properties of figures without regard to their final causes. This whole passage inveighs against "general prejudices," "superstitions," and those who "take refuge in the will of God, in other words the sanctuary of ignorance." The explanations commonly given of nature are "mere modes of imagining" and "misconceptions."

(2) The appendix to Part IV begins with a statement that the geometrical method of arranging the propositions can be replaced by a different manner, "so as to admit of being seen at one view." In fact, this appendix consists of some fine observations of a biographical character. For instance, that it is useful for men to associate and to do whatever serves to strengthen friendship, "but for this there is need for

skill and watchfulness." The last paragraph advises men to bear with an equal mind all that happens, "so long as we are conscious that we have done our duty and that the power which we possess is not sufficient to enable us to protect ourselves completely." Much more advice and exhortation is to be found in this summary of Spinoza's ethics. Free of the restraint of the geometrical manner, they flow spontaneously, vividly, and not without polemics.

(3) The preface to Part V discusses the power of reason, and makes its main target Descartes' doctrine of free will. It ridicules his view that the mind is united to a particular part of the brain by the "pineal gland" in such a way that every act of mental volition is connected to a certain given motion of the gland. Spinoza derides this doctrine and the conclusion that man can determine his action by joining any motion of the gland to any volition and thus acquire an absolute control over his passions. This doctrine, says Spinoza, "I could hardly believe to have proceeded from so great a man." Descartes, who had so often taken the Scholastics to task for wishing to explain obscurities through occult qualities, had done just the same by his doctrine of the pineal gland. The end of the preface reads like a playful satire: "For I am in ignorance, whether this gland can be agitated more slowly or more quickly by the mind than by the animal spirits . . . ." At the end Spinoza adds nonchalantly: "We may also add, that there is no gland discoverable in the midst of the brain . . . ."

(4) The note to Proposition 10 of Part V is an extensive exhortation in the course of which depersonalized terms lead into vivid personalistic instructions on how to frame a system of right conduct and apply it to particular circumstances. Unconcerned with rigid deduction from impersonal axioms, it describes human life as hazardous, full of follies, led by blind desires, where passions and reason are in constant struggle, and the law and ordinance of nature seem to be the rule of hatred and anger. Here Spinoza also gives direct instructions:

> Let him not think of its misuse, and its emptiness, and the fickleness of mankind, and the like, whereof no man thinks except through a morbidness of disposition; with thoughts like these do the most ambitious most torment themselves, when they despair of gaining the distinctions they hanker after, and in thus giving vent to their anger would fain appear wise.

The note to Proposition 20 continues the same topic, namely that the mind is able to command the emotions by certain "remedies." It teaches how the mind may exercise its power over the emotions and direct them toward the love of God as the most constant and powerful of all the motions. The clue to this guidance is the division between adequate and inadequate ideas, passive and active, weak and powerful, imperfect and perfect emotions. The "ought" aspect of Spinoza's philosophical theory is most paramount in these notes, although seemingly embedded in the "is" aspect of a natural process identified with self-preservation and power. The remarks here and elsewhere suggest that Spinoza considers socio-historical reality as woven by tears and hopes, passions and fanaticism relieved by only sporadic bursts of light. The "monistic" philosopher thought in terms of radical dichotomies, and the "negativity" of ignorance and passions was for him not the essence of man which in its becoming has ultimately to be reconciled with its "otherness" in an Hegelian absolute.[18] The "negativity" is for Spinoza merely a privation, a hole in the web of being, a nonbeing, which man has to fill by his acts of reason. L. S. Feuer believes that the ideas of Spinoza provided the French Revolution, especially Robespierre, with "the greatest single stimulus to articulate discontent."[19] Even if this view is somewhat exaggerated, the *Ethics* is undoubtedly the book of a radical dissenter. As H. A. Wolfson suggests, Spinoza would have become in our times "one of the first apostles of rebellion."[20]

(5) At almost the very end of the *Ethics*, the note to Proposition 41 launches a violent attack on "the general belief of the multitude" about religion and freedom. The language is obviously satirical: "Most people believe that they are free when they obey their lusts, that piety, religion and all ideas attributable to firmness of mind are burdens, which, after death, they hope to lay aside, in order to receive the reward of their bondage, that is for their piety and religion." This is a remarkably angry description of attitudes which can hardly be attributed to any believer instructed in his holy books. It uses the terms of a famous Rabbinical Tractat, "The Sayings of the Fathers," in order to denounce the Jewish and Christian creeds as vulgar teachings of fear and hope, fear of being horribly punished after death and hope for the consolations of after-life. The note is a viciously grotesque description of "human bondage" or of the "opiate of the people." It disregards totally the teachings of religious leaders who explicitly denounced these very features attributed by Spinoza to the creed of the multitude. Amidst the ecstatic descriptions of "blessedness" in which the "wise man" rejoices, the temper of this argumentation is unexpectedly assaulting.

These few examples, which could easily be multiplied, leave us with the conclusion that the geometrical method served the rebellious Marrano philosopher as a protective device against believers in religious authority, as well as against his own *agon*. In Spinoza's mind the geometrical rhetoric, the cautious, impersonal, and universally valid (*ex ipsa ratione*) method of deduction was a call, indeed, for tolerance, but also for *self*-discipline. The *ordo geometricus* and its representative and guarantor, namely *Deus* himself, the active nature (*natura naturans*), makes essential reality "benign." The *Ethics* intends to restore this "essential order" in all spheres of human endeavor, including the socio-political realm. Unlike Adam Smith, who believed in the proliferation of sects as an effective guarantee for religious toleration, Spinoza was afraid that even a society divided into a "thousand small sects,"[21] none of them too strong, can be very dangerous when not disciplined by the essential order of the divine cosmic necessity as reflected by the geometrical method.

NOTES

1. Henry Bergson, *The Creative Mind* (New York: The Philosophical Library, 1946), p. 60. Compare the historical and systematic explanations of the geometrical method and its uses in St. Dunin-Borkowski, S.J., *Der Junge De Spinoza* (Münster in Westfalen, 1910), pp. 398–416. See also the summary and bibliography in H.G. Hübberling, *Spinoza's Methodology* (Van Gorcum, 1964).

2. Sir Thomas Heath, *Euclid I*, Preface p. xxvi.

3. Descartes, *Discourse on Method* IV, in *Descartes' Philosophical Writings* tr. and ed. by Elizabeth Anscombe and Peter T. Geach (Indianapolis and New York, 1971) p. 46. Marx's comment is to be found in *Das Kapital* I, p. 408–409, and in note 3 in Marx-Engel's *Gesamtausgabe* 1. Abt. (Frankfurt a.M./Berlin 1927–32). Heidegger interpreted Descartes' statement as expressing a typical feature of Western metaphysics, namely the desire to organize and control the world in all its dimensions of being in an objective and impersonal way, which seduces man "to forget Being." See *Holzwege* (Frankfurt a.M. 1957) p. 102–103.

4. Halbert Hains Britan, *The Principles of Descartes' Philosophy by B. De Spinoza* (The Open Court, 1961), Introduction, p. x.

5. Britan, p. xv.

6. Harry A. Wolfson, *The Philosophy of Spinoza* (Cleveland and New York: The World Publishing Co., 1965), Vol. I, p. 55.

7. *Ibid.*, p. 44.

8. *Ibid.*, p. 59.

9. Britan, *op. cit.*, Preface, p. 1.

10. *Ibid.*, p. 3.

11. Wolfson, *op. cit.*, p. 59.

12. The well-known works of these authors are listed in the bibliography by E.M. Curley, in *Spinoza, Essays in Interpretation* (eds. E. Freeman and M. Mandelbaum: Open Court, 1975), pp. 265–316.

13. "Etenim hace certitudo Prophetica mathematica quidem non est, sed tantum moralis." (*TTP*, Gebhardt III, 30)

14. See the papers by A. Wolf and Francis S. Haserot on Spinoza's doctrine of attributes and on the status of universals, and those of David Savan and G.H.R. Parkinson on the problem of language and error, in P. Kashap (ed.), *Studies in Spinoza* (University of California Press, 1972).

15. William K. Frankena, "Spinoza's 'New Morality'," in *Spinoza, Essays in Interpretation*, pp. 85–100.

16. Leo Strauss, *Persecution and the Art of Writing* (New York: Free Press, 1952), pp. 142–201.

17. John Colerus, *The Life of Benedict de Spinoza* (The Hague, 1906), p. 61.

18. On the relations between Spinoza and Hegel, see Efraim Shmueli, "Hegel's Interpretation of Spinoza's Concept of Substance," *International Journal for Philosophy of Religion*, 1 (1970).

19. Lewis S. Feuer, *Spinoza and the Rise of Liberalism* (Beacon Press, Boston, 1958), p. 177.

20. H.A. Wolfson, *op. cit.*, Vol. II, p. 330.

21. Quoted by Feuer, *op. cit.*, p. 176.

On the Aims and Method of Spinoza's Philosophy

DOUGLAS LEWIS
University of Minnesota

> Granted then that there are countless individuals, at last is everything one, and the recognition of this unity forms the goal and end of all philosophy and all natural research.
> —Giordano Bruno, *De la Causa*, Dialogue 4.

Introduction

Generally speaking, in contemporary times philosophers despair of accomplishing philosophy's traditional task of giving an account of the whole of nature that satisfies the demands of reason. G. E. Moore is an exception. In *Some Main Problems of Philosophy*, a course of lectures delivered in 1910–1911, he says:

> The most important and interesting thing which philosophers have tried to do is no less than this; namely: To give a general description of the *whole* of the universe, mentioning all the most important kinds of things which we know to be in it, considering how far it is likely that there are in it important kinds of things which we do not absolutely *know* to be in it, and also considering the most important ways in which these various kinds of things are related to one another.[1]

By mentioning this basic question with which philosophers have grappled, Moore gives his listener some idea of the sort of problem he intends to pursue in the remainder of his lectures. By comparison, Albert Camus views philosophy's traditional quest as a hopeless one. In *The Myth of Sisyphus*, written in 1940, he calls the human situation absurd. By this he means that although, on the one hand, man longs to have a rational comprehension of the world that make sense of it, on the other, this longing is unsatisfiable. The person who is conscious of this longing while being aware that the world remains opaque to its demands has recognized the absurdity of the human condition. Bertrand Russell has also despaired of philosophy's ancient quest. In a short essay entitled "Philosophy's Ulterior Motives," published in

1950 in *Unpopular Essays,* he characterizes the philosophical tempera-
ment as combining "two somewhat conflicting characteristics: on the
one hand a strong desire to believe some general proposition about the
universe or human life; on the other hand, inability to believe con-
tentedly except on what appear to be intellectual grounds." That
Russell thinks all philosophical attempts to give an account of the
order of nature are intellectual rubbish is clear from the next sentence,
"The more profound the philosopher, the more intricate and subtile
must his fallacies be in order to produce in him the desired state of
intellectual acquiescence (italics mine)."[2] Russell extols, in contrast,
the virtues of the man of science, to whom general doctrines are merely
hypotheses, "to be tested by experiment."

Traditionally, the belief has been maintained that should men obtain
an account of the whole of nature that makes sense of it they would
experience a profound satisfaction. Camus reflects this traditional
belief. In the section of the *Myth of Sisyphus* entitled "Absurd Walls,"
he says: "If thought discovered in the shimmering mirrors of phenomena eternal relations capable of summing them up and summing themselves up in a single principle, then would be seen an intellectual joy of
which the myth of the blessed would be but a ridiculous imitation."[3]
Much earlier, in the eighteenth century, Hume had scoffed at this
belief. In the opening paragraph of section V of *An Enquiry Concerning Human Understanding,* he cautions:

> The passion for philosophy . . . may only serve, by imprudent manage-
> ment, to foster a predominant inclination. . . . It is certain that while
> we aspire to the magnanimous firmness of the philosophic sage, and
> endeavor to confine our pleasures altogether within our own minds,
> we may, at last, render our philosophy . . . only a more refined system
> of selfishness, and reason ourselves out of all virtue as well as social
> enjoyment.[4]

In the *Ethics,* Spinoza presents an account of the order of nature
which he maintains satisfies the demands of reason to have a consistent
and intelligible comprehension of the whole of it.[5] Unlike Russell, he
does not think there are any fallacies in his philosophy, nor does he
suffer the general despair of contemporary philosophy. Also, Spinoza
maintains that an account of the order of the whole of nature satisfying
the demands of reason, because it yields intuitive knowledge of God,
yields a satisfaction to the soul, which he calls man's highest happiness.
His philosophy is difficult and complex; it is stated in what is now an
archaic vocabulary. Yet, the ends it promises—however out of character
they may be with contemporary times—continue to exercise some hold

upon human interest and to sustain somewhat its attention. Some will certainly sympathize with Russell's view that all profound philosophy must involve fallacy. Others will understand and appreciate Hume's sentiment that one's philosophy may only foster a predominant inclination. Still, whether all profound philosophy involves fallacy seems to be a matter to be settled, not *a priori*, but by studying examples of it. And one can maintain, without undue prejudice, that it is not clearly *certain* that we may "reason ourselves out of all virtue as well as social enjoyment" by our philosophy. Were this certain, it would also be certain that no account of the order of nature would yield the satisfaction of which Spinoza speaks.

This paper does not attempt to resolve the issues just raised. It aims only to aid others in their understanding of Spinoza's attempted resolution.

I.

1. Spinoza has set himself three tasks in the *Ethics*. First, he aims to aid his reader in forming a conception of the order of the whole of nature, a conception which satisfies the demands of reason. These demands are consistency and completeness. That is, a rationally satisfying conception of the order of the whole of nature contains no internal contradictions, and every phenomenon of human experience finds a place and make sense in terms of it. Second, he aims to aid his reader in becoming master of his own emotions and desires, that is, in becoming free from the bondage of passive desires and emotions. This end is accomplished when one possesses a true knowledge of the nature of human emotions and desires. Third, he aims to make clear to his reader, on a reflective level, what constitutes the peace of mind springing from intuitive knowledge of God and of the essence of things.

The three tasks Spinoza has set himself are interrelated. The knowledge of the nature of human emotions and desires, from the possession of which one becomes master of his own emotions, involves a knowledge of the whole order of nature, of which man and his passions are a part. Without a conception of the order of the whole, a person is without the means for becoming master of his own emotions. Also, a person experiences the peace of mind springing from intuitive knowledge of God and of the essence of things *only when* his conception of the order of nature satisfies reason's demands.[6] Without such a conception, clarity as to what constitutes the peace of mind springing from intuitive knowledge would be wholly theoretical, abstract, and idle. Thus, accomplishing the second and third tasks is dependent upon accomplishing the first.

On the other hand, the first task is separable from the second and third, at least at preliminary stages. With respect to the second task: it is true that the knowledge of the nature of human emotions and desires, a knowledge that involves knowledge of the order of the whole of nature satisfying reason, serves as a means for becoming master of emotions; and it is also true that while actually subject to disturbances stemming from passive emotions and desires, a person is unable to form a conception of the order of the whole that makes sense of it. Nevertheless, one does not need to have become free from the bondage of the passions, that is, to have become master of his own emotions, in order to form this conception. One has one's moments; one is not always subject to disturbances stemming from the passions. Bondage to passive emotions and desires consists in a lack of capacity to prevent being caught up in disturbances, and the actions they imply, when circumstances engender them. Yet, even after having formed the rationally satisfying conception of the whole order of nature, if one is not master of his emotions, he is unable to sustain and maintain this conception in his own thoughts. In this way he is at the mercy of fortune. By becoming master of his own emotions, one becomes able to sustain this conception in face of circumstances that otherwise would overcome him. With respect to the third task: although forming a conception of the order of nature that makes sense of the whole of it is a condition of becoming clear—in a way that is not abstract—regarding what constitutes peace of mind, nevertheless one can form this conception without possessing this knowledge. Yet, when the mind does become clear, on a reflective level, regarding the constitution of the peace of mind springing from intuitive knowledge of God and of the essence of things, its capacity for maintaining its conception of the order of the whole is strengthened.

In setting himself these three tasks, Spinoza is undertaking the traditional work of philosophy. Throughout its history philosophers have attempted to form an account of nature that makes sense of the whole of it. Traditionally, the belief has been maintained that should this attempt be successful men would experience profound satisfaction. According to Spinoza, when a person has formed a rationally satisfying conception of the order of the whole of nature, he does not possess what one might think of as a conception of reason, or the rational faculty, *merely*; he possesses intuitive knowledge of God and of the essence of things from which peace of mind springs. Spinoza calls the peace of mind (*anima acquiescentia*) which springs from intuitive knowledge man's highest happiness.

The three tasks Spinoza has set himself in the *Ethics* determine its organization. Parts I and II present the conception of the whole order of nature Spinoza considers satisfies reason's demands. Parts III, IV, and V, through proposition 20, present his concept of the nature of human passive and active emotions and desires and explain what a person with this knowledge can do about them. Part V, from proposition 21, describes the characteristics ideas have in the order of the intellect;[7] and it gives an account of what constitutes the peace of mind—and also blessedness—which springs from the intuitive knowledge of God and the essence of things. A person experiences this peace when his mind contains the rationally satisfying conception of the whole order of nature.

2. The style Spinoza has chosen for presenting his philosophy has been a source of consternation to some. In the *Ethics*, he presents it in the manner of a geometer. Each of the five parts begins with definitions and axioms, and each contains propositions followed by demonstrations, interspersed with corollaries and notes. Definitions give the meanings of key terms; axioms state aspects of the philosophy not established on the basis of others. The demonstration following a proposition shows how that proposition is implied by earlier propositions, axioms, and definitions. Notes call attention to difficulties a reader may encounter and to confusions involved in competing views.

Frequently, commentators offer explanations for Spinoza's choice of the geometrical style for presenting philosophy. I will explain what I understand his reason to be. Two sorts of phenomena of human life hinder a person from forming that conception of the order of the whole of nature which is internally consistent and within which all phenomena of human experience find a place and make sense. One of these two sorts has already been indicated. *At the level of emotion,* disturbances stemming from passive emotion and desires, and ideas regarding good and evil connected with them, stand between a person and accomplishing this end. *On the intellectual plane,* six primary confused idea can be distinguished which have similar consequences. (These will be enumerated and discussed below.) Spinoza believes that from the definition of 'God' presented at the beginning of Part I of the *Ethics*, together with a few other definitions and some axioms, there can be inferred adequate ideas (1) of the essence, or nature, of God, (2) of the nature of the mundane system of which men are part— Spinoza calls this system the modes of substance—and (3) of the relationship of the mundane system to God. These adequate ideas constitute the conception (or idea) of the order of the whole of nature that satisfies the demands of reason. Also, they contrast with those confusions of thought on the intellectual plane which are among the phenomena of human life that hinder a person from forming this conception. Thus, should a person who is confused exercise and sharpen his capacity to reason—his capacity to deduce conclusions from premises—then, reflecting upon the given definition of 'God' and the propositions which follow from it, he would become aware of his confusions on the intellectual plane. Thereby, the difficulty involved in confused ideas on the intellectual plane would be circumvented.

In chapter 2 of *The Philosophy of Spinoza: Unfolding the Latent Processes of His Reasoning*, Harry A. Wolfson suggests three reasons why Spinoza may have chosen to present his philosophy in the geometrical manner, all of which are different from the one I characterized above. He says that the motives prompting Spinoza to depart from the old, established form of exposition "can be only conjectured."[8] He distinguishes a number of styles in which philosophy had frequently been written—dialogue, disputation and question, exegesis, autobiography—and mentions that Spinoza himself uses several of these in other philosophical works. Even the geometrical manner of presenting philosophical positions is precedented, for Descartes, among others, had written in this way. But no one had used this method as systematically as Spinoza does in the *Ethics*. Wolfson completely rejects the view that Spinoza chose to write philosophy in the style of a geometer because the content of his philosophy demands it. I agree with him on this point. He says, "It is these two principles—the denial of final causes in the universe and of freedom in human actions—that Spinoza wishes to illustrate by his use of mathematical analogies. It is only this, and nothing more, that his mathematical way of looking at things means."[9] Wolfson suggests that one reason for Spinoza's choice is pedagogy: "the geometrical form was believed to delineate the main features of an argument and to bring them into high relief."[10] Another reason may have been desire to return to a more rigorous form of presentation in reaction to fashionable renaissance literary styles, such as poetry, dialogue and rhetoric—the philosophy presented in these styles tended to be loose and unsystematic—without returning to the discredited disputation and question of the scholastics. And he suggests that there may have been still a third reason for Spinoza's use of the geometrical form. The scholastic method of writing philosophy "required that the various views held by opponents on each problem should be stated, that the pros and cons for each view should be reproduced, that refutations and rebuttals should be marshalled, and that only then the author's own view should be given and its superiority to those of others pointed out. Spinoza . . . did not want to go through all this formality."[11] Wolfson quotes him as expressing in a letter to Oldenburg reluctance to appear to be desirous of exposing the errors of others. While I think all these suggestions, especially the third, are illuminating, they miss Spinoza's reason for choosing to present his philosophy in the style of a geometer. His reason is indeed pedagogical, but not in the way noted by Wolfson.

Contrary to what Wolfson says, the motives prompting Spinoza to present his philosophy in the style of a geometer do not need to be conjectured. Spinoza explains his reason—along with discussion of other points—in the middle portion of Part II of the *Ethics*, from Propositions 14 through 47. After making a few comments about several human cognitive faculties (*E* II, P14–23,), Spinoza lists things of which human beings have only inadequate ideas. (*E* II, P24–31) He defines 'adequate idea' (*E* II, Df. 4) at the beginning of Part II. Human beings have only inadequate ideas of the parts of the human body, of external bodies, of the human body itself, of the human mind, and of the duration of our and external bodies. He emphasizes that although we have, and can have, only inadequate ideas of these things, we need not therefore be in states of confusion about them. Inadequate ideas—that is, ideas the agreement of which with their objects is not evident from consideration of the ideas themselves— are a source of confusion only when "they are referred to the human mind alone" (*E* II, P28, Dm.), that is, only when they are considered without relationship to God (or the idea of God) and to the order of the whole of nature. When they are considered with relationship to God and to the order of the whole of nature, it becomes clear why they are necessarily always inadequate in us. After saying a few things about the nature of truth and error (*E* II, P32–6), Spinoza mentions things of which human beings do, nevertheless, have adequate ideas: namely, what is common to all and equally in a part and in the whole. (*E* II, P37–40) Referring the reader to the lemmas on bodies, he gives the "notions called common" as examples of adequate ideas of these things. These adequate ideas, or common notions, are the basis of the human sciences of geometry and physics and provide human beings with contexts in which they can exercise their capacity of reasoning, deducing conclusions from premises. Finally, after distinguishing and commenting upon the varieties of knowledge human beings possess—knowledge formed from inadequate and adequate ideas alike—(*E* II, P40, S; *E* II, P41–4), Spinoza mentions one further idea, adequate in every human mind, yet different from the notions called common although derived from that which is common to all and equally in a part and in the whole: namely, the idea of the eternal and infinite essence of God (*E* II, P45–7). Of this idea he says, "we can from this knowledge infer many things, which we may adequately know." (*E* II, P47, S) Thus, should men be prevailed upon to exercise and sharpen their capacity to deduce conclusions from premises in the context of theological questions, as they have in the context of geometrical and physical ones, confusions on the intellectual plane concerning the nature of God and of the mundane system of which He is the cause would show their true colors clearly. By presenting the philosophy of the *Ethics* after the manner of geometry, Spinoza intends to make this additional context for exercising the human capacity to reason available to his readers, a context where exercising reason has salutary consequences.

The character of the difficulty presented by confused ideas on the intellectual plane can be illustrated by examples drawn from the level of emotion. Spinoza does this in the autobiographical section of *On the Improvement of Human Understanding*, an unfinished piece left with instructions to his executors to include with the posthumous publication of the *Ethics* as a kind of preface. He says that for a time he pursued the ends of riches, fame, and pleasures of the senses. These pursuits so occupy the mind that they render it nearly incapable of thinking of anything else. He mentions that while occupied with them he was unable to determine whether a true good yielding "continuous, supreme and unending happiness" even exists or whether he would be able to discover what constitutes it and attain it for himself. In order to determine that a true good exists and that he was able to discover its constituents and to attain it, he had first to turn his attention away from these ends. (*TdIE*, Elwes II, 3–6) The difficulty involved in confused ideas on the intellectual plane, the character of which is illustrated here by disturbances stemming from passions, is circumvented by presenting philosophy in the style of a geometer.

3. Spinoza regards several ideas (or beliefs) on the intellectual plane as hindrances to forming that conception of the order of the whole of nature which is internally consistent and within which all phenomena of human experience find a place and make sense. Setting aside ideas concerning good and evil, which are connected with the emotions, I think that of the primary ideas which can be distinguished on the intellectual plane, Spinoza considers six as having this consequence. Accordingly, (*a*) it is confused to think that it is questionable whether God exists. (*b*) There is confusion involved in thinking that God's nature is wholly spiritual and that matter (or, as Spinoza calls it, extension) is something wholly apart from God and does not pertain to His essence. (*c*) Belief that God acts by freedom of will and that He plans and designs the mundane system of which He is the cause is confused. (*d*) There is confusion involved in thinking that the mind of man is distinct and separable from the human body. (*e*) It is confused to

think that human beings have, or can form, adequate ideas of those particular things in nature with which they come into contact in their daily experience. (*f*) Belief that men act by freedom of the will, that is, that by the will they are set apart from other creatures of nature, is confused.

a. According to Spinoza, doubt whether God exists, or belief that God does not exist, is a symptom of confusion on the part of the doubter or disbeliever. This facet of his philosophy is brought out by his use of the word 'substance' in connection with God. God is, among other things, a substance. He defines substance as "that which is in itself, and is conceived through itself; in other words, that of which a conception can be formed independently of any other conception." (*E* I, Df. 3) To have perspicuously a conception of substance is already to know adequately of the existence of that which one conceives. For a concept of substance comes only from the substance of which it is the conception. Thus, a person who doubts whether God exists, or disbelieves that God exists, misunderstands to what Spinoza is referring with the word 'God'. Of course, through a long historical usage, images have come to be associated with 'God', images which correspond to no reality except the confusions, from which they have arisen, in terms of which human beings think of themselves. To doubt, or disbelieve, the existence of the referent of these images is not confused. This phenomenon does not provide a sufficient reason for abandoning the word, however.

b.-c. The belief that God, while wholly spiritual in His essence, creates matter, which is something wholly apart from His essence, is confused. Similarly, the belief that God designs and plans the mundane system of which He is the cause and of which men are part and that He exercises freedom of will in these activities is confused. Spinoza maintains that matter, or extension, is not less correctly ascribed to God's essence than spirituality, or thought. The human intellect—the human mind so far as it perceives things truly—perceives matter, or extension, as displaying the character of God's essence. Also, although the manner in which each part of the mundane system exists and acts, as well as the manner of existing and acting of the whole, is indeed a consequence of God's nature; it is neither designed nor planned, nor does God exercise any freedom of will in producing it.

d. According to Spinoza, the human mind (*mens*), or soul (*anima*), is neither distinct from, nor can it exist without, the human body. A corresponding point can be made, of course, for every other creature of nature. To borrow a phrase from Spinoza, the human mind is the idea of the human body; that is to say, the mind is the reflection or representation in thought of the organization or structure of the body.

In corollary 2 of Proposition 16 of Part II, Spinoza gives some indication as to how to take this statement. He says that the ideas we have of external things reflect as much the constitutions of our own bodies as of the external things of which they are the ideas. Without the human body, there would be nothing for the human mind to reflect or represent. On the other hand, to coin a phrase analogous to Spinoza's, the human body is the motion and rest of the human mind. The body is the reflection or representation in extension of the organization or structure of the mind. In Spinoza's philosophy, neither mind nor body is ontologically more primary than the other.

e. The belief that human beings have, or can form, adequate ideas of those particular things in nature with which they come into contact in their daily experience, or of the existence of which they learn from experience, is confused. This confused belief is perhaps a special one and is not likely to be a source of difficulty to many. Spinoza defines 'adequate idea' at the beginning of Part II of the *Ethics*: "By *an adequate idea*, I mean an idea which, in so far as it is considered in itself, without relation to the object, has all the properties or intrinsic marks of a true idea." (*E* II, Df. 4) This definition means that from reflection upon an adequate idea alone its agreement with its object, that is its truth, is evident. According to Spinoza, human beings do not have, nor can they form, adequate ideas of the parts of their own bodies, of external bodies, of their own bodies themselves, of their minds or of the duration of their own or other bodies. Of the agreements of our ideas with the various members of this array of things we cannot know simply from reflecting upon our ideas. Descartes, for example, had thought that we know of the nature of our own minds merely from reflecting upon the ideas we have of them. This belief of Descartes, his *sum res cogitans*, prevented him from forming a conception of the whole order of nature that was internally consistent and made sense of it.

f. Spinoza's doctrine of the denial of freedom of the will is susceptible of misunderstanding. He does not deny the existence of the phenomena of human life that fall generally under the term 'will'. Human beings formulate plans, choose among alternatives, make decisions, etc. But in formulating plans, choosing among alternatives, and making decisions, they exhibit and follow the laws of nature in accordance with which all creatures of nature exist and act. The plans human beings formulate, the alternatives they choose, the decisions they make have their causes exactly as all other phenomena of nature. Indeed, the fact of the existence in human life of the phenomena which fall generally under the term 'will' has its causes, which are understood by understanding the order of the whole of nature. The doctrine of the denial of freedom of will in Spinoza's philosophy denies that weight human beings lay upon planning, choosing, deciding, etc., when they think of these activities as signs of the separateness of man from other creatures of nature and of his ontological uniqueness.

Men are reinforced in thinking confusedly about themselves and about the order of the whole of nature when they accept the images, which have come to be associated with the word 'God,' enumerated under (b) and (c) above. By believing that God, while wholly spiritual in his essence, creates matter, which is something wholly apart from His essence, and that God acts by freedom of the will, planning and designing His creation, men are encouraged to believe that the mind or soul of man is distinct from and can exist without the human body and that the exercise of human will displays his ontological superiority to other creatures of nature. These four beliefs, together with the two others mentioned, stand between a person who thinks in terms of them and the forming of a conception of the order of the whole of nature that is internally consistent and within which all phenomena of human experience find a place and make sense. Nevertheless, Spinoza maintains that from his definition of 'God', in combination with the few other definitions and axioms, there can be inferred adequate ideas which (together with those that imply them) yield a conception of the order of nature that makes sense of the whole of it. This conception makes evident the confusions involved in confused ideas on the intellectual plane. Should men be prevailed upon to exercise their capacity to reason in connection with this definition, confusions on an intellectual plane concerning the nature of God and the nature of the mundane system of which human beings are part would be dispelled.

4. The idea of God which functions centrally in Spinoza's philosophy is a medieval one. In Spinoza's words, "By God, I mean a being absolutely infinite, that is, a substance consisting of infinite attributes, each of which expresses eternal and infinite essence." (E I, Df. 6) A brief acount of God as represented in his philosophy may be included here. (1) God is a substance, that is, something which is in itself and is conceived through itself (E I, Df. 4), the existence of which is implied by its essence. The concept of God is not formed through or by means of any other thing. (2) God consists of infinite attributes, that is, nothing which limits what an infinite intellect—a mind with an infinite capacity to think truly—perceives as constituting His essence.[12] (3) God is eternal, that is, He cannot be comprehended or conceived in terms of duration and time. (4) God is the cause of all things, is omnipotent and immutable; and He is also perfect, that is, He possesses

the capacity to maintain Himself in existence come what may. The words used here are among those traditionally spoken of as expressing God's attributes, but because Spinoza uses 'attribute' in a technical sense, they might better be spoken of as expressing true ascriptions.[13]

Spinoza believes that medieval philosophers were right when they conceived God as an infinite, eternal, omnipotent, and immutable being, the cause of all things. Nevertheless, they inconsistently and confusedly pictured God as wholly spiritual in His essence—with matter, or extension, as something apart from Him—and as acting from freedom of the will, planning and preparing a destiny for those things of which He is the cause. Spinoza also believes that medieval philosophers were right when they conceived God as the source of salvation, although he thinks that their view of this was intrinsically mysterious. In the note following proposition 36 of Part V, he uses the word 'salvation' for that peace of mind, or blessedness, which is experienced when, among other things, clarity has been obtained on a reflective level concerning what constitutes it.[14] When one looks at Spinoza's philosophy from the perspective of contemporary times, one might picture it as an attempt to avoid the horns of a dilemma. On the one hand, images derived from men's unenlightened views of themselves are associated with the word 'God'. These images are not only confused, but a source of confusion, and they tend to lead the more enlightened philosophers and others to abandon entirely the word and the idea it embodies. But on the other hand, to abandon that part of the medieval idea of God which constitutes an adequate idea would sacrifice the primary tool which enables philosophy to construct a rationally coherent account of the whole order of nature. Such a construction is philosophy's traditional work; success here is believed to yield men a profound satisfaction. One might imagine Spinoza to suppose that should a society ever form, the philosophy of which lacks this primary tool for accomplishing its traditional work, it would relegate philosophy to a position of only extrinsic and secondary importance.

Not only does the medieval idea of God function centrally in Spinoza's philosophy, he begins with it. According to him, God is first not only in the order of being, but also in the order of knowledge. One must have a clear understanding of the essence of God before going on to the systematic investigation of other, more mundane, matters. We have already noted several tasks which a person is unable to accomplish until he possesses a clear understanding of the order of the whole of nature. In a note following proposition 10 of Part II of the *Ethics*, Spinoza explains the difficulty one runs into if the concept (or idea) of

God is misplaced in the order of knowledge. There, he is presenting a hypothesis to explain a specific confusion of thought into which others have fallen, but this need not concern us. He says that those who have placed the investigation of natural phenomena before consideration of the essence of God, when they subsequently turn their attention to studying the divine essence, find they are unable to understand it properly. The first hypotheses with which they have overlaid natural phenomena confuse them. Because they have not understood the divine essence clearly beforehand, these hypotheses cannot be maintained. Spinoza says:

> While they are considering natural phenomena, they give no attention at all to the divine nature, and, when afterwards they apply their mind to the study of the divine nature, they are quite unable to bear in mind the first hypotheses, with which they have overlaid the knowledge of natural phenomena, inasmuch as such hypotheses are no help towards understanding the Divine nature. So that it is hardly to be wondered at, that these persons contradict themselves freely. (E II, P10, S2)

In chapter 2 of *The Philosophy of Spinoza*, Wolfson says that all of Spinoza's writing was directed toward one purpose: "to bring to its logical conclusion the reasoning of philosophers throughout history in their effort to reduce the universe to a unified and uniform whole governed by universal and unchangeable laws."[15] Wolfson demonstrates that Spinoza makes use of and relies heavily upon this reasoning. But his statement does not express accurately Spinoza's purpose. While all of Spinoza's writing is directed toward establishing the unity and uniformity present in the whole of the universe, and while the reasoning of philosophers throughout history is also directed toward this end, the establishing of this unity and uniformity is not its sole purpose. Among other purposes, Spinoza's writing aims to make clear to its reader, on a reflective level, the constitution of the peace of mind springing from intuitive knowledge of God and the essence of things, a peace of mind which a person experiences when his mind contains the idea reflecting the universe's unity and uniformity. If one wished to sum up the purpose of Spinoza's writing in a single statement, the following one would be more accurate: "Spinoza's writing aims to aid its reader in accomplishing the traditional end of philosophy: forming a conception of the order of the whole of nature satisfying the demands of reason and developing the capacity to maintain and sustain this conception in his own thoughts."

II.

I shall conclude this paper by discussing one place in Spinoza's philosophy where it may appear that his account of the order of the whole of nature is either not internally consistent or not complete, and I shall attempt to show that this appearance rests upon a misunderstanding. The difficulty occurs at the corollary following Proposition 25 of Part I of the *Ethics*. Wolfson uses the rubric, "how finite things arose from an infinite cause," for his discussion of it.[16]

Human beings are finite, individual things. Spinoza uses 'finite' in the sense of limited in capacity to think, to act and to continue in existence. That we are finite is something we know by experience, for experience teaches us that we are limited in what we can think and do and in the time during which we continue to exist. In *On the Improvement of Human Understanding*, Spinoza mentions men's death, which is an aspect of their finitude, as an example of something known by mere experience. (*TdIE*, Elwes II, 8) He calls the kind of knowledge that has its source in the suggestions of experience the first kind of knowledge, opinion, or imagination. (See E II, P40, S2.)

It may seem to some that there is an inconsistency involved in maintaining, on the one hand, that God is the cause of all things and is an absolutely infinite being and, on the other, that He numbers finite things among His effects. However, although he maintains that human beings, although finite, are effects of an absolutely infinite cause, Spinoza does not attempt to demonstrate the finitude of human beings or of any modes of substance from the definition of God, the other definitions and the axioms which open Part I of the *Ethics*. Rather, he maintains that the existence of finite modes cannot be demonstrated. Briefly, the argument runs: God is a substance; the conception of God is not formed through or by means of any other thing. Hence, God is something the existence of which is implied in His essence. Moreover, God is the cause of all things. The mundane system, of which man and all other things are parts, is the effect of which God is the cause. The mundane system, and every part of it, expresses God's essence after its own manner. For this reason it, and every part of it, is called a mode, or a modification, of substance. Furthermore, God never has been, and never will be, without the mundane system. As God is a cause, effects exist which express His essence. (See E I, A3.) Finally, God could never have been and can never be without the mundane system, because of His omnipotence. Consequently, the mundane system, considered as a whole, is infinite after its own kind and everlasting, continuing without beginning or end. However, because from God's essence considered absolutely—that is, as it is in itself and is conceived through itself—only infinite and everlasting modes follow, or can be inferred,[17] and because from God's essence considered as expressed in infinite and everlasting modes, only infinite and everlasting modes follow, or can be inferred, finite modes *cannot follow, and cannot be conceived as following,* from God's essence so considered.

According to Spinoza, from the definition of 'God' presented at the beginning of Part I of the *Ethics,* together with the few other definitions and the axioms, each of which expresses an adequate idea, there can be inferred other adequate ideas which yield a rationally satisfying conception of the whole order of nature. But from adequate ideas only adequate ideas can be inferred. Our knowledge that we are finite, and that other finite things exist, because it arises from the suggestions of experience, stems only from inadequate ideas, that is, from ideas the agreements of which with their objects is not evident from consideration of the ideas alone. That we are finite is not evident merely from reflecting upon the ideas involved in our knowledge, or opinion, that we are. Rather, our experience with other finite things teaches us that there are limits upon our thinking, actions, and the duration of our existence. Our knowledge that we are finite cannot, therefore, be inferred from the absolute conception of God as an absolutely infinite being, or from the conception of the order of the whole of nature that this conception (with others) yields.

It may seem that, if the above point is correct, the conception of the order of nature Spinoza presents is incomplete. But this appearance rests upon a misunderstanding. A conception of the whole order of nature is complete when every phenomenon of human experience finds a place and makes sense in terms of it. It is not a requirement that our knowledge that we are finite, or that other things are finite, can be inferred from the absolute conception of God as an absolutely infinite being, or from the rationally satisfying conception of the order of the whole of nature. In the *Ethics,* Spinoza has set himself the task of aiding his reader in forming a concept, satisfying reason, from within which his own place in the whole is clear and understood. He has not set himself the impossible task of proving to him that he, or anything else, is a finite individual. Two facts regarding finitude can be inferred from the general concept Spinoza presents: (1) if it is granted that one finite thing actually exists, infinitely many finite things actually exist; and (2) the knowledge each finite thing has that it is finite arises from its experience in contending with and making its way among other finite, individual things.

It is important to notice that I am distinguishing sharply between

231

the inadequacy of an idea and the confusion it may engender. Confused ideas on an intellectual plane hinder a person who thinks in terms of them from forming a conception of the order of the whole of nature that is internally consistent and within which every phenomenon of human experience finds a place and makes sense. A person who possesses a concept of the order of the whole is without *confused* ideas. However, such a person is not without *inadequate* ideas. Inadequate ideas are not *per se* confused; they are so only when they are fragmentary, that is, only when "they are referred to the human mind alone." (*E* II, P28, Dm.) When they are considered in relationship to God (or the idea of God) and to the order of the whole of nature, although they still remain inadequate in the human mind they do not give rise to confusion.[18] One then understands adequately why those ideas which are inadequate in men *are* inadequate. A person who has formed a rationally satisfying conception of the order of the whole of nature, although without confusion, knows as surely as anyone does that he is a finite individual.

As for the truth of our experience that we are limited in what we can think and do and in how long we can live—most of us do not doubt it. To use Spinoza's phrase, there is nothing (or little) to cause the imagination to waver.[19] Although the ideas involved in our knowledge that we are finite are inadequate, one cannot legitimately conclude that they are false. Spinoza's position on this point is clear from the example he uses to illustrate the three kinds of knowledge. (See *E* II, P40, S2.) According to this example, tradesmen know the fourth number in a proportion by both the first and second kinds of knowledge, but they can also know it by the third. Like most of us, Spinoza himself never doubted the fact of experience that human beings are finite.[20] Among other things, the consequences of being merely one finite individual amid infinitely many others were too evident.

NOTES

1. G.E. Moore, *Some Main Problems of Philosophy* (London: George Allen and Unwin Ltd., 1953), p. 1.

2. Bertrand Russell, *Unpopular Essays* (New York: Simon and Schuster, 1950), pp. 45–46.

3. Albert Camus, *The Myth of Sisyphus*, trans. J. O'Brien (London: Hamish Hamilton, 1955), p. 21.

4. David Hume, *Enquiries*, ed. L.A. Selby-Bigge, 2nd ed. (Oxford: Clarendon Press, 1902), p. 40.

5. All quotations from Spinoza's writings are given in Elwes' translations (see Elwes in Key to References).

6. The degree to which the rationally satisfying conception of the order of the whole of nature is articulate may vary. One may possess a concept of the whole

order of nature that in fact meets reason's requirements without being able to express it in a way which makes clear that it does. The activities involved in forming this concept make a difference in this respect.

7. The phrase 'order of the intellect' designates the order of ideas of the mind when it contains the concept indicated.

8. H. A. Wolfson, *The Philosophy of Spinoza: Unfolding the Latent Processes of His Reasoning*, 2 vols. (Cambridge: Harvard University Press, 1934), I, 58–59.

9. *Ibid.*, I, 53.

10. *Ibid.*, I, 55.

11. *Ibid.*, I, 58.

12. The human mind, or intellect, perceives only two things as constituting the essence of substance, thought and extension (spirituality and matter). *That it perceives less than infinite attributes* is a mark of its finitude. A thing can perceive, or be conscious of, only those things which affect it or through which it displays its essence. Only those things affect a thing which have something in common with it. The human mind can perceive, or be conscious of, only those things which affect human beings. By axiom 5 of Part II, which expresses a commonly accepted truth, human beings perceive only bodies and modes of thought. Once it is accepted that the human mind, or intellect, can only perceive less than infinite attributes, how many it perceives, or which ones, is a matter of no logical, but only practical, consequence.

13. God is also conscious of Himself and understands His own essence and all things that follow from His essence. The idea which constitutes God's understanding of His own essence and all things that follow from it is the idea of God, or the infinite intellect. But Spinoza does not speak of God's understanding of Himself as an attribute, or true ascription, constituting His essence. Rather, God's essence is the cause of which His own self-understanding is a necessary effect. (See *E* I, P31.)

14. According to Spinoza, the peace of mind that a person experiences when his mind has formed the rationally satisfying concept of the whole order of nature engenders love toward God, that is, joy accompanied by the idea of God as cause. (This peace of mind springs from intuitive knowledge of God and the essence of things.) The strength of this love toward God constitutes the strength of mind (*fortitudo*) by which a person with a true knowledge of the nature of human emotions and desires maintains mastery of his own emotions. Spinoza says of the person who experiences the peace of mind springing from intuitive knowledge of God and who possesses the strength that maintains mastery of the emotions that should he become clear, on a reflective level, about the constituents of peace of mind, he would be justifiably spoken of as truly blessed. (*E* V, P33) It is in this context that Spinoza uses the word 'salvation'.

15. Wolfson, I, 33.

16. *Ibid.*, I, 389. I am not discussing Wolfson's comments on this problem.

17. Spinoza calls these modes the immediate infinite and everlasting modes. An everlasting thing can be conceived in terms of the categories of duration and time, although it is without beginning or end. An eternal thing cannot be comprehended or conceived in terms of these categories. Whether the correct word here is 'everlasting' or 'eternal' I am not certain.

18. I understand the first portion of the first sentence in the note following *E* II, P29 as follows: "I say expressly that the mind has not an adequate but only a confused knowledge of itself, its own body, and of external bodies, whenever it

perceives things after the common order of nature; [when it does not perceive things after the common order of nature, though it still has inadequate knowledge of itself, its own body, and of external bodies, so far as they are actually existing things, its knowledge is not confused]." The addition in brackets is my own. The phrase 'common order of nature' contrasts with 'order of the intellect.' When a person perceives things after the common order of nature, the ideas of his mind are not arranged as they are when the mind contains the concept of the whole order of nature satisfying reason's demands. See footnote 7.

19. E II, P49, S. The discussion in this note concerns acquiescence in what is false, but not all knowledge (or opinion) of the first kind is false.

20. The fact that Spinoza's philosophy implies (assuming that it does), and led him to believe that there is something of the mind and of the body which is eternal, does not contradict this.

Contributors

THOMAS CARSON MARK is Assistant Professor of Philosophy at the University of California, San Diego. He is the author of *Spinoza's Theory of Truth* and of several papers on Spinoza.

G. H. R. PARKINSON is Professor of Philosophy at the University of Reading. He has written extensively on the rationalists and is the author of *Spinoza's Theory of Knowledge*.

S. PAUL KASHAP is Associate Professor of Philosophy at the University of California, Santa Cruz. He has written several papers on Spinoza, including "Thought and Action in Spinoza." He also edited *Studies in Spinoza: Critical and Interpretive Essays*.

DAVID R. LACHTERMAN is Assistant Professor of Philosophy at Swarthmore College. He is the author of "Selfhood and Self-Consciousness: An Inquiry into Kantian Themes" and translator of *Max Scheler: Selected Philosophical Essays*.

DAISIE RADNER is Assistant Professor of Philosophy at the State University of New York at Buffalo. She has published several papers on the rationalists, including "Spinoza's Theory of Ideas."

C. L. HARDIN is Associate Professor of Philosophy at Syracuse University and author of "Wittgenstein on Private Languages" and "An Empirical Refutation of the Ontological Argument."

WILLIAM SACKSTEDER is Professor of Philosophy at the University of Colorado. He has recently published "Spinoza Today: Some Commentary on Commentaries."

E. M. CURLEY is a Senior Research Fellow at the Australian National University. He has written several papers on Spinoza and on seventeenth-century philosophy in general, as well as *Spinoza's Metaphysics*.

RICHARD H. POPKIN is Professor of Philosophy at Washington University and editor of *Journal of the History of Philosophy*. In addition to many papers, he has written *The History of Scepticism from Erasmus to Descartes* and edited *The Philosophy of the Sixteenth and Seventeenth Centuries*.

EFRAIM SHMUELI is Professor Emeritus of Philosophy at Cleveland State University. The most recent of his papers on Spinoza is "Hegel's Interpretation of Spinoza's Concept of Substance."

DOUGLAS LEWIS is Associate Professor of Philosophy at the University of Minnesota. He has recently published "Spinoza on Extension."

Index

239

Suárez, Francisco: 108n.
Sub specie aeternitatis: 97, 134, 135 136
Substance: 20, 23, 30, 39, 47, 52n., 58, 76, 83, 107n., 132–33, 206, 225, 227, 230, 233n.; *see also* God
Sufficient reason, principle of: 163–64, 170–71, 174n.

Taylor, A.E.: 127n., 204
Thomasius, Jacob: 191, 195n.
Time: 60, 62–63, 129–32, 136–37, 138n., 200, 230
Truth: 11–14, 16–21, 23–30, 31n., 32n., 33n., 35–36, 38, 40–43, 45, 50 69, 140, 198, 200–202, 205–207, 226; *see also* idea, true
Tschirnhaus, L.W. von: 52n., 54n., 67, 77, 101, 103
Twain, Mark: 161

Velthuysen, Lambert van: 210
Vico, G.: 104n.
Voltaire, Francois-Marie Arouet de: 161

Wartofsky, Marx: 74, 104n.
Weinberg, Julius: 24, 33n.
White, Morton: 164
Will: 96, 166, 169–71, 207, 209, 224–28
Wolf, Abraham: 110n., 128n., 145, 159n., 214n.
Wolfson, H.A.: 103n., 123, 127n., 129, 137n., 181, 192n., 201–203, 213, 214n., 215n., 222–23, 229–30, 233n.